COLLECTED POEMS

This volume, brought out in the poet's fiftieth year, contains nearly all the verse he has published from 1929 up to the present. It is now possible to see how wide has been its range, how diverse its moods, and how resourceful is his poetic technique. Beneath each new venture in subject-matter and form, the reader can trace certain constant themes which, as Mr. Day Lewis says in his Preface, are the poet's 'one continuity, defining and preserving, through every change of language, every change of heart, what is essential to him.' These *Collected Poems* compose a most memorable *œuvre*, reflecting the stresses and hazards of the times through a highly personal sensibility, enriched by experience and strengthened by tradition.

COLLECTED POEMS
OF
C. DAY LEWIS

Collected Poems

of

C. DAY LEWIS

1954

JONATHAN CAPE

with

THE HOGARTH PRESS

THIS COLLECTION FIRST PUBLISHED 1954
BY
JONATHAN CAPE
30 BEDFORD SQUARE
WITH
THE HOGARTH PRESS
40-42 WILLIAM IV STREET
LONDON

SECOND IMPRESSION 1961

PRINTED IN GREAT BRITAIN IN THE CITY OF OXFORD
AT THE ALDEN PRESS
BOUND BY A. W. BAIN & CO. LTD., LONDON

CONTENTS

The first five of these books were published by the Hogarth Press, and re-issued in one volume, *Collected Poems 1929-1936*, in 1948. The remaining books were published by Jonathan Cape.

PREFACE

READING over my verse written during the last 25 years, I have felt both surprise and regret: regret, that so much energy should so often have run to waste; surprise, to hear a buried self speaking, now and then, with such urgency. Some poets can rewrite and improve their early work, years later. I wish I could do so: but the selves who wrote those poems are strangers to me, and I cannot resume their identities or go back into the world where they lived. There are certain themes, no doubt, linking these dead selves together. Perhaps these constant themes compose the personal tradition of a poet – his one continuity, defining and preserving, through every change of language, every change of heart, what is essential to him. At any rate, I could no more reconstruct an old poem than I could reassemble the self out of whom it was constructed: I can only write another poem, feeling my way along the same themes with the self I now am.

Where rewriting is impossible, selection seems desirable. But this involves criticism; and as a critic of his own work a poet is likely to be at once too limited and too detached, seeing all the poems he has written through the eyes of the new poem which is now on his mind, yet practically indifferent to them – as a man might feel towards a collection of old keys, when the doors he tried to open with them have vanished, or the locks been changed. In principle, I think a *Collected Poems* should offer everything one has written. In practice, I have excluded most of the last 14 pages of *A Time to Dance*, and all but two choruses of *Noah and the Waters*. Cuts might well have been made, too, in the first three books, particularly *The Magnetic Mountain*: but, since they were written as sequences, I decided to let them stand.

I should like to express my gratitude to Jonathan Cape and the Hogarth Press for making this volume possible by their collaboration.

C. DAY LEWIS

TRANSITIONAL POEM

To R. E. Warner

Transitional Poem

Part One

Ira brevis, longa est pietas, recidiva voluptas;
Et cum posse perit, mens tamen una manet.

MAXIMIAN

1

Now I have come to reason
And cast my schoolboy clout,
Disorder I see is without,
And the mind must sweat a poison
Keener than Thessaly's brew;
A pus that, discharged not thence,
Gangrenes the vital sense
And makes disorder true.
It is certain we shall attain
No life till we stamp on all
Life the tetragonal
Pure symmetry of brain.

I felt, in my scorning
Of common poet's talk,
As arrogant as the hawk
When he mounts above the morning.
'Behold man's droll appearance,
Faith wriggling upon his hooks,
Chin-deep in Eternal Flux
Angling for reassurance!'
I care not if he retorts –
'Of all that labour and wive
And worship, who would give
A fiddlestick for these thoughts

That sluggishly yaw and bend,
Fat strings of barges drawn
By a tug they have never seen
And never will comprehend?'

I sit in a wood and stare
Up at untroubled branches
Locked together and staunch as
Though girders of the air:
And think, the first wind rising
Will crack that intricate crown
And let the daylight down.
But there is naught surprising
Can explode the single mind: –
Let figs from thistles fall
Or stars from their pedestal,
This architecture will stand.

2

Come, soul, let us not fight
Like cynical Chinee
Beneath umbrella, nor wish to trade
Upon neutrality.
For the mind must cope with
All elements or none –
Bask in dust along with weevils,
Or criticize the sun.

Look, where cloud squadrons are
Stampeded by the wind,
A boy's kite sits as calm as Minos
If the string be sound:
But if there are no hands
To keep the cable tense
And no eyes to mark a flaw in it,
What use the difference

Between a gust that twitters
Along the wainscot at dawn
And a burly wind playing the zany
In fields of barleycorn?

The time has gone when we
Could sprawl at ease between
Light and darkness, and deduce
Omnipotence from our Mean.
For us the gregorian
Example of those eyes
That risked hell's blight and heaven's blinding
But dared not compromise.

3

That afternoon we lay on Lillington Common
The land wallowed around us in the sunlight;
But finding all things my strenuous sense included
Ciphers new-copied by the indefinite sunlight,
I fell once more under the shadow of my Sphinx.
The aimlessness of buttercup and beetle
So pestered me, I would have cried surrender
To the fossil certitudes of Tom, Dick, and Harry,
Had I known how or believed that such a surrender
Could fashion aught but a dead Sphinx from the live Sphinx.
Later we lit a fire, and the hedge of darkness –
Garnished with not a nightingale nor a glow-worm –
Sprang up like the beanstalk by which our Jack aspired once.
Then, though each star seemed little as a glow-worm
Perched on Leviathan's flank, and equally terrible
My tenure of this plateau that sloped on all sides
Into annihilation – yet was I lord of
Something: for, seeing the fall of a burnt-out faggot
Make all the night sag down, I became lord of
Light's interplay – stoker of an old parable.

4

Come up, Methuselah,
You doddering superman!
Give me an instant realized
And I'll outdo your span.

In that one moment of evening
When roses are most red
I can fold back the firmament,
I can put time to bed.

Abraham, stint your tally
Of concubines and cattle!
Give place to me – capitalist
In more intrinsic metal.

I have a lover of flesh
And a lover that is a sprite:
Today I lie down with finite,
Tomorrow with infinite.

That one is a constant
And suffers no eclipse,
Though I feel sun and moon burning
Together on her lips.

This one is a constant,
But she's not kind at all;
She raddles her gown with my despairs
And paints her lip with gall.

My lover of flesh is wild,
And willing to kiss again;
She is the potency of earth
When woods exhale the rain.

My lover of air, like Artemis
Spectrally embraced,
Shuns the daylight that twists her smile
To mineral distaste.

Twin poles energic, they
Stand fast and generate
This spark that crackles in the void
As between fate and fate.

5

My love is a tower.
Standing up in her
I parley with planets
And the casual wind.
Arcturus may grind
Against our wall: – he whets
A tropic appetite,
And decorates our night.
'What happier place
For Johnny Head-in-Air,
Who never would hear
Time mumbling at the base?'

I will not hear, for she's
My real Antipodes,
And our ingrowing loves
Shall meet below earth's spine
And there shall intertwine,
Though Babel falls above.
Time, we allow, destroys
All aërial toys:
But to assail love's heart
He has no strategy,
Unless he suck up the sea
And pull the earth apart.

6

Dismayed by the monstrous credibility
Of all antinomies, I climbed the fells
To Easedale Tarn. Could I be child again
And grip those skirts of cloud the matriarch sky
Draggled on mere and hillside? . . . ('So the dog
Returns to his vomit,' you protest. Well only
The dog can tell what virtue lies in his vomit.)
    Sleep on, you fells and profound dales: there's no
Material wind or rain can insulate
The mind against its own forked speculation,
When once that storm sets in: and then the flash
That bleakly enlightens a few sour acres leaves but
A more Egyptian darkness whence it came.
    Mountains are the musicians; they despise
Their audience: but the wind is a popular preacher
And takes more from his audience than he gives them.
How can I wear the clouds, who feel each mountain
Yearn from its flinty marrow to abdicate
Sublimity and globe-trot with the wind?
    By Easedale Tarn, where I sought a comforter,
I found a gospel sterner than repentance.
Prophetic earth, you need no lumber of logic
Who point your arguments alike with a primrose
And a sick sheep coughing among the stones:
And I have only words; yet must they both
Outsoar the mountain and lap up the wind.

7

Few things can more inflame
This far too combative heart
Than the intellectual Quixotes of the age
Prattling of abstract art.

18

No one would deny it –
But for a blind man's passion
Cassandra had been no more than a draggle-skirt,
Helen a ten-year fashion.
Yet had there not been one hostess
Ever whose arms waylaid
Like the tough bramble a princeling's journey, or
At the least no peasant maid
Redressing with rude heat
Nature's primeval wrong,
Epic had slumbered on beneath his blindness
And Helen lacked her song.

(So the antique balloon
Wobbles with no defence
Against the void but a grapnel that hops and ploughs
Through the landscape of sense.)

Phrase-making, dress-making –
Distinction's hard to find;
For thought must play the mannequin, strut in phrase,
Or gape with the ruck: and mind,
Like body, from covering gets
Most adequate display.
Yet time trundles this one to the rag-and-bone man,
While that other may
Reverberate all along
Man's craggy circumstance –
Naked enough to keep its dignity
Though it eye God askance.

Part Two

Do I contradict myself?
Very well then, I contradict myself;
I am large, I contain multitudes.

WALT WHITMAN

8

It is becoming now to declare my allegiance,
To dig some reservoir for my springtime's pain,
Bewilderment and pride, before their insurgence
Is all sopped up in this dry regimen.

Laughable dwarfs, you may twirl and tweak my heart, –
Have I not fought with Anakim at the crossways?
Once I was Cicero, though pedant fate
Now bids me learn the grammar of my days.

These, then, have my allegiance; they whose shining
Convicted my false dawn of flagrant night,
Yet ushered up the sun, as poets leaning
Upon a straw surmise the infinite.

You, first, who ground my lust to love upon
Your gritty humorous virginity,
Then yielding to its temper suddenly
Proved what a Danube can be struck from stone:
With you I ran the gauntlet for my prime,
Then living in the moment lived for all time.

Next the hawk-faced man, who could praise an apple
In terms of peach and win the argument. Quick
Was he to trip the shambling rhetoric
Of laws and lions: yet abstract turned the tables
And his mind, almost, with a whiff of air
Clothed first in a woman and after in a nightmare.

She next, sorrow's familiar, who turned
Her darkness to our light; that 'brazen leech'
Alleviating the vain cosmic itch
With fact coated in formulæ lest it burned
Our tongue. She who released my struggling days
Shall live in me, not memory, for always.

Last the tow-haired poet, never done
With cutting and planing some new gnomic prop
To jack his all too stable universe up: –
Conduct's Old Dobbin, thought's chameleon.
Single mind copes with split intelligence,
Breeding a piebald strain of truth and nonsense.

These have I loved and chosen, once being sure
Some spacious vision waved upon their eyes
That troubles not the common register;
And love them still, knowing it otherwise.

Knowing they held no mastership in wisdom
Or wit save by certificate of my love,
I have found out a better way to praise them –
Nestor shall die and let Patroclus live.

So I declare it. These are they who built
My house and never a stone of it laid agley.
So cheat I memory that works in gilt
And stucco to restore a fallen day.

9

I thought to have had some fame
As the village idiot
Condemned at birth to sit
Oracle of blind alleys:
Shanghaied aboard the galleys
I got reprieve and shame.

Tugging at his oar
This idiot who, for lack
Of the striped Zodiac,
Swore that every planet
Was truck, soon found some merit
In his own abject star.

Then there came disgust
Of the former loon who could
Elbow a bridge and brood
From Chaos to last Trump
Over the imbecile pomp
Of waters dribbling past.

For what can water be
But so much less or more
Gravamen to the oar? –
(Reasons our reformed dunce)
It is high time to renounce
This village idiocy.

10

How they would jeer at us –
Ulysses, Herodotus,
The hard-headed Phœnicians
Or, of later nations,
Columbus, the Pilgrim Fathers
And a thousand others
Who laboured only to find
Some pittance of new ground,
Merchandize or women.
Those rude and bourgeois seamen
Got glory thrown in
As it were with every ton
Of wave that swept their boat,
And would have preferred a coat
For keeping off the spray.

Since the heroes lie
Entombed with the recipe
Of epic in their heart,
And have buried – it seems – that art
Of minding one's own business
Magnanimously, for us
There's nothing but to recant
Ambition, and be content
Like the poor child at play
To find a holiday
In the sticks and mud
Of a familiar road.

11

If I bricked up ambition and gave no air
To the ancestral curse that gabbles there,
   I could leave wonder on the latch
   And with a whole heart watch
The calm declension of an English year.

I would be pedagogue – hear poplar, lime
And oak recite the seasons' paradigm.
   Each year a dynasty would fall
   Within my orchard wall –
I'd be their Tacitus, and they my time.

Among those pippin princes I could ease
A heart long sick for some Hesperides:
   Plainsong of thrushes in the soul
   Would drown that rigmarole
Of Eldorados, Auks, and Perilous Seas.

(The God they cannot see sages define
In a slow-motion. If I discipline
   My flux into a background still

And sure as a waterfall
Will not a rainbow come of that routine?)

So circumscribe the vampire and he'll die soon –
Lunacy and anæmia take their own.
   Grounded in temperate soil I'll stay,
   An orchard god, and say
My glow-worms hold a candle to the moon.

12

   Enough. There is no magic
   Circle nor prophylactic
   Sorcery of garlic
   Will keep the vampire in.
   See! – that authentic
   Original of sin
   Slides from his cabin
   Up to my sober trees
   And spits disease.
   Thus infected, they
   Start a sylvan rivalry,
   Poplar and oak surpass
   Their natural green, and race
   Each other to the stars.

   Since my material
   Has chosen to rebel,
   It were most politic –
   Ere I also fall sick –
   To escape this Eden.
   Indeed there has been no peace
   For any garden
   Or for any trees
   Since Priapus died,
   And lust can no more ride
   Over self-love and pride.

Leave Eden to the brutes:
For he who lets his sap
Run downward to the roots
Will wither at the top
And wear fool's-cap.
I am no English lawn
To build a smooth tradition
Out of Time's recession
And centuries of dew . . .
Adam must subdue
The indestructible serpent,
Outstaring it: content
If he can transplant
One slip from paradise
Into his own eyes.

13

Can the mole take
A census of the stars?
Our firmament will never
Give him headache.

The man who nuzzles
In a woman's lap
Burrows toward a night
Too deep for puzzles:

While he, whose prayer
Holds up the starry system
In a God's train, sees nothing
Difficult there.

So I, perhaps,
Am neither mole nor mantis;
I see the constellations,
But by their gaps.

14

In heaven, I suppose, lie down together
Agonized Pilate and the boa-constrictor
That swallows anything: but we must seize
One horn or the other of our antitheses.
When I consider each independent star
Wearing its world of darkness like a fur
And rubbing shoulders with infinity,
I am content experience should be
More discontinuous than the points pricked
Out by the mazy course of a derelict,
Iceberg, or Flying Dutchman, and the heart
Stationary and passive as a chart.
In such star-frenzy I could boast, betwixt
My yester and my morrow self are fixed
All the birds carolling and all the seas
Groaning from Greenwich to the Antipodes.

But an eccentric hour may come, when systems
Not stars divide the dark; and then life's pistons
Pounding into their secret cylinder
Begin to tickle the most anchorite ear
With hints of mechanisms that include
The man. And once that rhythm arrests the blood,
Who would be satisfied his mind is no
Continent but an archipelago?
They are preposterous paladins and prance
From myth to myth, who take an Agag stance
Upon the needle points of here and now,
Where only angels ought to tread. Allow
One jointure feasible to man, one state
Squared with another – then he can integrate
A million selves and where disorder ruled
Straddle a chaos and beget a world.

Peals of the New Year once for me came tumbling
Out of the narrow night like clusters of humming-
Birds loosed from a black bag, and rose again
Irresponsibly to silence: but now I strain
To follow them and see for miles around
Men square or shrug their shoulders at the sound.
Then I remember the pure and granite hills
Where first I caught an ideal tone that stills,
Like the beloved's breath asleep, all din
Of earth at traffic: silence's first-born,
Carrying over each sensual ravine
To inform the seer and uniform the seen.
So from this ark, this closet of the brain,
The dove emerges and flies back again
With a Messiah sprig of certitude –
Promise of ground below the sprawling flood.

15

Desire is a witch
And runs against the clock.
It can unstitch
The decent hem
Where space tacks on to time:
It can unlock
Pandora's privacies.

It puffs in these
Top-gallants of the mind,
And away I stand
On the elemental gale
Into an ocean
That the liar Lucian
Had never dared retail.

When my love leans with all
Her shining breast and shoulder,

I know she is older
Than Ararat the hill,
And yet more young
Than the first daffodil
That ever shews a spring.

When her eyes delay
On me, so deep are they
Tunnelled by love, although
You poured Atlantic
In this one and Pacific
In the other, I know
They would not overflow.

Desire clicks back
Like cuckoo into clock;
Leaves me to explain
Eyes that a tear will drown
And a body where youth
Nor age will long remain
To implicate the truth.

It seems that we must call
Anything truth whose well
Is deep enough;
For the essential
Philosopher-stone, desire,
Needs no other proof
Than its own fire.

16

Remembering how between
Embrace and ultimate bone
Always have interposed
Strata undiagnosed
In Love's geology;

And even memory
Is bullied by the flesh
Out of its usual dish;
I railed upon desire,
The silly self-betrayer
Whose Cronic appetite
Gobbles up all his brood;
And I found, in body's despite,
A moral to clinch the mood.

They say that a mathematician
Once fell to such a passion
For x and y, he locked
His door to keep outside
Whatever might distract
Him from his heavenly bride:
And presently died
In the keenest of blisses
With a dozen untasted dishes
Outside his door.
          O man,
Feed Cronos with a stone.
He's easily decoyed
Who, perched on any throne,
Happily gnaws the void.

From this theoric tower
Corn-land and city seem
A lovely skiagram:
You could not guess what sour
Contagion has outworn
Those streets of men and corn.
Let body doubt: the pure
Shadow will reassure,
For shadow gives a free
Licence to lunacy. –

29

And yet fools say it is
The heart that's credulous . . .
For once, O sceptic heart,
Will you not play your part?

17

When nature plays hedge-schoolmaster,
Shakes out the gaudy map of summer
And shows me charabanc, rose, barley-ear
And every bright-winged hummer,

He only would require of me
To be the sponge of natural laws
And learn no more of that cosmography
Than passes through the pores.

Why must I then unleash my brain
To sweat after some revelation
Behind the rose, heedless if truth maintain
On the rose-bloom her station?

When bullying April bruised mine eyes
With sleet-bound appetites and crude
Experiments of green, I still was wise
And kissed the blossoming rod.

Now summer brings what April took,
Riding with fanfares from the south,
And I should be no Solomon to look
My Sheba in the mouth.

Charabancs shout along the lane
And summer gales bay in the wood
No less superbly because I can't explain
What I have understood.

30

Let logic analyse the hive,
Wisdom's content to have the honey:
So I'll go bite the crust of things and thrive
While hedgerows still are sunny.

Part Three

*But even so, amid the tornadoed Atlantic of
my being, do I myself still centrally disport
in mute calm.*

HERMAN MELVILLE

18

On my right are trees and a lank stream sliding
Impervious as Anaconda to the suns
Of autumn; and the boughs are vipers writhing
To slough the summer from their brittle bones.
Here is the Trojan meadow, here Scamander;
And I, the counterfeit Achilles, feel
A river-god surge up to tear me asunder,
A serpent melancholy bruise my heel.

On my left is the city famed for talk
And tolerance. Its old men run about
Chasing reality, chasing the Auk
With butterfly-nets. Its young men swell the rout
Gaping at Helen in the restaurant,
Mocking at Helen from monastic towers.
Boy Achilles, who has known Helen too long
To scold or worship, stands outside and glowers.

Between the stream and city a rubbish heap
Proclaims the pleasant norm with smouldering stenches.
See! the pathetic pyre where Trojans keep
Well out of sight the prey of time's revenges;

31

Old butterfly-nets, couches where lovers lay –
All furniture out of fashion. So the fire
Guts the proud champions of the real: so Troy
Cremates her dead selves and ascends to higher.

Grecians awake, salute the happy norm!
Now may Achilles find employment still;
And once again the blood-lust will grow warm,
Gloating on champions he could never kill.
And if Scamander rears up and pursues,
This ring of rubbish fire will baffle all
His rage. Hero, you're safe, in the purlieus
Of God's infernal acre king and thrall.

19

When April comes alive
Out of the small bird's throat,
Achilles in the sunshine
Kept on his overcoat.
Trojan and Greek at battle,
Helen wantoning –
None but heroic metal
Could ignore the spring.

When honeysuckle and summer
Suffocate the lane,
That sulky boil was broken
And I at last a man.
I'd have stripped off my skin to
The impacts of hate and love –
Rebel alone because I
Could not be slave enough.

Bodies now, not shadows,
Intercept the sun:
It takes no rod to tell me

That discipline's begun.
Seeking the fabled fusion
From love's last chemical,
I found the experiment
Makes monads of us all;

For love still keeps apart,
And all its vanities
But emphasize higher heaven,
As February trees
When rooks begin their noisy
Coronation of the wood
Are turreted with folly
Yet grow toward some good.

I thought, since love can harness
Pole with contrary pole,
It must be earthed in darkness
Deeper than mine or mole.
Now that I have loved
A while and not gone blind,
I think love's terminals
Are fixed in fire and wind.

20

How often, watching the windy boughs
Juggle with the moon, or leaning
My body against a wind
That sets all earth careening;
Or when I have seen flames browsing
On the prairie of night and tossing
Their muzzles up at Orion;
Or the sun's hot arsenal spent
On a cloud salient
Till the air explodes with light;
How often have I perceived a delight

33

Which parallels the racing mind,
But never rides it off the course.

Another fire, another wind
Now take the air, and I
Am matched with a stricter ecstasy.
For he whom love and fear enlist
To comb his universe
For what Protagoras missed,
Needs be reborn hermaphrodite
And put himself out to nurse
With a siren and a sibyl.
So the spider gradually,
Drawing fine systems from his belly,
Includes creation with a thread
And squats on the navel of his world.
Yet even that arch-fakir must feed
Austerity on warm blood.

The tracks of love and fear
Lead back till I disappear
Into that ample terminus
From which all trains draw out
Snorting towards an Ultima Thule.
Nothing is altered about
The place, except its gloom is newly
Lacquered by an unaccustomed eye,
Yet cannot blunt mine eyes now
To the clear finality
Of all beginnings.
                Outside
In the diamond air of day
The engines simmer with delay,
Desiring a steely discipline
No less, though now quite satisfied
They travel a loop-line.

21

My lover is so happy, you well might say
One of the Hellene summers had lost its way
And taken shelter underneath her breast.
None but its proper fear can now arrest
Our meteoric love: but still we grieve
That curves of mind and body should outlive
All expectation, and the heart become
A blunt habitual arc, a pendulum
Wagged by the ghost of its first impetus.
Love keeps the bogey slave to admonish us
Of vanity, yet through this fear we scrawl
Our sky with love's vain comets ere it fall.

And then, up on High Stoy standing alone,
We saw the excellence of the serious down
That shakes the seasons from its back, and bears
No obligation but to wind and stars.
What paroxysm of green can crack those huge
Ribs grown from Chaos, stamped by the Deluge?

Later, within the wood sweetly reclining
On bluebell and primrose, we loved; whose shining
Made a poor fiction of the royal skies,
But were to love alone repositories
Of what by-product wonder it could spare
From lips and eyes. Yet nothing had such power
As prattle of small flowers within the brake
To mount the panic heart and rein it back
From the world's edge. For they, whose virtue lies
In a brief act of beauty, summarize
Earth's annual passion and leave the naked earth
Still dearer by their death than by their birth.
So we, who are love's hemispheres hiding
Beneath the coloured ordeal of our spring,
Shall be disclosed, and I shall see your face
An autumn evening certain of its peace.

22

It is an easier thing
To give up great possessions
Than to forego one farthing
Of the rare unpossessed.

But I've been satellite
Long enough to this moon,
The pharisee of night
Shining by tradition.

There's no star in the sky
But gazing makes it double
And the infatuate eye
Can breed dilemmas on it.

Wiser it were to sheath
My burning heart in clay
Than by this double breath
To magnify the tomb.

I'd live like grass and trees,
Familiar of the earth,
Proving its basalt peace
Till I was unperturbed

By synod of the suns
Or a moon's insolence
As the ant when he runs
Beneath sky-scraping grass.

23

You've trafficked with no beast but unicorn
Who dare hold me in scorn
For my dilemmas. Nor have you perceived
The compass-point suggest

An east by pointing to the west,
Or you'd not call me thus deceived
For fixing my desire
On this magnetic north to gyre
Under the sheer authority of ice.

I have seen what impertinence
Stokes up the dingy rhetoric of sense:
I've seen your subaltern ambitions rise
Yellow and parallel
As smoke from garden cities that soon fades
In air it cannot even defile. Poor shades,
Not black enough for hell,
Learn of this poplar which beyond its height
Aspires not, and will bend beneath the thumb
Of every wind; yet when the stars come
It is an omen darker than the night.

The rest may go. No satisfaction lies
In such. And you alone shall hear
My pride, whose love's the accurate frontier
Of all my enterprise.
While your beauties' succession
Holds my adventure in a flowery chain
As the spring hedgerows hold the lane,
How can I care whether it ends upon
Marsh or metropolis?

But look within my heart, see there
The tough stoic ghost of a pride was too severe
To risk an armistice
With lesser powers than death; but rather died
Welcoming that iron in the soul
Which keeps the spirit whole,
Since none but ghosts are satisfied
To see a glory passing and let it pass.

For I had been a modern moth and hurled
Myself on many a flaming world,
To find its globe was glass.
In you alone
I met the naked light, by you became
Veteran of a flame
That burns away all but the warrior bone.
And I shall know, if time should falsify
This star the company of my night,
Mine is the heron's flight
Which makes a solitude of any sky.

24

Farewell again to this adolescent moon;
   I say it is a bottle
For papless poets to feed their fancy on.
   Once mine sucked there, and I dreamed
The heart a record for the gramophone –
   One scratch upon the surface,
And the best music of that sphere is gone.
   So I put passion away
In a cold storage and took its tune on trust,
   While proper men with church-bells
Signal a practised or a dreamt-of lust . . .
   No fear could sublimate
The ennui of a tomb where music slept
   In artificial frost,
Nor could it long persuade me to accept
   Rigidity for peace.
Moon-stricken I worked out a solitude
   Of sand and sun, believing
No other soil could bear the genuine rood.
   But nothing grew except
The shadow at my heels. Now I confess
   There's no virtue in sand:
It is the rose that makes the wilderness.

I thought integrity
Needed a desert air; I saw it plain,
A chimney of stone at evening,
A monolith on the skyline after rain.
Instead, the witless sun
Fertilized that old succubus and bred
A skeleton in a shadow.
Let cactus spring where hermits go to bed
With those they come to kill.
Three-legged I ran with that importunate curse,
Till I guessed (in the sexual trance
Or playing darts with drunken schoolmasters)
The integrity that's laid bare
Upon the edge of common furniture.
Now to the town returning
I accept the blind collisions that ensure
Soul's ektogenesis.

25

Where is the true, the central stone
That clay and vapour zone,
That earthquakes budge nor vinegar bites away,
That rivets man against Doomsday?

You will not find it there, although
You sink a shaft below
Despair and see the roots of death close-curled
About the kernel of your world.

Where is the invaluable star
Whose beams enlacèd are
The scaffolding of truth, whose stages drawn
Aside unshutter an ideal dawn?

It is well hid. You would not find
It there, though far you mined

Up through the golden seams that cram the night
And walked those galleries of light.

Above, below, the Flux tight-packed
Stages its sexual act –
An ignominious scuffling in the dark
Where brute encounters brute baresark.

Keep to the pithead, then, nor pry
Beyond what meets the eye,
Since household stuff, stone walls, mountains and trees
Placard the day with certainties.

For individual truth must lie
Within diversity;
Under the skin all creatures are one race,
Proved integers but by their face.

So he, who learns to comprehend
The form of things, will find
They in his eye that purest star have sown
And changed his mind to singular stone.

26

Chiefly to mind appears
That hour on Silverhowe
When evening's lid hung low
And the sky was about our ears.
Buoyed between fear and love
We watched in eastward form
The armadas of the storm
And sail superbly above;
So near, they'd split and founder
On the least jag of sense,
One false spark fire the immense
Broadside the confounding thunder.

They pass, give not a salvo,
And in their rainy wash
We hear the horizons crash
With monitors of woe.

Only at highest power
Can love and fear become
Their equilibrium,
And in that eminent hour
A virtue is made plain
Of passionate cleavage
Like the hills' cutting edge
When the sun sets to rain.
This is the single mind,
This the star-solved equation
Of life with life's negation.
A deathless cell designed
To demonstrate death's act,
Which, the more surely it moves
To earth's influence, but proves
Itself the more intact.

27

With me, my lover makes
   The clock assert its chime:
But when she goes, she takes
   The mainspring out of time.

Yet this time-wrecking charm
   Were better than love dead
And its hollow alarum
   Hammered out on lead.

Why should I fear that Time
   Will superannuate
These workmen of my rhyme –
   Love, despair and hate?

Fleeing the herd, I came
  To a graveyard on a hill,
And felt its mould proclaim
  The bone gregarious still.

Boredoms and agonies
  Work out the rhythm of bone: –
No peace till creature his
  Creator has outgrown.

Passion dies from the heart
  But to infect the marrow;
Holds dream and act apart
  Till the man discard his narrow

Sapience and folly
  Here, where the graves slumber
In a green melancholy
  Of overblown summer.

Part Four

The hatches are let down
And the night meets the day
The spirit comes to its own
The beast to its play.
                                      W. H. AUDEN

28

In the beginning was the Word.
  Under different skies now, I recall
  The childhood of the Word.
                              Before the Fall,

Was dancing on the green with sun and moon:
And the Word was with God.
Years pass, relaxed in a faun's afternoon.
And the Word was God.

 For him rise up the litanies of leaves
From the tormented wood, and semi-breves
Of birds accompany the simple dawn.
Obsequious to his mood the valleys yawn,
Nymphs scamper or succumb, waterfalls part
The hill-face with vivacious smiles. The heart,
Propped up against its paradise, records
Each wave of godhead in a sea of words.
He grows a wall of sunflower and moonflower blent
To protest his solitude and to prevent
Wolf or worm from trespassing on his rule.
Observe how paradise can make a fool:
They can't get in; but he – for a god no doubt
Is bound by his own laws – cannot get out.
And the Word was made flesh,

 Under different skies now,
Wrenching a stony song from a scant acre,
The Word still justifies its Maker.

 Green fields were my slippers,
  Sky was my hat,
 But curiosity
  Killed the cat.
 For this did I burst
  My daisy band –
 To be clapped in irons
  By a strange hand?

Nevertheless, you are well out of Eden:
For there's no wonder where all things are new;
No dream where all is sleep; no vision where
Seer and seen are one; nor prophecy
Where only echo waits upon the tongue.
 Now he has come to a country of stone walls,

Breathes a precarious air.
Frontiers of adamant declare
A cold autonomy. There echo starves;
And the mountain ash bleeds stoically there
Above the muscular stream.
What cairn will show the way he went?
A harrow rusting on defeated bones?
Or will he leave a luckier testament –
Rock deeply rent,
Fountains of spring playing upon the air?

29

Those Himalayas of the mind
Are not so easily possessed:
There's more than precipice and storm
Between you and your Everest.

You who declare the peak of peaks
Alone will satisfy your want,
Can you distil a grain of snow?
Can you digest an adamant?

Better by far the household cock
Scratching the common yard for corn,
Whose rainy voice all night at will
Can signify a private dawn.

Another bird, sagacious too,
Circles in plain bewilderment
Where shoulder to shoulder long waves march
Towards a magnetic continent.

'What are these rocks impede our pomp?'
Gesticulating to the sun
The waves part ranks, sidle and fume,
Then close behind them and march on.

44

The waves advance, the Absolute Cliffs
Unaccountably repel:
They linger grovelling; where assault
Has failed, attrition may tell.

The bird sees nothing to the point;
Shrugs an indifferent wing; proceeds
From rock to rock in the mid-ocean
Peering for barnacles and weeds.

30

In the chaotic age
    This was enough for me –
Her beauty walked the page
    And it was poetry.

Now that the crust has cooled,
    The floods are kept in pen,
Mountains have got their mould
    And air its regimen.

Nothing of heat remains
    But where the sacred hill
Conserves within her veins
    The fiery principle.

Fire can no longer shake
    Stars from their sockets down;
It burns now but to make
    Vain motions above the town.

This glum canal, has lain
    Opaque night after night,
One hour will entertain
    A jubilee of light,

And show that beauty is
A motion of the mind
By its own dark caprice
Directed or confined.

31

Where is the fool would want those days again
Whose light was globed in pain
And danced upon a point of wire?
When the charged batteries of desire
Had licence but to pass
Into a narrow room of frosted glass?

The globe was broken and the light made free
Of a king's territory.
Artemis then, that huntress pale,
Flung her black dogs upon the trail:
So with one glance around
The hunted lightning ran and went to ground.

Safer perhaps within that cell to stay
Which qualified its ray
And gave it place and period,
Than be at liberty where God
Has put no firmament
Of glass to prove dark and light different.

But Artemis leaps down. At her thin back
Wheel the shades in a pack.
At once that old habit of fire
Jumps out, not stopping to inquire
Whether it follows or flies,
Content to use the night for exercise.

And I, when at the sporting queen's halloo
The light obedient flew

46

Blazing its trail across the wild —
Resigned now but not reconciled,
That ancient Sphinx I saw
Put moon and shades like mice beneath its paw.

32

The red nor'-easter is out:
Trees in the covert strain
Like dogs upon a leash
And snuff the hurricane.
Another wind and tree now
Are constant to their west:
The breath that scours the midday
Unseen, is manifest
In this embittered thorn —
Forcing the stubborn frame
To grow one way and point
His constancy and aim.

This wind that fills the hollow
Sky, of a vacuum
Was purely bred. The thorn once
In modest seed lay mum
That squats above the Atlantic
Promontoried on pride.
For my tenacious tree
Requires not, to decide
That he has roots somewhere,
A tropic foliage;
Since that the leaf recurs
Is a sufficient gauge.

Again, what of this glass
Whereby the formulæ
Of sense should all be solved?
It cannot enlarge a flea

47

Nor accurately define
The features of a star.
Gazing through it I saw
Nothing particular
Distant or close. A summer
Accident it was
Explained its property.

It is a burning-glass
Which interrupts the sun
To make him more intense,
And touch to a single flame
The various heap of sense.

33

Seventeen months ago
We came to the mine on the moor. A crow
Sees more than meets the eye –
What marrow in fleshless bones may lie.
And now I passed by a forbidding coast
Where ironworks rust
On each headland: goats crop the salted grass:
Steam oozes out of the mud. Earth has
No promise for proprietors. I from far
Came, and passing saw something oracular.
Put down the tripod here.

I stretched a line from pole to pole
To hang my paper lanterns on. Poor soul,
By such a metaphysical conceit
Thinking to make ends meet!
This line, spun from the blind heart –
What could it do but prove the poles apart?
More expert now, I twist the dials, catch
Electric hints, curt omens such
As may be heard by one tapping the air

That belts an ambiguous sphere.
Put down the tripod here.

This is the interregnum of my year;
All spring except the leaf is here,
All winter but the cold.
Bandage of snow for the first time unrolled
Lays bare the wounds given when any fate
And most men's company could humiliate:
Sterilized now; yet still they prick
And pulse beneath the skin, moving me like
An engine driven on
By sparks of its own combustion.
There are going to be some changes made today.

Then add to this that I
Have known, and shall again, the greedy thigh;
Browned by that sun, but not betrayed,
Which puts the Dog-Star in the shade:
For though my world at one Equator meet,
These Arctic zones are still complete.
Baring my skin to every bruise
Love gives, I'll love the more; since they're but dues
That flesh must pay to bone
Till each is overthrown.
There are going to be some changes made today.

34

The hawk comes down from the air.
Sharpening his eye upon
A wheeling horizon
Turned scrutiny to prayer.

He guessed the prey that cowers
Below, and learnt to keep
The distance which can strip
Earth to its blank contours.

Then trod the air, content
With contemplation till
The truth of valley and hill
Should be self-evident.

Or as the little lark
Who veins the sky with song,
Asking from dawn to dark
No revenues of spring:

But with the night descends
Into his chosen tree,
And the famed singer ends
In anonymity.

So from a summer's height
I come into my peace;
The wings have earned their night,
And the song may cease.

FROM FEATHERS TO IRON

To The Mother

D

From Feathers to Iron

Do thoughts grow like feathers, the dead end of life?

W. H. AUDEN

We take but three steps from feathers to iron.

JOHN KEATS

1

Suppose that we, tomorrow or the next day,
Came to an end – in storm the shafting broken,
Or a mistaken signal, the flange lifting –
Would that be premature, a text for sorrow?

Say what endurance gives or death denies us.
Love's proved in its creation, not eternity:
Like leaf or linnet the true heart's affection
Is born, dies later, asks no reassurance.

Over dark wood rises one dawn felicitous,
Bright through awakened shadows fall her crystal
Cadenzas, and once for all the wood is quickened.
So our joys visit us, and it suffices.

Nor fear we now to live who in the valley
Of the shadow of life have found a causeway;
For love restores the nerve and love is under
Our feet resilient. Shall we be weary?

Some say we walk out of Time altogether
This way into a region where the primrose
Shows an immortal dew, sun at meridian
Stands up for ever and in scent the lime tree.

This is a land which later we may tell of.
Here-now we know, what death cannot diminish
Needs no replenishing; yet certain are, though
Dying were well enough, to live is better.

Passion has grown full man by his first birthday.
Running across the bean-fields in a south wind,
Fording the river mouth to feel the tide-race —
Child's play that was, though proof of our possessions.

Now our research is done, measured the shadow,
The plains mapped out, the hills a natural boundary.
Such and such is our country. There remains to
Plough up the meadowland, reclaim the marshes.

2

Let's leave this town. Mutters of loom
Nor winding gear disturb
The flat and residential air —
A city all suburb.

Go not this road, for arc-lamps cramp
The dawn; sense fears to take
A mortal step, and body obeys
An automatic brake.

Ah, leave the wall-eyed town, and come
Where heaven keeps open house;
Watch not the markets but the stars;
Get shares of gilt-edged space.

For what we have in hand is no
Business of shop and street.
This is our strait, our Little Minch
Where wind and tide meet.

You are the tides running for ever
Along their ancient groove:
Such winds am I, pause not for breath
And to fresh shores will move.

3

Back to the countryside
That will not lose its pride
When the green flags of summer all are taken,
Having no mind to force
The seasons from their course
And no remorse for a front line forsaken.

Look how the athletic field
His flowery vest has peeled
To wrestle another fall with rain and sleet.
The rock will not relent
Nor desperate earth consent
Till the spent winter blows his long retreat.

Come, autumn, use the spur!
Let us not still defer
To drive slow furrows in the impatient soil:
Persuade us now these last
Silk summer shreds to cast
And fasten on the harsh habit of toil.

The swallows are all gone
Into the rising sun.
You leave tonight for the Americas.
Under the dropping days
Alone the labourer stays
And says that winter will be slow to pass.

4

Come on, the wind is whirling our summer away,
And air grows dizzy with leaves.
It is time to lay up for a winter day,
Conserve earth's infant energy, water's play,
Bind the sun down in sheaves.

Contact of sun and earth loads granary;
Stream's frolic will grind flour;
Tree's none the worse for fruit. Shall we
Insulate our strong currents of ecstasy
Or breed units of power?

Bodies we have, fabric and frame designed
To take the stress of love,
Buoyant on gust, multi-engined.
Experiment's over. We must up and find
What trade-routes are above.

This is no pleasure trip. We carry freight
To a certain end; not whirled
Past earth's pull, nosing at no star's gate.
We'll have fresh air; will serve, perhaps, the state;
Surely, enlarge our world.

Or, think. Tightens the darkness, the rails thrum
For night express is due.
Glory of steam and steel strikes dumb;
Sense sucked away swirls in the vacuum.
So passion passes through.

Here is love's junction, no terminus.
He arrives at girl or boy.
Signal a clear line and let us
Give him the run of life: we shall get thus
A record of our joy.

5

Beauty's end is in sight,
Terminus where all feather joys alight.
Wings that flew lightly
Fold and are iron. We see
The thin end of mortality.

We must a little part,
And sprouting seed crack our cemented heart.
Who would get an heir
Initial loss must bear:
A part of each will be elsewhere.

What life may now decide
Is past the clutch of caution, the range of pride.
Speaking from the snow
The crocus lets me know
That there is life to come, and go.

6

Now she is like the white tree-rose
That takes a blessing from the sun:
Summer has filled her veins with light,
And her warm heart is washed with noon.

Or as a poplar, ceaselessly
Gives a soft answer to the wind:
Cool on the light her leaves lie sleeping,
Folding a column of sweet sound.

Powder the stars. Forbid the night
To wear those brilliants for a brooch
So soon, dark death, you may close down
The mines that made this beauty rich.

Her thoughts are pleiads, stooping low
O'er glades where nightingale has flown:
And like the luminous night around her
She has at heart a certain dawn.

7

Rest from loving and be living.
Fallen is fallen past retrieving
The unique flyer dawn's dove
Arrowing down feathered with fire.

Cease denying, begin knowing.
Comes peace this way here comes renewing
With dower of bird and bud knocks
Loud on winter wall on death's door.

Here's no meaning but of morning.
Naught soon of night but stars remaining,
Sink lower, fade, as dark womb
Recedes creation will step clear.

8

HE We whom a full tornado cast up high,
    Two years marooned on self-sufficiency,
    Kissing on an island out of the trade-routes
    Nor glancing at horizon, – we'll not dare
    Outstay the welcome of our tropic sun.

SHE Here is the dark Interior, noon yet high,
    Light to work by and a sufficiency
    Of timber. Build then. We may reach the trade-routes
    We'll take the winds at their word; yes, will dare
    Wave's curling lip, the hot looks of the sun.

HE Hull is finished. Now must the foraging eye
Take in provisions for a long journey:
Put by our summertime, the fruits, the sweet roots,
The virgin spring moss-shadowed near the shore,
And over idle sands the halcyon.

SHE No mark out there, no mainland meets the eye.
Horizon gapes; and yet must we journey
Beyond the bays of peace, pull up our sweet roots,
Cut the last cord links us to native shore,
Toil on waters too troubled for the halcyon.

BOTH Though we strike a new continent, it shall be
Our islet; a new world, our colony.
If we miss land, no matter. We've a stout boat
Provisioned for some years: we need endure
No further ill than to be still alone.

9

Waning is now the sensual eye
Allowed no flaw upon the skin
And burnt away wrinkle and feature,
Fed with pure spirit from within.

Nesciently that vision works.
Just so the pure night-eye, the moon,
Labours, a monumental mason,
To gloss over a world of stone.

Look how she marbled heath and terrace,
Effacing boundary and date.
She took the sky; earth was below her
A shining shell, a featherweight.

No more may pupil love bend over
A plane theorem, black and white.
The interlocking hours revolve,
The globe goes lumbering into light.

Admiral earth breaks out his colours
Bright at the forepeak of the day;
Hills in their hosts escort the sun
And valleys welcome him their way.

Shadow takes depth and shape turns solid:
Far-ranging, the creative eye
Sees arable, marsh, enclosed and common,
Assents to multiplicity.

10

Twenty weeks near past
Since the seed took to earth.
Winter has done his worst.
Let upland snow ignore;
Earth wears a smile betrays
What summer she has in store.
She feels insurgent forces
Gathering at the core,
And a spring rumour courses
Through her, till the cold extreme
Sleep of grove and grass is
Stirred, begins to dream.
So, when the violins gather
And soar to a final theme,
Broadcast on winds of ether
That golden seed extends
Beneath the sun-eye, the father,
To ear at the earth's ends.

11

There is a dark room,
The locked and shuttered womb,
Where negative's made positive.
Another dark room,
The blind, the bolted tomb,
Where positives change to negative.

We may not undo
That or escape this, who
Have birth and death coiled in our bones.
Nothing we can do
Will sweeten the real rue,
That we begin, and end, with groans.

12

As one who wanders into old workings
Dazed by the noonday, desiring coolness,
Has found retreat barred by fall of rockface;
Gropes through galleries where granite bruises
Taut palm and panic patters close at heel;
Must move forward as tide to the moon's nod,
As mouth to breast in blindness is beckoned.
Nightmare nags at his elbow and narrows
Horizon to pinpoint, hope to hand's breadth.
Slow drip the seconds, time is stalactite,
For nothing intrudes here to tell the time,
Sun marches not, nor moon with muffled step.
He wants an opening, – only to break out,
To see the dark glass cut by day's diamond,
To relax again in the lap of light.

But we seek a new world through old workings,
Whose hope lies like seed in the loins of earth,

Whose dawn draws gold from the roots of darkness.
Not shy of light nor shrinking from shadow
Like Jesuits in jungle we journey
Deliberately bearing to brutish tribes
Christ's assurance, arts of agriculture.
As a train that travels underground track
Feels current flashed from far-off dynamos,
Our wheels whirling with impetus elsewhere
Generated we run, are ruled by rails.
Train shall spring from tunnel to terminus,
Out on to plain shall the pioneer plunge,
Earth reveal what veins fed, what hill covered.
Lovely the leap, explosion into light.

13

But think of passion and pain.
Those absolute dictators will enchain
The low, exile the princely parts:
They close a door between the closest hearts:
Their verdict stands in steel,
From whose blank rigour kings may not appeal.

When in love's airs we'd lie,
Like elms we leaned together with a sigh
And sighing severed, and no rest
Had till that wind was past:
Then drooped in a green sickness over the plain
Wanting our wind again.

Now pain will come for you,
Take you into a desert without dew,
Labouring through the unshadowed day
To blast the sharp scarps, open up a way
There for the future line.
But I shall wait afar off and alone.

Small comfort may be found,
Though our embraced roots grope in the same ground;
Though on one permanent way we run,
Yes, under the same sun.
Contact the means, but travellers report
The ends are poles apart.

14

Now the full-throated daffodils,
Our trumpeters in gold,
Call resurrection from the ground
And bid the year be bold.

Today the almond tree turns pink,
The first flush of the spring;
Winds loll and gossip through the town
Her secret whispering.

Now too the bird must try his voice
Upon the morning air;
Down drowsy avenues he cries
A novel great affair.

He tells of royalty to be;
How with her train of rose
Summer to coronation comes
Through waving wild hedgerows.

Today crowds quicken in a street,
The fish leaps in the flood:
Look there, gasometer rises,
And here bough swells to bud.

For our love's luck, our stowaway,
Stretches in his cabin;
Our youngster joy barely conceived
Shows up beneath the skin.

Our joy was but a gusty thing
Without sinew or wit,
An infant flyaway; but now
We make a man of it.

15

I have come so far upon my journey.
This is the frontier, this is where I change,
And wait between two worlds to take refreshment.
    I see the mating plover at play
Blowing themselves about over the green wheat,
And in a bank I catch
The shy scent of the primrose that prevails
Strangely upon the heart. Here is
The last flutter of the wind-errant soul,
Earth's first faint tug at the earthbound soul.
    So, waiting here between winter and summer,
Conception and fruition, I
Take what refreshment may be had from skies
Uncertain as the wind, prepare
For a new route, a change of constitution.

Some change of constitution, where
Has been for years an indeterminate quarrel
Between a fevered head and a cold heart;
Rulers who cannot rule, rebels who will not
Rebel; an age divided
Between tomorrow's wink, yesterday's warning.
    And yet this self, contains
Tides continents and stars – a myriad selves,
Is small and solitary as one grass-blade
Passed over by the wind
Amongst a myriad grasses on the prairie.
    You in there, my son, my daughter,
Will you become dictator, resolve the factions?
Will you be my ambassador
And make my peace with the adjacent empires?

16

More than all else might you,
My son, my daughter,
Be metal to bore through
The impermeable clay
And rock that overlay
The living water.

Through that artesian well
Myself may out,
Finding its own level.
This way the waste land turns
To arable, and towns
Are rid of drought.

17

Down hidden causeways of the universe
Through space-time's cold
Indifferent airs I strolled,
A pointless star: till in my course
I happened on the sun
And in a spurt of fire to her did run.

That heavenly body as I neared began
To make response,
And heaved with fire at once.
One wave of gathered heat o'er-ran
Her all and came to a head,
A mountain based upon an ardent bed.

(Faith may move mountains; but love's twice as strong,
For love can raise
A mountain where none was:
Also can prove astronomers wrong
Who deem the stars too hot
For life: – here is a star that has begot.)

Soon from the mother body torn and whirled
By tidal pull
And left in space to cool
That mountain top will be a world
Treading its own orbit,
And look to her for warmth, to me for wit.

18

It is time to think of you,
Shortly will have your freedom.
As anemones that renew
Earth's innocence, be welcome.
Out of your folded sleep
Come, as the western winds come
To pasture with the sheep
On a weary of winter height.
Lie like a pool unwrinkled
That takes the sky to heart,
Where stars and shadows are mingled
And suns run gold with heat.
Return as the winds return,
Heir to an old estate
Of upland, flower and tarn.

But born to essential dark,
To an age that toes the line
And never o'ersteps the mark.
Take off your coat: grow lean:
Suffer humiliation:
Patrol the passes alone,
And eat your iron ration.
Else, wag as the world wags –
One more mechanical jane
Or gentleman in wax.
Is it here we shall regain

Championship? Here awakes
A white hope shall preserve
From flatterers, pimps and fakes
Integrity and nerve?

19

Do not expect again a phœnix hour,
The triple-towered sky, the dove complaining,
Sudden the rain of gold and heart's first ease
Tranced under trees by the eldritch light of sundown.

By a blazed trail our joy will be returning:
One burning hour throws light a thousand ways,
And hot blood stays into familiar gestures.
The best years wait, the body's plenitude.

Consider then, my lover, this is the end
Of the lark's ascending, the hawk's unearthly hover:
Spring season is over soon and first heatwave;
Grave-browed with cloud ponders the huge horizon.

Draw up the dew. Swell with pacific violence.
Take shape in silence. Grow as the clouds grew.
Beautiful brood the cornlands, and you are heavy;
Leafy the boughs – they also hide big fruit.

20

Sky-wide an estuary of light
Ebbs amid cloud-banks out of sight.
At her star-anchorage shall swing
Earth, the old freighter, till morning.

Ride above your shadow and trim
Cargo till the stars grow dim:
Weigh then from the windless river;
You've a treasure to deliver.

Behold the incalculable seas
Change face for every cloud and breeze:
But a prime mover works inside,
The constant the integral tide.

Though black-bordered fancies vex
You and veering moods perplex,
Underneath's a current knowing
Well enough what way it's going.

Stroked by their windy shadows lie
The grainlands waving at the sky.
That golden grace must all be shed
To fill granaries, to make bread.

Do not grieve for beauty gone.
Limbs that ran to meet the sun
Lend their lightness to another;
Child shall recreate the mother.

21

Your eyes are not open. You are alone.
You then, to be my first-born, this is for you.
    May know, as I, sleet from a bland sky falling,
Perfidious landmark, false dawn:
Look out through panes at a spoilt holiday,
And weep, taking eternity to bed.
    When the hair grows, perceive a world
Officered by semi-cads and second baboons,
Be stood in the far corner.
    Later, after each dream of beauty ethereal,
Bicycling against wind to see the vicar's daughter,
Be disappointed.
    And yet there is yet worse to come:
Desire worn to the bone leaves room for pride's attrition.
For they shall ride in bloody uniform,

Offering choice of a sooner death or a later;
Mark you to ground, stop the earths,
Jog home to supper under a bland sky.
    Yes, you may know, as I do, self foreshortened,
Blocked out with blackness finally all the works of days.
O you who turn the wheel and look to both sides,
Consider Phlebas, who shall be taller and handsomer than you.
    One shall rub shoulders with the firmfoot oak
And with all shifting shade join hands:
Shall have the heels of time, shall shoot from afar
And find the loopholes of the armoured train.
    When the machine's run in, will get
Free play, better no doubt for the contracting
Of an indeterminate world.
    Day and night will make armistice for this one,
Entering the walled garden who knows the hour of spirit
Reconciled to flesh.
    Then falling leaf falls to renew
Acquaintance with old contours, with a world in outline.
Is time now to set house in order, bury
The dead and count the living, consolidate
The soul against proved enemies:
Time with the lengthening shadow to grow tall.
    Thus the free spirit emerges, in courts at ease,
Content with standing-room, pleased in a small allotment.

22

In this sector when barrage lifts and we
Are left alone with death,
There'll be no time to question strategy.
But now, midsummer offensive not begun,
We wait and draw mutinous breath,
Wondering what to gain
We stake these fallow fields and the good sun.

This has happened to other men before,
Have hung on the lip of danger
And have heard death moving about next door.
Yet I look up at the sky's billowing,
Surprised to find so little change there,
Though in that ample ring
Heaven knows what power lies coiled ready to spring.

What were we at, the moment when we kissed –
Extending the franchise
To an indifferent class, would we enlist
Fresh power who know not how to be so great?
Beget and breed a life – what's this
But to perpetuate
Man's labour, to enlarge a rank estate?

Planted out here some virtue still may flower,
But our dead follies too –
A shock of buried weeds to turn it sour.
Draw up conditions – will the heir conform?
Or thank us for the favour, who
Inherits a bankrupt firm,
Worn-out machinery, an exhausted farm?

23

This was not the mind's undertaking,
But as outrageous heat
Breaking in thunder across hills
Sweetens our aching dust.

Such is not answerable to mind,
Is random as a flake
Blindly down-dancing here or clouds
That take their windy course.

Thin from thin air reason issues;
We live on living earth
Whose trees enlarge their fruit without
Misgiving or excuse.

Reason is but a riddle of sand;
Its substance shifts in storm.
Space-spanned, God-girdled, love will keep
Its form, being planned of bone.

24

Speak then of constancy. Thin eyelids weakly thus
Batted to beauty, lips that reject her, is not this;
Nor lust of eye (Christ said it) denied the final kiss.

Rather a set response, metal-to-magnet affair;
Flows with the tidal blood, like red of rose or fire
Is a fast dye outlasts the fabric of desire.

Happy this river reach sleeps with the sun at noon,
Takes dews and rains to her wide bed, refusing none
That full-filled peace, yet constant to one sea will run.

So melt we down small toys to make each other rich,
Although no getting or spending can extend our reach
Whose poles are love, nor close who closer lie than leech.

For think – throbbing our hearts linked so by endless band,
So geared together, need not otherwise be bound.

25

And since, though young, I know
Not to expect much good,
Our dreams from first to last
Being treacherous underfoot;

Best I dare wish for you,
That once (my son, my daughter)
You may get home on rock
Feet tired of treading water.

Lucky, will have also
An outward grace to ease
The axles of your world
And keep the parts at peace:

Not the waste random stuff
That stops the gannet's wing;
I mean, such oil ensures
A turbine's smooth running.

26

Beauty breaks ground, oh, in strange places.
Seen after cloudburst down the bone-dry watercourses,
In Texas a great gusher, a grain-
Elevator in the Ukraine plain;
To a new generation turns new faces.

Here too fountains will soon be flowing.
Empty the hills where love was lying late, was playing,
Shall spring to life: we shall find there
Milk and honey for love's heir,
Shadow from sun also, deep ground for growing.

My love is a good land. The stranger
Entering here was sure he need prospect no further.
Acres that were the eyes' delight
Now feed another appetite.
What formed her first for seed, for crop must change her.

This is my land. I've overheard it
Making a promise out of clay. All is recorded –
Early green, drought, ripeness, rainfall,
Our village fears and festivals,
When the first tractor came and how we cheered it.

And as the wind whose note will deepen
In the upgrowing tree, who runs for miles to open
His throat above the wood, my song
With that increasing life grew strong,
And will have there a finished form to sleep in.

27

Dropping the few last days, are drops of lead,
Heavier hang than a lifetime on the heart.
Past the limetrees that drug the air jackdaws
Slanting across a sluggish wind go home:
On either side of the Saltway fields of clover
Cling to their sweetness under a threatening sky.
Numb with crisis all, cramped with waiting.
Shallowly breathes the wind or holds his breath,
As in ambush waiting to leap at convoy
Must pass this way – there can be no evasions.
Surly the sky up there and means mischief;
The parchment sky that hourly tightens above us,
Screwed to storm-pitch, where thunder shall roll and roll
Intolerably postponing the last movement.

Now the young challenger, too tired to sidestep,
Hunches to give or take decisive blow.
The climbers from the highest camp set out
Saying goodbye to comrades on the glacier,
A day of rock between them and the summit
That will require their record or their bones.
Now is a charge laid that will split the hill-face,

Tested the wires, the plunger ready to hand.
For time ticks nearer to a rebel hour,
Charging of barricades, bloodshed in city:
The watcher in the window looking out
At the eleventh hour on sun and shadow,
On fixed abodes and the bright air between,
Knows for the first time what he stands to lose.

Crisis afar deadens the nerve, it cools
The blood and hoods imagination's eye,
Whether we apprehend it or remember.
Is fighting on the frontier: little leaks through
Of possible disaster, but one morning
Shells begin to drop in the capital.
So I, indoors for long enough remembering
The round house on the cliff, the springy slopes,
The well in the wood, nor doubting to revisit
But if to see new sunlight on old haunts
Swallows and men come back *but if* come back
From lands *but if* beyond our view *but if*
She dies? Why then, here is a space to let,
The owner gone abroad, never returning.

28

Though bodies are apart
The dark hours so confine
And fuse our hearts, sure, death
Will find no way between.

Narrow this hour, that bed;
But room for us to explore
Pain's long-drawn equator,
The farthest ice of fear.

74

Storm passes east, recurs:
The beaked lightnings stoop:
The sky falls down: the clouds
Are wrung to the last drop.

Another day is born now.
Woman, your work is done.
This is the end of labour.
Come out into the sun!

29

Come out in the sun, for a man is born today!
Early this morning whistle in the cutting told
Train was arriving, hours overdue, delayed
By snow-drifts, engine-trouble, Act of God, who cares now? –
For here alights the distinguished passenger.
Take a whole holiday in honour of this!

Kipfer's back from heaven, Bendien to Holland,
Larwood and Voce in the Notts eleven.
Returning also the father the mother,
Chastened and cheered by underworld excursion,
Alive returning from the black country,
Take a whole holiday in honour of this.

Now shall the airman vertically banking
Out of the blue write a new sky-sign;
The nine tramp steamers rusting in the estuary
Get up full pressure for a trade revival;
The crusty landlord renew the lease, and everyone
Take a whole holiday in honour of this.

Today let director forget the deficit,
Schoolmaster his handicap, hostess her false face:
Let phantasist take charge of flesh-and-blood situation,
Petty-officer be rapt in the Seventh Symphony.
For here a champion is born and commands you
Take a whole holiday in honour of this.

Wherever radiance from ashes arises –
Willowherb glowing on abandoned slagheaps,
Dawn budding scarlet in a bed of darkness,
Life from exhausted womb outstriving –
There shall the spirit be lightened and gratefully
Take a whole holiday in honour of this.

EPILOGUE

LETTER TO W. H. AUDEN

A mole first, out of riddling passages
You came up for a breather into my field,
Then back to your engineering; a scheme conjectured
From evidence of earth not cast at random.
The surly vegetable said 'What's this
Butting through sand for unapparent reasons?'
The animal said 'This fellow is no runner.'
Mineral said 'Brother, you like the dark.'
What are you at down there, nosing among
Saxon skulls, roots of our genealogies?
This is the field of ghosts. There are no clues here;
But dead creators packed in close fibre.
Perhaps you are going straight to some point, straighter
And further than these furrows I drive in daylight.

Daffodils now, the pretty debutantes,
Are curtsying at the first court of the year:
Their schoolgirl smell unmans young lechers. You
Preferred, I remember, the plump boy, the crocus.
Enough of that. They only lie at your feet.
But I, who saw the sapling, prophesied
A growth superlative and branches writing
On heaven a new signature. For I
Looked at no garden shrub, chantry of thrushes;
But such a tree as, gripping its rock perch
On a northern fell within the sound of hammers,
Gives shadow to the stonechat and reminder
Of chastity to men: grown venerable
Will give its name to that part of the country.
This was the second time that you had pulled
The rusty trigger summoning the stragglers.
Once more the bird goes packing, the skeleton
Sets teeth against a further dissolution.
And what have we to hope for who are bound,
Though we strip off the last assurance of flesh
For expedition, to lay our bones somewhere?
Say that a rescue party should see fit
To do us some honour, publish our diaries,
Send home the relics – how should we thank them?
The march is what we asked for; it is ended.
Still, let us wear the flesh away and leave
Nothing for birds, anatomy to men.

THE MAGNETIC MOUNTAIN

To W. H. Auden

The Magnetic Mountain

Part One

Come, then, companions, this is the spring of blood,
Heart's heyday, movement of masses, beginning of good.

R. E. WARNER

1

Now to be with you, elate, unshared,
My kestrel joy, O hoverer in wind,
Over the quarry furiously at rest
Chaired on shoulders of shouting wind.

Where's that unique one, wind and wing married,
Aloft in contact of earth and ether;
Feathery my comet, Oh too often
From heaven harried by carrion cares.

No searcher may hope to flush that fleet one
Not to be found by gun or glass,
In old habits, last year's hunting-ground,
Whose beat is wind-wide, whose perch a split second.

But surely will meet him, late or soon,
Who turns a corner into new territory;
Spirit mating afresh shall discern him
On the world's noon-top purely poised.

Void are the valleys, in town no trace,
And dumb the sky-dividing hills:
Swift outrider of lumbering earth
Oh hasten hither my kestrel joy!

2

But Two there are, shadow us everywhere
And will not let us be till we are dead,
Hardening the bones, keeping the spirit spare,
Original in water, earth and air,
Our bitter cordial, our daily bread.

Turning over old follies in ante-room,
For first-born waiting or for late reprieve,
Watching the safety-valve, the slackening loom,
Abed, abroad, at every turn and tomb
A shadow starts, a hand is on your sleeve.

O you, my comrade, now or tomorrow flayed
Alive, crazed by the nibbling nerve; my friend
Whom hate has cornered or whom love betrayed,
By hunger sapped, trapped by a stealthy tide,
Brave for so long but whimpering in the end:

Such are the temporal princes, fear and pain,
Whose borders march with the ice-fields of death,
And from that servitude escape there's none
Till in the grave we set up house alone
And buy our liberty with our last breath.

3

Somewhere beyond the railheads
Of reason, south or north,
Lies a magnetic mountain
Riveting sky to earth.

No line is laid so far.
Ties rusting in a stack
And sleepers – dead men's bones –
Mark a defeated track.

Kestrel who yearly changes
His tenement of space
At the last hovering
May signify that place.

Iron in the soul,
Spirit steeled in fire,
Needle trembling on truth –
These shall draw me there.

The planets keep their course,
Blindly the bee comes home,
And I shall need no sextant
To prove I'm getting warm.

Near that miraculous mountain
Compass and clock must fail,
For space stands on its head there
And time chases its tail.

There's iron for the asking
Will keep all winds at bay,
Girders to take the leaden
Strain of a sagging sky.

Oh there's a mine of metal,
Enough to make me rich
And build right over chaos
A cantilever bridge.

4

Make no mistake, this is where you get off,
Sue with her suckling, Cyril with his cough,
Bert with a blazer and a safety razor,
Old John Braddleum and Terence the toff.

And now, may I ask, have you made any plans?
You can't go further along these lines;
Positively this is the end of the track;
It's rather late and there's no train back.
So if you are wanting to get anywhere
You must use your feet or take to the air,
The penny-a-liner, the seven-course-diner,
Prebendary Cute and the water-diviner –
Are you sure you don't want to go somewhere?
'Is it mountain there or mirage across the sand?'
That's Terra Incognita, Bogey-Man's-Land:
Why not give it a trial? You might go further
And fare much worse. 'No, no, that's going rather
Too far; besides, the whole thing may just be a sell.'
Then book your bed-sitter at the station hotel
Or stay at the terminus till you grow verminous,
Eating chocolate creams from the slot-machines;
But don't blame me when you feel unwell.
Line was a good line, ballasted on grit,
Surveyors weren't fools, platelayers didn't quit,
Viaduct for river, embankment for marsh,
Cutting for tough rock, signal for smash.
Can you keep the system going? Can you replace
Rolling stock? Is everything all right at the base?
Supposing they cut your communications
Can you live on here without any rations?
Then don't blame me when you're up the tree,
No trains coming through and you're feeling blue,
When you're left high and dry and you want to cry,
When you're in the cart and you've got a weak heart,
When you're up the pole and you can't find your soul,
When the shops are all looted and you've run out of coal.
   So it's me for the mountain. But before I begin
I'm taking a light engine back along the line
For a last excursion, a tour of inspection,
To clear the head and to aid the digestion.

Then I'll hit the trail for that promising land;
May catch up with Wystan and Rex my friend,
Go mad in good company, find a good country,
Make a clean sweep or make a clean end.

5

Let us be off! Our steam
Is deafening the dome.
The needle in the gauge
Points to a long-banked rage,
And trembles there to show
What a pressure's below.
Valve cannot vent the strain
Nor iron ribs refrain
That furnace in the heart.
Come on, make haste and start
Coupling-rod and wheel
Welded of patient steel,
Piston that will not stir
Beyond the cylinder
To take in its stride
A teeming countryside.

A countryside that gleams
In the sun's weeping beams;
Where wind-pump, byre and barrow
Are mellowed to mild sorrow,
Agony and sweat
Grown over with regret.
What golden vesper hours
Halo the old grey towers,
What honeyed bells in valleys
Embalm our faiths and follies!
Here are young daffodils
Wind-wanton, and the hills

Have made their peace with heaven.
Oh lovely the heart's haven,
Meadows of endless May,
A spirit's holiday!

Traveller, take care,
Pick no flowers there!

Part Two

Drive your cart and your plough over the bones of the dead.
WILLIAM BLAKE

6

Nearing again the legendary isle
Where sirens sang and mariners were skinned,
We wonder now what was there to beguile
That such stout fellows left their bones behind.

Those chorus-girls are surely past their prime,
Voices grow shrill and paint is wearing thin,
Lips that sealed up the sense from gnawing time
Now beg the favour with a graveyard grin.

We have no flesh to spare and they can't bite,
Hunger and sweat have stripped us to the bone;
A skeleton crew we toil upon the tide
And mock the theme-song meant to lure us on:

No need to stop the ears, avert the eyes
From purple rhetoric of evening skies.

7

First Defendant speaks
I that was two am one,
We that were one are two.

Warm in my walled garden the flower grew first,
Transplanted it ran wild on the estate.
Why should it ever need a new sun?
Not navel-string in the cold dawn cut,
Nor a weaned appetite, nor going to school
That autumn did it. Simply, one day
He crossed the frontier and I did not follow:
Returning, spoke another language.
Blessed are they that mourn,
That shear the spring grass from an early grave:
They are not losers, never have known the hour
When an indifferent exile
Passes through the metropolis *en route*
For Newfoundland.

   Mother earth, understand me. You send up
So many leaves to meet the light,
So many flights of birds,
That keep you all their days in shade and song;
And the blown leaf is part of you again
And the frozen blackbird falls into your breast.
Shall not the life-giver be life-receiver?
Am I alone to stand
Outside the natural economy?
Pasteurize mother's milk,
Spoon out the waters of comfort in kilogrammes,
Let love be clinic, let creation's pulse
Keep Greenwich time, guard creature
Against creator, and breed your supermen!
But not from me: for I
Must have life unconditional, or none.
So, like a willow, all its wood curtailed,
I stand by the last ditch of narrowing world,
And stir not, though I see
Pit-heads encroach or glacier crawl down.

8

This was your world and this I owe you,
Room for growing, a site for building,
The braced sinew, the hands agreeing,
Mind foreseeing and nerve for facing.
You were my world my breath my seasons
Where blood ran easy and springs failed not,
Kind was clover to feet exploring
A broad earth and all to discover.
Simple that world, of two dimensions,
Of stone mansions and good examples;
Each image actual, nearness was no
Fear and distance without a mirage.
Dawn like a greyhound leapt the hill-tops,
A million leaves held up the noonday,
Evening was slow with bells pealing,
And night compelling to breast and pillow.
This was my world, Oh this you gave me,
Safety for seed, petal uncurled there;
Love asked no proving nor price, a country
Sunny for play, for spring manœuvres.

Woman, ask no more of me;
Chill not the blood with jealous feud:
This is a separate country now,
Will pay respects but no tribute.
Demand no atavistic rites,
Preference in trade or tithe of grain;
Bound by the limiting matrix I
Increased you once, will not again.
My vision's patented, my plant
Set up, my constitution whole;
New fears, old tunes cannot induce
Nostalgia of the sickly soul.
Would you prolong your day, transfuse
Young blood into your veins? Beware

Lest one oppressed by autumn's weight
May thrill to feel death in the air.
Let love be like a natural day
That folds her work and takes to bed;
Ploughland and tree stand out in black,
Enough memorial for the dead.

9

Second Defendant speaks
Let us now praise famous men,
Not your earth-shakers, not the dynamiters,
But who in the Home Counties or the Khyber,
Trimming their nails to meet an ill wind,
Facing the Adversary with a clean collar,
Justified the system.
Admire the venerable pile that bred them,
Bones are its foundations,
The pinnacles are stone abstractions,
Whose halls are whispering-galleries designed
To echo voices of the past, dead tongues.
White hopes of England here
Are taught to rule by learning to obey,
Bend over before vested interests,
Kiss the rod, salute the quarter-deck;
Here is no savage discipline
Of peregrine swooping, of fire destroying,
But a civil code; no capital offender
But the cool cad, the man who goes too far.
Ours the curriculum
Neither of building birds nor wasteful waters,
Bound in book not violent in vein:
Here we inoculate with dead ideas
Against blood-epidemics, against
The infection of faith and the excess of life.
Our methods are up to date; we teach
Through head and not by heart,

Language with gramophones and sex with charts,
Prophecy by deduction, prayer by numbers.
For honours see prospectus: those who leave us
Will get a post and pity the poor;
Their eyes glaze at strangeness;
They are never embarrassed, have a word for every-
                         thing,
Living on credit, dying when the heart stops;
Will wear black armlets and stand a moment in silence
For the passing of an era, at their own funeral.

10

You'll be leaving soon and it's up to you, boys,
Which shall it be? You must make your choice.
There's a war on, you know. Will you take your stand
In obsolete forts or in no-man's-land?
That ancestral castle, that picturesque prestige
Looks well on paper but will it stand a siege?
All modern conveniences – still, I should change
Position now the enemy knows the range.
Blockade may begin before you're much older –
Will you tighten the belt and shrug the shoulder
Or plough up the playing-fields, sow new soil,
Build a reservoir and bore for oil?
'Take a sporting chance', they tell you. But will it suffice
To wear a scrum-cap against falling skies?
'Play the game': but supposing the other chap kicks,
You'd like to have learnt some rough-house tricks.
It boils down to this – do you really want to win
Or prefer the fine gesture of giving in?
Are you going to keep or to make the rules,
Die with fighters or be dead with fools?
Men are wanted who will volunteer
To go aloft and cut away tangled gear;
Break through to blocked galleries below pit-head,
Get in touch with living and raise from the dead:

Men to catch spies, fly aeroplanes,
Harrow derelict acres and mend the drains.
There'll be work for you all if you're fain without
                                  feigning
To give up toys and go into training.
But you'll have to forget a great deal you've learnt,
The licence of Saturn, lacerations of Lent,
Self-abuse, your dignity, the Bad and the Good,
Heroism in phantasy and fainting at blood.
And you'll have to remember a great deal you've forgotten,
How to love a girl and how to sew a button,
Tiger's shock-tactics, elephant's defence,
The integral spirit and the communal sense.
Can you sing at your work? Enforce discipline
Without insignia? Then you've still a chance to win.

11

Third Defendant speaks
I have always acted for the best.
My business is the soul: I have given it rope,
Coaxed it heavenward, but would not let it escape me.
The peoples have sought a Ruler:
I conjured one for each after his own image;
For savage a Dark Demon, for Hebrew a Patriot,
For Christian a Comforter, for atheist a Myth.
The rulers have sought an Ally:
I have called down thunders on the side of authority,
Lightnings to galvanize the law;
Promising the bread of heaven to the hungry of earth,
Shunting the spirit into grassy sidings,
I have served the temporal princes.
There have been men ere now, disturbers of the peace,
Leaders out of my land of milk and honey,
Prescribing harder diet;
Whom I thrashed, outlawed, slew, or if persisting

Deified, shelving them and their dynamite doctrines
Up in the clouds out of the reach of children.
I have always acted for the best:
Hung on the skirts of progress, the tail of revolution,
Ready to drug the defeated and bless the victor.
I am a man apart
Who sits in the dark professing a revelation:
Exploiting the Word with the letter I turn
Joy into sacraments, the Holy Ghost to a formula.
But an impious generation is here,
Let in the light, melt down my mysteries,
Commission the moon to serve my altars
And make my colleagues village entertainers.
That tree of Grace, for years I have tended,
Is a slow-grower, not to be transplanted,
They'll cut it down for pit-props;
That harvest of Faith, not without blood ripened,
They have ploughed in; their dynamos chant
Canticles of a new power: my holy land is blasted,
The crust crumbles, the veins run vinegar.

12

Oh subterranean fires, break out!
Tornadoes, pity not
The petty bourgeois of the soul,
The middleman of God!

Who ruins farm and factory
To keep a private mansion
Is a bad landlord, he shall get
No honourable mention.

Who mobbed the kestrel out of the air,
Who made the tiger tame,
Who lost the blood's inheritance
And found the body's shame;

Who raised his hands to brand a Cain
And bless a submarine—
Time is up: the medicine-man
Must take his medicine.

The winter evening holds her peace
And makes a crystal pause;
Frozen are all the streams of light,
Silent about their source.

Comrade, let us look to earth,
Be stubborn, act and sleep:
Here at our feet the lasting skull
Keeps a stiff upper lip:

Feeling the weight of a long winter,
Grimaces underground;
But never again will need to ask
Why spirit was flesh-bound.

And we whom winter days oppress
May find some work to hand,
Perfect our plans, renew parts,
Break hedges down, plough land.

So when primroses pave the way
And the sun warms the stone,
We may receive the exile spirit
Coming into its own.

13

Fourth Defendant speaks
To sit at head of one's own table,
To overlook a warm familiar landscape,
Have large cupboards for small responsibilities –

Surely that does outweigh
The rent veil and the agonies to follow?
Me the Almighty fixed, from Eve fallen,
Heart-deep in earth, a pointer to star fields,
Suffering sapflow, fruitage, early barrenness;
Changeable reputed, but to change constant,
Fickle of fashion no more than the months are;
Daily depend on surroundings for sustenance,
On what my roots reach, what my leaves inhale here.
Grant me a rich ground, wrapped in airs temperate,
Not where nor'-easters threaten the flint scarps;
Consequence then shall I have, men's admiration
Now, and my bones shall be fuel for the future.
Yet have I always failed.
For he, who should have been my prime possession,
Was not to be possessed.
I leant o'er him, a firmament of shadow,
But he looked up through me and saw the stars.
I would have bound him in the earth-ways,
Fluid, immediate, the child of nature.
But he made bricks of earth, iron from fire,
Turned waves to power, winds to communication;
Setting up Art against Chaos, subjecting
My flux to the synthetic frost of reason.
I am left with a prone man,
Virtue gone out of him; who in the morning
Will rise to join Crusades or assist the Harlequins.
Though I persuade him that his stars are mine eyes'
Refraction, that wisdom's best expressed in
The passive mood, – here's no change for the better:
I was the body's slave, am now the spirit's.
Come, let me contemplate my own
Mysteries, a dark glass may save my face.

Live you by love confined,
There is no nearer nearness;
Break not his light bounds,
The stars' and seas' harness:
There is nothing beyond,
We have found the land's end.
We'll take no mortal wound
Who felt him in the furnace,
Drowned in his fierceness,
By his midsummer browned:
Nor ever lose awareness
Of nearness and farness
Who've stood at earth's heart careless
Of suns and storms around,
Who have leant on the hedge of the wind,
On the last ledge of darkness.

We are where love has come
To live: he is that river
Which flows and is the same;
He is not the famous deceiver
Nor early-flowering dream.
Content you. Be at home
In me. There's but one room
Of all the house you may never
Share, deny or enter.
There, as a candle's beam
Stands firm and will not waver
Spire-straight in a close chamber,
As though in shadowy cave a
Stalagmite of flame,
The integral spirit climbs
The dark in light for ever.

Consider. These are they
Who have a stake in earth
But risk no wing on air,
Walk not a planet path.

Theirs the reward of all
That live by sap alone,
Flourishing but to show
Which way the wind has gone.

While oaks of pedigree
Stand over a rich seam,
Another sinks the shaft,
Fills furnace, gets up steam.

These never would break through
The orbit of their year,
Admit no altered stress,
Decline a change of gear.

The tree grips soil, the bird
Knows how to use the wind;
But the full man must live
Rooted yet unconfined.

Part Three

Never yield before the barren.
D. H. LAWRENCE

16

Look west, Wystan, lone flyer, birdman, my bully boy!
Plague of locusts, creeping barrage, has left earth bare:
Suckling and centenarian are up in air,
No wing-room for Wystan, no joke for kestrel joy.

Sky-scrapers put high questions that quench the wind's breath,
Whose shadow still comes short of truth, but kills the grass:
Power-house chimneys choke sun, ascetic pylons pass
Bringing light to the dark-livers, charged to deal death.

Firework fêtes, love displays, levitation of dead,
Salvation writ in smoke will reassure the town,
While comfy in captive balloons easily brought down
Sit frail philosophers, gravity gone to the head.

Gain altitude, Auden, then let the base beware!
Migrate, chaste my kestrel, you need a change of air!

17

First Enemy speaks
Begin perhaps with jokes across the table,
Bathing before breakfast, undressing frankly,
Trials of strength, innocent invasions;
Concealing velvet hand in iron grip
Play the man, let woman wait indoors.
I do like doing things with you.

Shoot home the bolt, draw close the silken cordon:
Regrets for youth, malice at mutual friends,
Excluding company with a private smile,
Longer looks noting, change of tune. Ah, now
To find one's touch, anticipate the last movement!
You are so different from the others.

This is my act, who can play Cleopatra,
Can hear state secrets, see the guarded plans:
A man my empire, darling I proclaim
Through sultry eyes dominion appetites –
To be called a queen, be a subject for sonnets.
You can't really think me beautiful?

Then set the stage, lights for a final tableau –
I never shall love the dark since Maurice died –
Buzzards are wheeling above, horns blowing around;
We come to a point, circle the trembling prey
In sunny fern or many-mirrored bedroom.
I love to watch your face.

Now am I in the very lists of love,
Clutching the terminals may surely hope
To make a contact. Feel, body, Oh fail not!
Shall the harsh friction the gritted teeth of lust
Not generate a spark, bring me to life?
I've never felt like this before.

So, so again. And he that was alive
Is dead. Or sleeps. A stranger to these parts.
Nerve insulated, flesh unfused, this is
No consummation; yet a dear achievement:
Reach for the powder-puff, I have sinned greatly.
I suppose you hate me, now.

18

Not hate nor love, but say
Refreshment after rain,
A lucid hour; though this
Need not occur again.

You shall no further feast
Your pride upon my flesh.
Cry for the moon: here's but
An instantaneous flash.

My wells, my rooted good
Go deeper than you dare:
Seek not my sun and moon,
They are centred elsewhere.

I know a fairer land,
Whose furrows are of fire,
Whose hills are a pure metal
Shining for all to share.

And there all rivers run
To magnify the sea,
Whose waves recur for ever
In calm equality.

Hands off! The dykes are down.
This is no time for play.
Hammer is poised and sickle
Sharpened. I cannot stay.

19

Second Enemy speaks
Now sir, now madam, we're all plain people here,
Used to plain speaking: we know what is what,
How to stretch a point and where to draw the line.

You want to buy. I have the goods.
  Read about rector's girls
  Duke's disease synthetic pearls
  Latest sinners tasty dinners
  Plucky dogs shot Sinn Feiners
  Flood in China rape in Wales
  Murderer's tears scenes at sales
  That's the stuff aren't you thrilled
  Sit back and see the world.
Yet, though abiding by the law and the profits,
I have a solemn duty and shall not shirk it
Who stand *in loco parentis* to the British Public,
We must educate our bastards.
  Professor Jeans spills the beans
  Dean Inge tells you a thing
  A man in a gown gives you the low-down
  A man with a beard says something weird
  Famous whore anticipates war
  Woman mayor advises prayer
  A grey-haired gaga says leave it to mother
  Run off and play no more lessons today.
And thirdly, brethren, you must be saved from yourselves,
From that secret voice, that positive contagion.
I'll have no long faces on this ship while I'm captain.
And you know what happens to mutineers.
  Is the boss unkind? Have you dropped a stitch?
  Smile! All together! You'll soon be better.
  Have you got a grouch? Do you feel an itch?
  There, there! Sit down and write uncle a letter.
  Lock the front door, here are your slippers,
  Get out your toys and don't make a noise;
  Don't tease the keepers, eat up your kippers,
  And you'll have a treat one day if you're good boys.

Fireman and farmer, father and flapper,
I'm speaking to you, sir, please drop that paper;
Don't you know it's poison? Have you lost all hope?
Aren't you ashamed, ma'am, to be taking dope?
There's a nasty habit that starts in the head
And creeps through the veins till you go all dead:
Insured against accident? But that won't prove
Much use when one morning you find you can't move.

They tell you all's well with our lovely England
And God's in our capital. Isn't it grand
Where the offal of action, the rinsings of thought
From a stunted peer for a penny can be bought?
It seems a bargain, but in the long run
Will cost you your honour, your crops and your son.
They're selling you the dummy, for God's sake don't buy it!
Baby, that bottle's not clean, don't try it!

You remember that girl who turned the gas on –
They drove her to it, they couldn't let her alone.
That young inventor – you all know his name –
They used the plans and he died of their fame.
Careful, climber, they're getting at your nerve!
Leader, that's a bribe, they'd like you to serve!
Bull, I don't want to give you a nightmare,
But, keep still a moment, are you quite sure you're there?

As for you, Bimbo, take off that false face!
You've ceased to be funny, you're in disgrace.
We can see the spy through that painted grin;
You may talk patriotic but you can't take us in.
You've poisoned the reservoirs, released your germs
On firesides, on foundries, on tubes and on farms.
You've made yourself cheap with your itch for power
Infecting all comers, a hopeless whore.

Scavenger barons and your jackal vassals,
Your pimping press-gang, your unclean vessels,
We'll make you swallow your words at a gulp
And turn you back to your element, pulp.
Don't bluster, Bimbo, it won't do you any good;
We can be much ruder and we're learning to shoot.
Closet Napoleon, you'd better abdicate,
You'd better quit the country before it's too late.

21

Third Enemy speaks
God is a proposition,
And we that prove him are his priests, his chosen.
From bare hypothesis
Of strata and wind, of stars and tides, watch me
Construct his universe,
A working model of my majestic notions,
A sum done in the head.
Last week I measured the light, his little finger;
The rest is a matter of time.

God is an electrician,
And they that worship him must worship him
In ampere and in volt.
Scrap sun and moon, your twilight of false gods:
X. is not here or there;
Whose lightning scrawls brief cryptograms on sky,
Easy for us to solve;
Whose motions fit our formulae, whose temple
Is a pure apparatus.

God is a statistician:
Offer him all the data; tell him your dreams.
What is your lucky number?
How do you react to bombs? Have you a rival?

Do you really love your wife?
Get yourself taped. Put soul upon the table:
Switch on the arc-lights; watch
Heart's beat, the secret agents of the blood.
Let every cell be observed.

God is a Good Physician,
Gives fruit for hygiene, crops for calories.
Don't touch that dirty man,
Don't drink from the same cup, sleep in one bed:
You know He would not like it.
Young men, cut out those visions, they're bad for the eyes:
I'll show you face to face
Eugenics, Eupeptics and Euthanasia,
The clinic Trinity.

22

Where is he, where? How the man stares!
Do you think he is there, buttoned up in your stars?
Put by that telescope;
You can't bring him nearer, you can't, sir, you haven't a hope.
Is he the answer to your glib equations,
The lord of light, the destroyer of nations?
To be seen on a slide, to be caught on a filter? The Cause
Limed in his own laws?
Analyst, you've missed him. Or worse and worst
You've got him inside? You must feel fit to burst.
Here, there, everywhere
Or nowhere. At least you know where. And how much do you
care?

Where then, Oh where? In earth or in air?
The master of mirth, the corrector of care?
Nightingale knows, if any,

And poplar flowing with wind; and high on the sunny
Hill you may find him, and low on the lawn
When every dew-drop is a separate dawn.
In the moment before the bombardment, poised at peace
He hides. And whoever sees
The cloud on the sky-line, the end of grief,
Dust in the distance that spells a relief,
Has found. Shall have his share
Who naked emerges on the far side of despair.

This one shall hear, though from afar,
The clear first call of new life, through fear
Piercing and padded walls:
Shall arise, shall scatter his heirlooms, shall run till he falls.
That one is slower, shall know by growing,
Not aware of his hour, but suddenly blowing
With leaves and roses, living from springs of the blood.
These ones have found their good:
Facing the rifles in a blind alley
Or stepping through ruins to sound reveille
They feel the father here,
They have him at heart, they shake hands, they know he is near.

23

Fourth Enemy speaks
I'm a dreamer, so are you.
See the pink sierras call,
The ever-ever land of dew,
Magic basements, fairy coal.
There the youngest son wins through,
Wee Willie can thrash the bully,
Living's cheap and dreams come true;
Lying manna tempts the belly;
Crowns are many, claims are few.

Come along then, come away
From the rush hour, from the town:
Blear and overcast today
Would put a blackcap out of tune,
Spoil the peacock's June display.
Rigid time of driving-belts
Gives no rest for grace-notes gay:
Fear and fever, cables, bolts
Pin the soul, allow no play.

You're a poet, so am I:
No man's keeper, intimate
Of breeding earth and brooding sky,
Irresponsible, remote,
A cool cloud, creation's eye.
Seek not to turn the winter tide
But to temperate deserts fly:
Close chain-mail of solitude
Must protect you or you die.

Come away then, let us go;
Lose identity and pass
Through the still blockade of snow,
Fear's frontier, an age of ice:
Pierce the crust and pass below
Towards a red volcanic core,
The warm womb where flesh can grow
Again and passion sleep secure
In creative ebb and flow.

24

Tempt me no more; for I
Have known the lightning's hour,
The poet's inward pride,
The certainty of power.

Bayonets are closing round.
I shrink; yet I must wring
A living from despair
And out of steel a song.

Though song, though breath be short,
I'll share not the disgrace
Of those that ran away
Or never left the base.

Comrades, my tongue can speak
No comfortable words,
Calls to a forlorn hope,
Gives work and not rewards.

Oh keep the sickle sharp
And follow still the plough:
Others may reap, though some
See not the winter through.

Father, who endest all,
Pity our broken sleep;
For we lie down with tears
And waken but to weep.

And if our blood alone
Will melt this iron earth,
Take it. It is well spent
Easing a saviour's birth.

25

Consider these, for we have condemned them;
Leaders to no sure land, guides their bearings lost
Or in league with robbers have reversed the signposts,
Disrespectful to ancestors, irresponsible to heirs.

Born barren, a freak growth, root in rubble,
Fruitlessly blossoming, whose foliage suffocates,
Their sap is sluggish, they reject the sun.

The man with his tongue in his cheek, the woman
With her heart in the wrong place, unhandsome, unwholesome;
Have exposed the new-born to worse than weather,
Exiled the honest and sacked the seer.
These drowned the farms to form a pleasure-lake,
In time of drought they drain the reservoir
Through private pipes for baths and sprinklers.

Getters not begetters; gainers not beginners;
Whiners, no winners; no triers, betrayers;
Who steer by no star, whose moon means nothing.
Daily denying, unable to dig:
At bay in villas from blood relations,
Counters of spoons and content with cushions
They pray for peace, they hand down disaster.

They that take the bribe shall perish by the bribe,
Dying of dry rot, ending in asylums,
A curse to children, a charge on the state.
But still their fears and frenzies infect us;
Drug nor isolation will cure this cancer:
It is now or never, the hour of the knife,
The break with the past, the major operation.

Part Four

He comes with work to do, he does not come to coo.

GERARD MANLEY HOPKINS

26

Junction or terminus – here we alight.
A myriad tracks converge on this moment,
This man where all ages and men are married,
Who shall right him? Who shall determine?

Standing astonished at the close of day
We know the worst, we may guess at good:
Geared too high our power was wasted,
Who have lost the old way to the happy ending.

A world behind us the west is in flames,
Devastated areas, works at a standstill;
No seed awakes, wary is no hunter,
The tame are ruined and the wild have fled.

Where then the saviour, the stop of illness?
Hidden the mountain was to steel our hearts.
Is healing here? An untrodden territory
Promises no coolness, invites but the brave.

But see! Not far, not fiction, a real one,
Vibrates like heat-haze full in the sun's face
Filling the heart, that chaste and fleet one,
Rarely my kestrel, my lucky star.

O man perplexed, here is your answer.
Alone who soars, who feeds upon earth –
Him shall you heed and learn where joy is
The dance of action, the expert eye.

Now is your moment, O hang-fire heart;
The ice is breaking, the death-grip relaxes,
Luck's turned. Submit to your star and take
Command, Oh start the attacking movement!

27

Wystan, Rex, all of you that have not fled,
This is our world, this is where we have grown
Together in flesh and live; though each alone
Shall join the enclosed order of the dead,
Enter the silent brotherhood of bone.

All you that have a cool head and safe hands
Awaken early, there is much to do;
Hedges to raze, channels to clear, a true
Reckoning to find. The other side commands
Eternity. We have an hour or two.

Let us speak first against that ancient firm
Who sell an armament to any cause,
Fear and Pain brothers: call them bullies and curs
Who take us into corners and make us squirm,
Finding the weak spot, fumbling at secret doors.

Let us tell them plainly now they haven't a chance,
We are going about together, we've mingled blood,
Taken a tonic that's set us up for good;
Their disguises are tabled, their movements known in advance,
We have found out who hides them and gives them food.

Lipcurl, Swiveleye, Bluster, Crock and Queer,
Mister I'll-think-it-over, Miss Not-to-day,
Young Who-the-hell-cares and old Let-us-pray,
Sir Après-moi-le-déluge. It is here
They get their orders. These will have to pay.

Hear, the ice-wall of winter at our back,
Spring's first explosions throbbing across the plain,
Earth's diastole, flood-tide of heart and vein:
Collect your forces for a counter-attack,
New life is on the way, the relief train.

28

Though winter's barricade delays,
Another season's in the air;
We'll sow the spring in our young days,
Found a Virginia everywhere.

Look where the ranks of crocuses
Their rebel colours will display
Coming with quick fire to redress
The balance of a wintry day.

Those daffodils that from the mould
Drawing a sweet breath soon shall flower,
With a year's labour get their gold
To spend it on a sunny hour.

They from earth's centre take their time
And from the sun what love they need:
The proud flower burns away its prime,
Eternity lies in the seed.

Follow the kestrel, south or north,
Strict eye, spontaneous wing can tell
A secret. Where he comes to earth
Is the heart's treasure. Mark it well.

Here he hovers. You're on the scent;
Magnetic mountain is not far,
Across no gulf or continent,
Not where you think but where you are.

Stake out your claim. Go downwards. Bore
Through the tough crust. Oh learn to feel
A way in darkness to good ore.
You are the magnet and the steel.

Out of that dark a new world flowers.
There in the womb, in the rich veins
Are tools, dynamos, bridges, towers,
Your tractors and your travelling-cranes.

29

But winter still rides rough-shod upon us,
Summer comes not for wishing nor warmth at will:
Passes are blocked and glaciers pen us
Round the hearth huddled, hoping for a break,
Playing at patience, reporting ill.
Aware of changed temperature one shall wake
And rushing to window arouse companions
To feel frost surrender, an ice age finished;
Whose strength shall melt from the mountains and run
Riot, careering down corries and canyons.
What floods will rise then through rivers replenished,
Embankments broken, and bluffs undone,
Laid low old follies, all landmarks vanished.
Is it ready for launching, the Argo, the Ark,
Our transport, our buoyant one, our heart of oak?

Make haste, put through the emergency order
For an overtime day, for double shifts working:
Weather is breaking, tomorrow we must board her,
Cast off onto chaos and shape a course.
Many months have gone to her making,
Wood well-seasoned for watertight doors,
The old world's best in her ribs and ballast,
White-heat, high pressure, the heart of a new

In boiler, in gadget, in gauge, in screw.
Peerless on water, Oh proud our palace,
A home for heroes, the latest of her line;
A beater to windward, obedient to rudder,
A steamer into storm, a hurricane-rider,
Foam-stepper, star-steerer, freighter and fighter –
Name her, release her, anoint her with wine!

Whom shall we take with us? The true, the tested,
Floods over to find a new world and man it,
Sure-foot, Surveyor, Spark and Strong,
Those whom winter has wasted, not worsted,
Good at their jobs for a break-down gang:
Born haters will blast through debris or granite,
Willing work on the permanent ways,
And natural lovers repair the race.
As needle to north, as wheel in wheel turning,
Men shall know their masters and women their need,
Mating and submitting, not dividing and defying,
Force shall fertilize, mass shall breed.
Broad let our valleys embrace the morning
And satisfied see a good day dying,
Accepting the shadows, sure of seed.

30

You who would come with us,
Think what you stand to lose –
An assured income, the will
In your favour and the feel
Of firmness underfoot.
For travellers by this boat
Nothing to rest the eyes on
But a migrant's horizon,
No fixtures or bric-à-brac –
Wave walls without a break.

Old acquaintance on the quay
Have come to clutch your knee –
Merry-Andrew and Cassandra,
Squeamish, Sponge and Squanderer,
The Insurance Agent, the Vicar,
Hard Cheese the Confidence-Tricker,
Private Loot, General Pride,
And Lust the sultry-eyed.
Others you hate to leave
Wave with autumnal grief,
The best of what has been,
Props of an English scene;
A day we may not recover,
A camp you must quit for ever.

Now, if you will, retract.
For we are off to act
Activity of young
And cut the ravelled string.
Calm yourselves, you that seek
The flame, and whose flesh is weak
Must keep it in cold storage:
For we shall not encourage
The would-be hero, the nervous
Martyr to rule or serve us.
Stand forward for volunteers
Who have tempered their loves and fears
In the skilled process of time,
Whose spirit is blown to a flame
That leaves no mean alloys.
You who have heard a voice –
The siren in the morning
That gives the worker warning,
The whisper from the loam
Promising life to come,
Manifesto of peace

Read in an altered face –
Who have heard; and believe it true
That new life must break through.

31

In happier times
When the heart is whole and the exile king returned
We may sing shock of opposing teams
And electric storms of love again.

Our voices may be tuned
To solo flight, to record-breaking plane;
Looking down from hill
We may follow with fresh felicities
Wilful the light, the wayward motion of trees,
In happier times when the heart is whole.

In happier times
When the land is ours, these springs shall irrigate
Good growing soil until it teems,
Redeemed from mortgage, drilled to obey;
But still must flow in spate.
We'll focus stars again; though now must be
Map and binoculars
Outlining vision, bringing close
Natural features that will need no glass
In happier times, when the land is ours.

Make us a wind
To shake the world out of this sleepy sickness
Where flesh has dwindled and brightness waned!
New life multiple in seed and cell
Mounts up to brace our slackness.
Oppression's passion, a full organ swell
Through our throats welling wild
Of angers in unison arise

And hunger haunted with a million sighs,
Make us a wind to shake the world!

Make us the wind
From a new world that springs and gathers force,
Clearing the air, cleaning the wound;
Sets masses in motion and whips the blood.
Oh they shall find him fierce
Who cling to relics, dead wood shall feel his blade.
Rudely the last leaves whirled,
A storm on fire, dry ghosts, shall go in
Fear and be laid in the red of their own ruin.
Make us the wind from a new world!

32

You that love England, who have an ear for her music,
The slow movement of clouds in benediction,
Clear arias of light thrilling over her uplands,
Over the chords of summer sustained peacefully;
Ceaseless the leaves' counterpoint in a west wind lively,
Blossom and river rippling loveliest allegro,
And the storms of wood strings brass at year's finale:
Listen. Can you not hear the entrance of a new theme?

You who go out alone, on tandem or on pillion,
Down arterial roads riding in April,
Or sad beside lakes where hill-slopes are reflected
Making fires of leaves, your high hopes fallen:
Cyclists and hikers in company, day excursionists,
Refugees from cursed towns and devastated areas;
Know you seek a new world, a saviour to establish
Long-lost kinship and restore the blood's fulfilment.

You who like peace, good sorts, happy in a small way
Watching birds or playing cricket with schoolboys,

Who pay for drinks all round, whom disaster chose not;
Yet passing derelict mills and barns roof-rent
Where despair has burnt itself out – hearts at a standstill,
Who suffer loss, aware of lowered vitality;
We can tell you a secret, offer a tonic; only
Submit to the visiting angel, the strange new healer.

You above all who have come to the far end, victims
Of a run-down machine, who can bear it no longer;
Whether in easy chairs chafing at impotence
Or against hunger, bullies and spies preserving
The nerve for action, the spark of indignation –
Need fight in the dark no more, you know your enemies.
You shall be leaders when zero hour is signalled,
Wielders of power and welders of a new world.

33

Come for a walk in our pleasant land:
We must wake up early if we want to understand
The length and breadth and depth of decay
Has corrupted our vowels and clogged our bowels,
Impaired our breathing, eaten pride away.
What do they believe in – these yellow yes-men,
Pansies, politicians, prelates and pressmen,
Boneless wonders, unburstable bouncers,
Back-slappers, cheer-leaders, bribed announcers
Broadcasting All-Clear as the raiders draw near;
Would mend a burst dam with sticking-plaster
And hide with shocked hand the yawn of disaster –
What do they believe in? A god of gold,
A gilt-edged proposition; but it seems they've been sold.
All you fine ladies, once you were flowers
England was proud of, rich blooms, good growers;
But overblown now; and we can't afford you
Your missions and fashions, your synthetic passions;
We don't want to bed you and we'd rather not board you:

Weedy, greedy, unsatisfied, unsexed,
You're not living in this world, and as for the next –
You could hand white feathers on the judgment day
And give the damned a charity matinée.
Our holy intellectuals – what are they at?
Filling in hard times with literary chat,
Laying down the law where no one listens,
Finding the flaw in long-scrapped systems
And short cuts to places no more on the map:
Though off their feed now and inclined to mope.
Nasties, nudists, bedlamites, buddhists,
Too feeble to follow, unable to guide,
It's time we asked them to step aside.
Children of the sahib, the flag and the mater,
Grim on golf-courses and haggard on horses
They try to live but they've ceased to matter:
Who'll give a penny to the poor old guy?
These were the best that money could buy
And it isn't good enough. For what can they fight? –
The silver spoon, the touched hat, the expensive seat:
Marching at the orders of a mad physician
Down private roads to common perdition.
Where is the bourgeois, the backbone of our race?
Bent double with lackeying, the joints out of place;
Behind bluffs and lucky charms hiding to evade
An overdue audit, anæmic, afraid.
Trimmers and schemers, pusillanimous dreamers,
At cinemas, shop-windows and arenas we've found them
Bearing witness to a life beyond them.
They're paying for death on the instalment plan
Who hoped to go higher and failed to be men.
We'd like to fight but we fear defeat,
We'd like to work but we're feeling too weak,
We'd like to be sick but we'd get the sack,
We'd like to behave, we'd like to believe,
We'd like to love, but we've lost the knack.

34

(for Frances Warner)

What do we ask for, then?
Not for pity's pence nor pursy affluence,
Only to set up house again:
Neither a coward's heaven, cessation of pain,
Nor a new world of sense,
But that we may be given the chance to be men.
For what, then, do we hope?
Not longer sight at once but enlarged scope;
Miraculous no seed or growth of soul, but soil
Cleared of weed, prepared for good:
We shall expect no birth-hour without blood
Nor fire without recoil.

Publish the vision, broadcast and screen it,
Of a world where the will of all shall be raised to highest power,
Village or factory shall form the unit.
Control shall be from the centres, quick brain, warm heart,
And the bearings bathed in a pure
Fluid of sympathy. There possessions no more shall be part
Of the man, where riches and sacrifice
Are of flesh and blood, sex, muscles, limbs and eyes.
Each shall give of his best. It shall seem proper
For all to share what all produced.
Men shall be glad of company, love shall be more than a guest
And the bond no more of paper.

Open your eyes, for vision
Is here of a world that has ceased to be bought and sold
With traitor silver and fairy gold;
But the diamond of endurance, the wrought-iron of passion
Is all their currency.
As the body that knows through action they are splendid,
Feeling head and heart agree;

Young men proud of their output, women no longer stale
With deferred crisis; the old, a full day ended,
Able to stand down and sit still.
Only the exploiter, the public nuisance, the quitter
Receive no quarter.

Here they do not need
To flee the birthplace. There's room for growing and working.
Bright of eye, champions for speed,
They sing their own songs, they are active, they play not watch:
Happy at night talking
Of the demon bowler cracked over the elm-trees,
The reverse pass that won the match.
At festivals knowing themselves normal and well-born
They remember the ancestors that gave them ease,
Harris who fought the bully at Melbourne,
What Wainwright wrote with his blood, Rosa in prison –
All who sucked out the poison.

35

In these our winter days
Death's iron tongue is glib
Numbing with fear all flesh upon
A fiery-hearted globe.

An age once green is buried,
Numbered the hours of light;
Blood-red across the snow our sun
Still trails his faint retreat.

Spring through death's iron guard
Her million blades shall thrust;
Love that was sleeping, not extinct,
Throw off the nightmare crust.

Eyes, though not ours, shall see
Sky-high a signal flame,
The sun returned to power above
A world, but not the same.

36

Now raise your voices for a final chorus,
Lift the glasses, drink tomorrow's health –
Success to the doctor who is going to cure us
And those who will die no more in bearing wealth.
On our magnetic mountain a beacon burning
Shall sign the peace we hoped for, soon or late,
Clear over a clean earth, and all men turning
Like infants' eyes like sunflowers to the light.

Drink to the ordered nerves, the sight restored;
A day when power for all shall radiate
From the sovereign centres, and the blood is stirred
To flow in its ancient courses of love and hate:
When the country vision is ours that like a barn
Fills the heart with slow-matured delight,
Absorbing wind and summer, till we turn
Like infants' eyes like sunflowers to the light.

For us to dream the birthday, but they shall act it –
Bells over fields, the hooters from the mine,
On New Year's Eve under the bridegroom's attic
Chorus of coastguards singing Auld Lang Syne.
Now at hope's horizon that day is dawning,
We guess at glory from a mountain height,
But then in valley towns they will be turning
Like infants' eyes like sunflowers to the light.

Beckon O beacon, and O sun be soon!
Hollo, bells, over a melting earth!
Let man be many and his sons all sane,
Fearless with fellows, handsome by the hearth.
Break from your trance: start dancing now in town,
And, fences down, the ploughing match with mate.
This is your day: so turn, my comrades, turn
Like infants' eyes like sunflowers to the light.

A TIME TO DANCE

Learning to Talk

See this small one, tiptoe on
The green foothills of the years,
Views a younger world than yours;
When you go down, he'll be the tall one.

Dawn's dew is on his tongue –
No word for what's behind the sky,
Naming all that meets the eye,
Pleased with sunlight over a lawn.

Hear his laughter. He can't contain
The exquisite moment overflowing.
Limbs leaping, woodpecker flying
Are for him and not hereafter.

Tongue trips, recovers, triumphs,
Turning all ways to express
What the forward eye can guess –
That time is his and earth young.

We are growing too like trees
To give the rising wind a voice:
Eagles shall build upon our verse,
Our winged seeds are tomorrow's sowing.

Yes, we learn to speak for all
Whose hearts here are not at home,
All who march to a better time
And breed the world for which they burn.

Though we fall once, though we often,
Though we fall to rise not again,
From our horizon sons begin;
When we go down, they will be tall ones.

Moving In

Is it your hope, hope's hearth, heart's home, here at the lane's
end?
Deeds are signed, structure is sound though century-old;
Redecorated throughout, all modern convenience, the cable
extended;
Need grope no more in corners nor cower from dark and cold.

Who between town and country dreams of contact with the two
worlds
Earthquake will wake, a chasm at his feet, crack of doom overhead.
What deeds can survive, what stone can shoulder the shock of a
new world?
Dark and cold, dancing no spark, when the cable is dead.

Fear you not ghosts of former tenants, a fell visitation
From them whose haunts you have sealed, whose secrets you
haled to light?
Gay as grass are you? Tough as granite? But they are patient,
Waiting for you to weaken, awaiting a sleepless night.

You have cut down the yews, say you, for a broader view? No
churchyard
Emblems shall bind or blind you? But see, the imperative brow
Frowns of the hills, offers no compromise, means far harder
Visions than valley steeples call to, a stricter vow.

Though your wife is chaste, though your children lustily throng,
                                                though laughing
Raise you a record crop, yet do you wrong your powers,
Flattered no longer by isolation nor satisfied loving.
Not box hedge where the birds nest, not embankments of flowers

Guard from regret. No private good will let you forget all
Those, time's accessories, whose all is a leaden arc
Between work and sleep; who might have been men, brighter
                                                metal,
Proudly reaped the light, passed peacefully into dark.

The Conflict

I sang as one
Who on a tilting deck sings
To keep men's courage up, though the wave hangs
That shall cut off their sun.

As storm-cocks sing,
Flinging their natural answer in the wind's teeth,
And care not if it is waste of breath
Or birth-carol of spring.

As ocean-flyer clings
To height, to the last drop of spirit driving on
While yet ahead is land to be won
And work for wings.

Singing I was at peace,
Above the clouds, outside the ring:
For sorrow finds a swift release in song
And pride its poise.

Yet living here,
As one between two massing powers I live
Whom neutrality cannot save
Nor occupation cheer.

None such shall be left alive:
The innocent wing is soon shot down,
And private stars fade in the blood-red dawn
Where two worlds strive.

The red advance of life
Contracts pride, calls out the common blood,
Beats song into a single blade,
Makes a depth-charge of grief.

Move then with new desires,
For where we used to build and love
Is no man's land, and only ghosts can live
Between two fires.

Losers

Those are judged losers and fortune-flouted
Whose flighted hopes fell down short of satisfaction;
The killed in action, the blasted in beauty, all choosers

Of the wrong channel for love's seasonal spate:
Cheerless some amid rock or rank forest life-long
Laboured to hew an estate, but they died childless:

Those within hail of home by blizzard o'ertaken;
Those awakening from vision with truth on tongue, struck
              dumb:
Are deemed yet to have been transfigured in failure.

Men mourn their beauty and promise, publish the diaries;
Medals are given; the graves are evergreen with pity:
Their fire is forwarded through the hearts of the living.

What can we say of these, from the womb wasted,
Whose nerve was never tested in act, who fell at the start,
Who had no beauty to lose, born out of season?

Early an iron frost clamped down their flowing
Desires. They were lost at once: they failed and died in the
                                                    whirling
Snow, bewildered, homeless from first to last.

Frightened we stop our ears to the truth they are telling
Who toil to remain alive, whose children start from sleep
Weeping into a world worse than nightmares.

Splendour of cities they built cannot ennoble
The barely living, ambitious for bread alone. Pity
Trails not her robe for these and their despairs.

In Me Two Worlds

In me two worlds at war
Trample the patient flesh,
This lighted ring of sense where clinch
Heir and ancestor.

This moving point of dust
Where past and future meet
Traces their battle-line and shows
Each thrust and counterthrust.

The armies of the dead
Are trenched within my bones,
My blood's their semaphore, their wings
Are watchers overhead.

Their captains stand at ease
As on familiar ground,
The veteran longings of the heart
Serve them for mercenaries.

Conscious of power and pride
Imperially they move
To pacify an unsettled zone –
The life for which they died.

But see, from vision's height
March down the men to come,
And in my body rebel cells
Look forward to the fight.

The insolence of the dead
Breaks on their solid front:
They tap my nerves for power, my veins
To stain their banners red.

These have the spirit's range,
The measure of the mind:
Out of the dawn their fire comes fast
To conquer and to change.

So heir and ancestor
Pursue the inveterate feud,
Making my senses' darkened fields
A theatre of war.

A Warning to those who Live on Mountains

You inhabit the mountains, half-way to heaven;
Wind carries your wishes like winged seeds
Over the valley, not sowing in vain:
Breathe rarest air, with the pure red rowan
Have graceful grown and calm as glaciers.
You are proud of the view; on plateau and peak
Rampant your telescopes rake the horizon,
Make nothing of the distance to nearest or next world.
You have made your mark on the stony-hearted massif,
Galleried granite and worked for gold
Till a solid world turned to fantastic tracery:
In snow-line receding your power we see,
Your heraldic pride hewn on the hillface.

Remember the ringed ammonite, running
Crazy, was killed for being too clever.

Impatient grow the peoples of the plain,
They wait for a word, the helio winking
As it talks of truce, the exile's return.
Labouring aloft you forget plain language,
Simple the password that disarms suspicion:
Starved are your roots, and still would you strain
The tie between brain and body to breaking-point?
Your power's by-products have poisoned their streams,
Their vision grows short as your shadow lengthens,
And your will walls them in. Beware, for a heavy
Charge is laid against you, Oh little longer
Will the hand be withheld that hesitates at the wire's end,
And your time totters like a tenement condemned.

Famous that fall, or shall they tell how in the final
Moment remaining you changed your mind?

Johnny Head-In-Air

It was an evening late in the year
When the frost stings again,
Hard-bitten was the face of the hills
And harsh breathed the plain.

Along a stony watershed
Surly and peaked with cold
I saw a company straggling over,
Over an endless wold.

The plain breathed up in smoke: its breath
Like a dying curse did freeze:
The fingers of the fog reached up
And took them by the knees.

Cruel, cruel look the stars
Fixed in a bitter frown:
Here at our feet to left and right
The silly streams run down.

We have left the ice-fields far behind,
Jungle, desert and fen;
We have passed the place of the temperate race
And the land of the one-eyed men.

The road reels back a million miles,
It is high time we came
Dropping down to the rich valleys
Where each can stake his claim.

Iron, iron rang the road,
All iron to the tread:
Heaven's face was barred with steel
Star-bolted overhead.

The well, the ill, on foot or on wheel,
The shattered, the shamed, the proud –
And limousines like painted queans
Went curving through the crowd.

What are these shapes that drive them on?
Is it the ravenous host
Of the dead? Or are they the shadows of children
Not born, nipped by the frost?

The viaduct's broken down behind:
They cannot turn again.
Telegraph poles stride on before them
Pacing out their pain.

Where are you going, you wan hikers,
And why this ganglion gear?
What are those packs that on your backs
Through frost and fog you bear?

Through frost and fog, by col and crag
Leads on this thoroughfare
To kingdom-come: it is our gods
That on our backs we bear.

True they had travelled a million miles
If they had travelled one:
They walked or rode, each with his load,
A leaden automaton:

But never the sun came out to meet them
At the last lap of land,
Nor in the frore and highest heaven
Did the flint-eyed stars unbend.

Now they have come to night's massif;
Those sheer, unfissured walls
Cry halt, and still the following shadows
Rustle upon their heels.

They have come to the crisis of the road,
They have come without maps or guides:
To left and right along the night
The cryptic way divides.

I looked and I saw a stark signpost
There at the road's crest,
And its arms were the arms of a man pointing,
Pointing to east and west.

His face was pure as the winnowed light
When the wild geese fly high,
And gentle as on October evenings
The heron-feathered sky.

The mists grovelled below his feet
And the crowd looked up to pray:
From his beacon eyes a tremendous backwash
Of darkness surged away.

Speak up, speak up, you skyward man,
Speak up and tell us true;
To east or west – which is the best,
The through-way of the two?

The heaven-wind parts your hair, the sun
Is wintering in your eyes;
Johnny Head-In-Air, tell us
Which way our good luck lies.

Wirily stirred the stiffening grasses
With a chitter of migrant birds:
Wearily all that horde fell silent
Waiting for his words.

Each way the blindly spearing headlights
Were blunted on the gloom:
Only his eyes like keen X-rays
Saw into the night's womb.

I look to right, to right, comrades,
I look to right and I see
A smooth decline past rowan and pine
That leads to a low country.

Roses cling to a second summer
There, and the birds are late
To bed; the dying sun has left it
A legacy of light:

Winds browse over the unreaped corn,
Rivers flow on gems,
Shades dream in the dust of glory, and steeples
Hum with remembered chimes.

But go you now or go you then,
Those ferlies you'll not behold
Till the guardians of that valley have crossed
Your hand with fairy gold.

Who takes that gold is a ghost for ever
And none shall hear his cries,
He never shall feel or heat or hail,
He never shall see sun rise.

I look to left, to left, comrades,
I look to left, and there —
Put off those gods, put off those goods
That on your backs you bear —

For he must travel light who takes
An eagle's route, and cope
With canyons deeper than despair
And heights o'ertopping hope:

Only the lifting horizon leads him
And that is no man's friend:
Only his duty breath to whisper
All things come to an end.

But all shall be changed, all shall be friends
Upon that mountainside;
They shall awake with the sun and take
Hilltops in their stride.

Out of their crimson-hearted east
A living day shall dawn,
Out of their agonies a rare
And equal race be born.

His arms were stretched to the warring poles,
The current coursed his frame:
Over the hill-crest, niched in night,
They saw a man of flame.

Come down, come down, you suffering man,
Come down, and high or low
Choose your fancy and go with us
The way that we should go.

That cannot be till two agree
Who long have lain apart:
Traveller, know, I am here to show
Your own divided heart.

The Ecstatic

Lark, skylark, spilling your rubbed and round
Pebbles of sound in air's still lake,
Whose widening circles fill the noon; yet none
Is known so small beside the sun:

Be strong your fervent soaring, your skyward air!
Tremble there, a nerve of song!
Float up there where voice and wing are one,
A singing star, a note of light!

Buoyed, embayed in heaven's noon-wide reaches –
For soon light's tide will turn – Oh stay!
Cease not till day streams to the west, then down
That estuary drop down to peace.

Poem for an Anniversary

Admit then and be glad
Our volcanic age is over.
A molten rage shook earth from head to toe,
Seas leapt from their beds,
World's bedrock boiling up, the terrible lava.
Now it is not so.

Remember, not regret
Those cloudy dreams that trod on air
How distantly reflecting fire below:
The mating in air, the mute
Shuddering electric storms, the foul or fair
Love was used to know.

Admire, no more afraid,
Country made for peace. Earth rent,
Rocks like prayers racked from the heart, are now
Landmarks for us and shade:
Hotfoot to havoc where the lava went,
Cooler rivers flow.

Survey what most survives –
Love's best, climate and contour fine:
We have trained the giant lightning to lie low
And drive our linked lives;
Those clouds stand not in daydream but for rain,
And earth has grain to grow.

Sonnet

This man was strong, and like a seacape parted
The tides. There were not continents enough
For all his fledged ambitions. The hard-hearted
Mountains were moved by his explosive love.
Was young: yet between island and island
Laid living cable and whispered across seas:
When he sang, our feathery woods fell silent:
His smile put the fidgeting hours at ease.

See him now, a cliff chalk-faced and crumbling,
Eyes like craters of volcanoes dead;
A miser with the tarnished minutes fumbling,
A queasy traveller from board to bed:
The voice that charmed spirits grown insane
As the barking of dogs at the end of a dark lane.

Two Songs

I've heard them lilting at loom and belting,
Lasses lilting before dawn of day:
But now they are silent, not gamesome and gallant –
The flowers of the town are rotting away.

There was laughter and loving in the lanes at evening;
Handsome were the boys then, and girls were gay.
But lost in Flanders by medalled commanders
The lads of the village are vanished away.

Cursed be the promise that takes our men from us –
All will be champion if you choose to obey:
They fight against hunger but still it is stronger –
The prime of our land grows cold as the clay.

The women are weary, once lilted so merry,
Waiting to marry for a year and a day:
From wooing and winning, from owning or earning
The flowers of the town are all turned away.

Come, live with me and be my love,
And we will all the pleasures prove
Of peace and plenty, bed and board,
That chance employment may afford.

I'll handle dainties on the docks
And thou shalt read of summer frocks:
At evening by the sour canals
We'll hope to hear some madrigals.

Care on thy maiden brow shall put
A wreath of wrinkles, and thy foot
Be shod with pain: not silken dress
But toil shall tire thy loveliness.

Hunger shall make thy modest zone
And cheat fond death of all but bone –
If these delights thy mind may move,
Then live with me and be my love.

A Carol

Oh hush thee, my baby,
Thy cradle's in pawn:
No blankets to cover thee
Cold and forlorn.
The stars in the bright sky
Look down and are dumb
At the heir of the ages
Asleep in a slum.

The hooters are blowing,
No heed let him take;
When baby is hungry
'Tis best not to wake.
Thy mother is crying,
Thy dad's on the dole:
Two shillings a week is
The price of a soul.

A Time to Dance

In memory of

L. P. HEDGES

For those who had the power
    of the forest fires that burn
Leaving their source in ashes
    to flush the sky with fire:
Those whom a famous urn
    could not contain, whose passion
Brimmed over the deep grave
    and dazzled epitaphs:
For all that have won us wings
    to clear the tops of grief,
My friend who within me laughs
    bids you dance and sing.

Some set out to explore
    earth's limit, and little they recked if
Never their feet came near it
    outgrowing the need for glory:
Some aimed at a small objective
    but the fierce updraught of their spirit
Forced them to the stars.
    Are honoured in public who built
The dam that tamed a river;
    or holding the salient for hours
Against odds, cut off and killed,
    are remembered by one survivor.

All these. But most for those
    whom accident made great,
As a radiant chance encounter
    of cloud and sunlight grows
Immortal on the heart:

whose gift was the sudden bounty
Of a passing moment, enriches
   the fulfilled eye for ever.
Their spirits float serene
   above time's roughest reaches,
But their seed is in us and over
   our lives they are evergreen.

*   *   *

Let us sing then for my friend not a dirge, not a funeral anthem,
But words to match his mirth, a theme with a happy end;
A bird's buoyancy in them, over the dark-toned earth
To hold a sustained flight, a tune sets death to dancing;
The stormcock's song, the ecstatic poise of the natural fighter,
And a beat as of feet advancing to glory, a lilt emphatic.

*   *   *

Sing we the two lieutenants, Parer and M'Intosh,
After the War wishing to hie them home to Australia,
Planned they would take a high way, a hazardous crazy air-way:
Death their foregone conclusion, a flight headlong to failure,
We said. For no silver posh
Plane was their pigeon, no dandy dancer quick-stepping through
                heaven,
But a craft of obsolete design, a condemned D.H. nine;
Sold for a song it was, patched up though to write an heroic
Line across the world as it reeled on its obstinate stoic
Course to that southern haven.

On January 8th, 1920, their curveting wheels kissed
England goodbye. Over Hounslow huddled in morning mist
They rose and circled like buzzards while we rubbed our sleepy
                eyes:
Like a bird scarce-fledged they flew, whose flying hours are
                few –
Still dear is the nest but deeper its desire unto the skies –
And they left us to our sleeping.

They felt earth's warning tug on their wings: vain to advance
Asking a thoroughfare through the angers of the air
On so flimsy a frame: but they pulled up her nose and the earth
went sloping
Away, and they aimed for France.

Fog first, a wet blanket, a kill-joy, the primrose-of-morning's
blight,
Blotting out the dimpled sea, the ample welcome of land,
The gay glance from the bright
Cliff-face behind, snaring the sky with treachery, sneering
At hope's loss of height. But they charged it, flying blind;
They took a compass-bearing against that dealer of doubt,
As a saint when the field of vision is fogged gloriously steels
His spirit against the tainter of air, the elusive taunter:
They climbed to win a way out,
Then downward dared till the moody waves snarled at their
wheels.

Landing at last near Conteville, who had skimmed the crest of
oblivion,
They could not rest, but rose and flew on to Paris, and there
Trivially were delayed – a defective petrol feed –
Three days: a time hung heavy on
Hand and heart, till they leapt again to the upper air,
Their element, their lover, their angel antagonist.
Would have taken a fall without fame, but the sinewy frame-
work the wrist
Of steel the panting engine wrestled well: and they went
South while the going was good, as a swallow that guide nor goad
Needs on his sunny scent.

At Lyons the petrol pump failed again, and forty-eight hours
They chafed to be off, the haughty champions whose breathing-
space
Was an horizon span and the four winds their fan.

Over Italy's shores
A reverse, the oil ran out and cursing they turned about
Losing a hundred miles to find a landing-place.
Not a coast for a castaway this, no even chance of alighting
On sward or wind-smooth sand:
A hundred miles without pressure they flew, the engine fighting
For breath, and its heart nearly burst before they dropped to land.

And now the earth they had spurned rose up against them in
          anger,
Tier upon tier it towered, the terrible Apennines:
No sanctuary there for wings, not flares nor landing-lines,
No hope of floor and hangar.
Yet those ice-tipped spears that disputed the passage set spurs
To their two hundred and forty horse power; grimly they gained
Altitude, though the hand of heaven was heavy upon them,
The downdraught from the mountains: though desperate eddies
          spun them
Like a coin, yet unkindly tossed their luck came uppermost
And mastery remained.

Air was all ambushes round them, was avalanche earthquake
Quicksand, a funnel deep as doom, till climbing steep
They crawled like a fly up the face of perpendicular night
And levelled, finding a break
At fourteen thousand feet. Here earth is shorn from sight:
Deadweight a darkness hangs on their eyelids, and they bruise
Their eyes against a void: vindictive the cold airs close
Down like a trap of steel and numb them from head to heel;
Yet they kept an even keel,
For their spirit reached forward and took the controls while
        their fingers froze.

They had not heard the last of death. When the mountains
        were passed,

He raised another crest, the long crescendo of pain
Kindled to climax, the plane
Took fire. Alone in the sky with the breath of their enemy
Hot in their face they fought: from three thousand feet they
tilted
Over, side-slipped away – a trick for an ace, a race
And running duel with death: flame streamed out behind,
A crimson scarf of, as life-blood out of a wound, but the wind
Of their downfall stanched it; death wilted,
Lagged and died out in smoke – he could not stay their pace.

A lull for a while. The powers of hell rallied their legions.
On Parer now fell the stress of the flight; for the plane had been
bumped,
Buffeted, thrashed by the air almost beyond repair:
But he tinkered and coaxed, and they limped
Over the Adriatic on into warmer regions.
Erratic their course to Athens, to Crete: coolly they rode her
Like a tired horse at the water-jumps, they jockeyed her over
seas,
Till they came at last to a land whose dynasties of sand
Had seen Alexander, Napoleon, many a straddling invader,
But never none like these.

England to Cairo, a joy-ride, a forty-hour journey at most,
Had cost them forty-four days. What centuried strata of life
Fuelled the fire that haled them to heaven, the power that held
them
Aloft? For their plane was a laugh,
A patch, brittle as matchstick, a bubble, a lift for a ghost:
Bolts always working loose of propeller, cylinder, bearer;
Instruments faulty; filter, magneto, each strut unsound.
Yet after four days, though we swore she never could leave the
ground,
We saw her in headstrong haste diminish towards the east –
That makeshift, mad sky-farer.

Aimed they now for Baghdad, unwritten in air's annals
A voyage. But theirs the fate all flights of logic to refute,
Who obeyed no average law, who buoyed the viewless channels
Of sky with a courage steadfast, luminous. Safe they crossed
Sinai's desert, and daring
The Nejd, the unneighbourly waste of Arabia, yet higher soar-
ing
(Final a fall there for birds of passage, limed and lost
In shifty the sand's embrace) all day they strove to climb
Through stormy rain: but they felt her shorten her stride and
falter,
And they fell at evening time.

Slept that night beside their machine, and the next morning
Raider Arabs appeared reckoning this stranded bird
A gift: like cobras they struck, and their gliding shadows athwart
The sand were all their warning.
But the aeronauts, knowing iron the coinage here, had brought
Mills bombs and revolvers, and M'Intosh held them off
While Parer fought for life –
A spark, the mechanic's right answer, and finally wrought
A miracle, for the dumb engine spoke and they rose
Convulsively out of the clutch of the desert, the clench of their
foes.

Orchestrate this theme, artificer-poet. Imagine
The roll, crackling percussion, quickening tempo of engine
For a start: the sound as they soar, an octave-upward slur
Scale of sky ascending:
Hours-held note of level flight, a beat unhurried,
Sustaining undertone of movement never-ending:
Wind shrill on the ailerons, flutes and fifes in a flurry
Devilish when they dive, plucking of tense stays.
These hardly heard it, who were the voice, the heavenly air
That sings above always.

We have seen the extremes, the burning, the freezing, the
                                        outward face
Of their exploit; heroic peaks, tumbling-to-zero depressions:
Little our graph can show, the line they traced through space,
Of the heart's passionate patience.
How soft drifts of sleep piled on their senses deep
And they dug themselves out often: how the plane was a weight
                                        that hung
And swung on their aching nerve; how din drilled through the
                                        skull
And sight sickened – so slow earth filtered past below.
Yet nerve failed never, heart clung
To height, and the brain kept its course and the hand its skill.

Baghdad renewed a propeller damaged in desert. Arid
Baluchistan spared them that brought down and spoilt with thirst
Armies of Alexander. To Karachi they were carried
On cloud-back: fragile as tinder their plane, but the winds were
                                        tender
Now to their need, and nursed
Them along till teeming India made room for them to alight.
Wilting her wings, the sweltering suns had moulted her bright
Plumage, rotten with rain
The fabric: but they packed her with iron washers and tacked her
Together, good for an hour, and took the air again.

Feats for a hundred flights, they were prodigal of: a fairest
Now to tell – how they foiled death when the engine failed
Above the Irrawaddy, over close-woven forest.
What shoals for a pilot there, what a snarled passage and dark
Shelves down to doom and grip
Of green! But look, balanced superbly, quick off the mark
Swooping like centre three-quarter whose impetus storms a gap –
Defenders routed, rooted their feet, and their arms are mown
Aside, that high or low aim at his overthrow –
M'Intosh touched her down.

And they picked her up out of it somehow and put her at the
air, a
Sorry hack for such steeplechasing, to leap the sky.
'We'll fly this bloody crate till it falls to bits at our feet,'
Said the mechanic Parer.
And at Moulmein soon they crashed; and the plane by their
spirit's high
Tension long pinned, girded and guarded from dissolution,
Fell to bits at their feet. Wrecked was the undercarriage,
Radiator cracked, in pieces, compasses crocked;
Fallen all to confusion.
Their winged hope was a heap of scrap, but unsplintered their
courage.

Six weeks they worked in sun-glare and jungle damps, assemb-
ling
Fragments to make airworthy what was worth not its weight in
air,
As a surgeon, grafter of skin, as a setter of bones tumbling
Apart, they had power to repair
This good for naught but the grave: they livened her engine
and gave
Fuselage faith to rise rejuvenated from ruin.
Went with them stowaways, not knowing what hazard they
flew in –
Bear-cubs, a baby alligator, lizards and snakes galore;
Mascots maybe, for the plane though twice she was floored again
Always came up for more.

Till they came to the pitiless mountains of Timor. Yet these,
untamed,
Not timorous, against the gradient and Niagara of air they climbed
Scarce-skimming the summits; and over the shark-toothed
Timor sea

Lost their bearings, but shirked not the odds, the deaths that
lurked
A million to one on their trail:
They reached out to the horizon and plucked their destiny.
On for eight hours they flew blindfold against the unknown,
And the oil began to fail
And their flying spirit waned – one pint of petrol remained
When the land stood up to meet them and they came into their
own.

Southward still to Melbourne, the bourn of their flight, they
pressed
Till at last near Culcairn, like a last fretted leaf
Falling from brave autumn into earth's breast,
D.H. nine, their friend that had seen them to the end,
Gave up her airy life.
The Southern Cross was splendid above the spot where she fell,
The end of her rainbow curve over our weeping day:
And the flyers, glad to be home, unharmed by that dizzy fall,
Dazed as the dead awoken from death, stepped out of the broken
Body and went away.

What happened then, the roar
and rave of waving crowds
That fêted them, was only
an afterglow of glory
Reflected on the clouds
where they had climbed alone,
Day's golden epilogue:
and them, whose meteor path
Lightened our eyes, whose great
spirit lifted the fog
That sours a doubtful earth,
the stars commemorate.

In February, a world of hard light,
A frosty welcome, the aconites came up
Lifting their loving cups to drink the sun:
Spring they meant, mounting and more of hope.
And I thought of my friend, like these withered too soon,
Who went away in a night
Before the spring was ready, who left our town
For good. Like aconites he pledged the spring
Out of my grief-bound heart, and he made me sing
The spirit of life that nothing can keep down.

But yesterday, in May, a storm arose
Clouding the spring's festivities, and spoilt
Much would have been admired and given us shade.
We saw this year's young hopes beat down and soiled,
Blossoms not now for fruit, boughs might have made
Syringa's wreath of snows.
A fortune gone time held for us in trust.
And I knew no bold flourish of flowers can write
Off the dead loss, when friends dissolve in night
Changing our dear-invested love to dust.

Strange ways the dead break through. Not the Last Post
Brings them, nor clanging midnight: for then is the inner
Heart reinforced against assault and sap.
On break-up day or at the cricket-club dinner
Between a word and a word they find the gap,
And we know what we have lost.
Sorrow is natural thirst: we are not weaned
At once. Though long withdrawn the sickening blade,
Deeply we remember loss of blood
And the new skin glosses over an active wound.

Remember that winter morning – no maroon
Warned of a raid; death granted no farewell speech,
Acted without prologue, was a bell and a line

Speaking from far of one no more within reach.
Blood ran out of me. I was alone.
How suddenly, how soon,
In a moment, while I was looking the other way,
You hid yourself where I could never find you –
Too dark the shadows earth sheeted around you.
So we went home: that was the close of play.

Still I hoped for news. Often I stood
On promontories that straining towards the west
Fret their hearts away. Thence on a clear
Day one should glimpse the islands of the blest,
And he, if any, had a passport there.
But no, it was no good.
Those isles, it proved, were broken promises,
A trick of light, a way wishes delude:
Or, if he lived out there, no cable was laid
To carry his love whispering over seas.

So I returned. Perhaps he was nearer home
And I had missed him. Here he was last seen
Walking familiar as sunlight a solid road;
Round the next turn, his door. But look, there has been
Landslide: those streets end abruptly, they lead
The eye into a tomb.
Scrabble for souvenirs. Fit bone to bone;
Anatomy of buried joys you guess,
But the wind jeers through it. Assemble the shattered glass;
A mirror you have, but the face there is your own.

Was so much else we could have better spared –
Churches, museums, multiple stores: but the bomb
Fell on the power-house: total that eclipse.
He was our dynamo, our warmth, our beam
Transmitter of mirth – it is a town's collapse
Not easily repaired.
Or as a reservoir that, sharing out

Rain hoarded from heaven, springs from the valley,
Refreshment was for all: now breached and wholly
Drained, is a barren bed, a cup of drought.

Then to the hills, as one who dies for rain,
I went. All day the light makes lovely passes
There, whose hands are healing, whose smile was yours,
And eloquent winds hearten the dry grasses.
They have come to terms with death: for them the year's
Harvest, the instant pain,
Are as clouds passing indifferent over
Their heads, but certain givers in the end.
Downright these hills, hiding nothing they stand
Firm to the foot and comfort the eye for ever.

They say, 'Death is above your weight, too strong
For argument or armies, the real dictator:
He never was one to answer the question, Why?
He sends for you tomorrow, for us later:
Nor are you that Orpheus who could buy
Resurrection with a song.
Not for long will your chalk-faced bravado
Stand the erosion of eternity:
Learn from us a moment's sanity –
To be warm in the sun, to accept the following shadow.

In my heart's mourning underworld I sang
As miners entombed singing despair to sleep –
Their earth is stopped, their eyes are reconciled
To night. Yet here, under the sad hill-slope
Where I thought one spring of my life for ever was sealed,
The friend I had lost sprang
To life again and showed me a mystery:
For I knew, at last wholly accepting death,
Though earth had taken his body and air his breath,
He was not in heaven or earth: he was in me.

Now will be cloudburst over a countryside
Where the tongues of prophets were dry and the air was aching:
Sky-long the flash, the thunder, the release,
Are fresh beginning, the hour of the weather breaking.
Sing, you watercourses, bringers of peace!
Valleys, open wide
Your cracked lips! You shall be green again
And ease with flowers what the sun has seared.
Waking tomorrow we'll find the air cleared,
Sunny with fresh eloquence after rain.

For my friend that was dead is alive. He bore transplanting
Into a common soil. Strongly he grows
Upon the heart and gives the tentative wing
Take-off for flights, surety for repose.
And he returns not in an echoing
Regret, a hollow haunting,
Not as a shadow thrown across our day;
But radiant energy, charging the mind with power
That all who are wired to receive him surely can share.
It is no flying visit: he comes to stay.

His laughter was better than birds in the morning: his smile
Turned the edge of the wind: his memory
Disarms death and charms the surly grave.
Early he went to bed, too early we
Saw his light put out: yet we could not grieve
More than a little while,
For he lives in the earth around us, laughs from the sky.
Soon he forgave – still generous to a fault –
My crippling debt of sorrow, and I felt
In grief's hard winter earth's first melting sigh.

Think. One breath of midsummer will start
A buried life – on sunday boys content
Hearing through study windows a gramophone,

Sweet peas arrested on a morning scent –
And the man sighs for what he has outgrown.
He wastes pity. The heart
Has all recorded. Each quaver of distress,
Mirth's every crotchet, love's least tremolo –
Scarce-noted notes that to full movements flow –
Have made their mark on its deep tenderness.

Much more should he, who had life and to spare,
Be here impressed, his sympathy relayed
Out of the rich-toned past. And is. For through
Desert my heart he gives a fiery lead,
Unfolding contours, lengthening the view.
He is a thoroughfare
Over all sliding sands. Each stopping-place
Wears his look of welcome. May even find,
When I come to the snow-line, the bitter end,
His hand-holds cut on death's terrific face.

Distant all that, and heaven a hearsay word –
Truth's fan-vaulting, vision carved in flight
Perhaps, or the last delirium of self-loving.
But now a word in season, a dance in spite
Of death: love, the affirmative in all living,
Blossom, dew or bird.
For one is dead, but his love has gone before
Us, pointing and paving a way into the future;
Has gone to form its very flesh and feature,
The air we shall breathe, the kindling for our fire.

Nothing is lost. There is a thrifty wife,
Conceives all, saves all, finds a use for all.
No waste her deserts: limited rock, lightnings
And speedwell that run riot, seas that spill
Over, grass and man – whatever springs
From her excess of life

Is active and passive, spending and receipt.
And he took after her, a favourite son
In whom she excelled, through whom were handed on
Dewy her morning and her lasting heat.

Now we have sorrow's range, no more delaying –
Let the masked batteries of spring flash out
From ridge and copse, and flowers like shrapnel burst
Along the lanes, and all her land-mines spout
Quick and hanging green. Our best, our boast,
Our mood and month of maying,
For winter's bleak blockade is broken through
And every street flies colours of renaissance.
Today the hawk goes up for reconnaissance,
The heart beats faster having earth's ends in view.

Leave to the mercies of the manifold grass,
Will cover all earth's faults, what in his clay
Were but outcrops of volcanic life.
You shall recall one open as the day,
Many-mooded as the light above
English hills where pass
Sunlight and storm to a large reconciling.
You shall recall how it was warmth to be
With him – a feast, a first of June; that he
Was generous, that he attacked the bowling.

Lay laurels here, and leave your tears to dry –
Sirs, his last wishes were that you should laugh.
For those in whom was found life's richest seam
Yet they asked no royalty, one cenotaph
Were thanks enough – a world where none may scheme
To hoard, while many die,
Life; where all lives grow from an equal chance.
Tomorrow we resume building: but this
Day he calls holiday, he says it is
A time to dance, he calls you all to dance.

Today the land that knew him shall do him honour,
Sun be a spendthrift, fields come out with gold,
Severn and Windrush be Madrigal and Flowing,
Woodlarks flash up like rockets and unfold
In showers of song, cloud-shadows pace the flying
Wind, the champion runner.
Joy has a flying start, our hopes like flames
Lengthen their stride over a kindled earth,
And noon cheers all, upstanding in the south.
Sirs, be merry: these are his funeral games.

EPILOGUE

For those who had the power,
Unhesitating whether to kill or cure:
Those who were not afraid
To dam the estuary or start the forest fire:
Whose hearts were filled
With enthusiasm as with a constant wind
That, lifting the fog, the pall of vision, unveiled
Their own memorial, the stars:
There need be neither obituary nor wreath,
Accomplices of death.
These disappeared into the darkness ahead.
Followers shall find
Them walking larger than legends in that virgin land,
Their spirit shall be blowing out of the sunrise,
Their veins our rivers, their bones our bread.

Others, too, will die hard.
Spenders of life, they dealt freely with danger:
These could not learn to hoard,
To count the cost or to examine the change.

A hungry soul
Urged them to try new air-routes, and their skill
Raftered the sky with steel:
They took the field with laughter, they attacked the bowling.
In the machine's heart, regularly breathing,
We hear their hearts still beat,
Inherit their strength and swiftness through the turbine:
Pausing between shifts or in the pub at evening
We feel their generous heat;
We remember them as the glowing fruit remembers
Sap-flow and sunshine.

from NOAH AND THE WATERS

To Charles Fenby

PROLOGUE

This curve of ploughland, one clean stroke
Defining earth's nature constant to four seasons,
Fixes too for ever her simple relationship
With the sky and all systems imaginable there.

This clean red stroke, like a heart-beat of the earth's heart
Felt here under the sunlight's velvet hand,
Draws something simple and perfect as breath – that leaves
No more to be said,
And yet implies what wonders beyond, what breathing cities,
Pasture broad and untainted prairies of air.

This curve – the naked breasts of woman exalted for love,
Cradle both and summit of your superb ambition,
Move not more certainly to that far-flying
Among star-fields above even the wind's excitement,
And exhausted eddying down to peace.

Lover's eye is hawk's eye, on the whole earth
Spread for him seeing only the point of desire.
And then there is the poet's –
His gaze that like the moonlight rests on all
In level contemplation, making roof and ruin
Treachery scorn and death into silver syllables
And out of worn fragments a seamless coat.

These I must have; but more
To see this ploughland curve as a graph of history,
The unregarded sweat that has made it fertile,
Reading between the furrows a desperate appeal
From all whose share in them was bitter as iron,

Hearing the young corn whisper
The wishes of men that had no other voice.

Only then am I able to know the difficult
Birth of our new seed and bear my part of the harvest.

FIRST CHORUS

Stand with us here
On the south-western cliff of the great Jurassic escarpment,
A common for rare wood-larks, a place where wind-pumps veer
Constant as your necessity, drinking that reservoir
Free to all: invisible the veins it is life to open,
The lake only your death may look on.

Stand with us now and hear
Only the wood-lark's irrelevant song, the shepherd's whistle,
And seven-league footfall of wind striding through dry grasses.
For as yet the torrents to come are but a roaring in the ear

Of prophets, or the raving fancy of one delirious with thirst.
Pacific the sky, a delight for shepherds and hikers; though a seer
Might behold over the cities to north and north-east spreading
A stain, clouds not white, the coaling-up of wrath.

Stand with us here.
Feel underfoot the linked vertebræ of your land
Stretching north to the far fells, the head of rivers.
Prehistory sleeps below in many beds. Before
Man set a value on his thoughts or made a prison for fear,
These hills were grown up, to the sky happily married,
That now are wrinkled with the rains of more than mortal years,
Old enough to remember the first birds and the great reptiles.

Stand with us. Far and near
See history unfolded in the scrolled hills, her secret
Indelible as hieroglyphs stamped on their stone, clear
To the eye but hard for you to interpret. The green barrows
Of Britons. The high camps where Roman eagles kept watch
On Wales unblinking. The manors, cosy in combes. Dear
The dewponds, and still black the circles of Jubilee bonfires.

Stand with us here,
The past at your feet, your fingers nervous like the lark's wing
To be up and doing. And now, for today's sun goes higher,
Let your hearts grow warm as wax to take note of the future:
Let him step forward, if one there be wise to weather,
From behaviour of martens or altered tones of the smooth-voiced
                                                            weir
Able to learn and to beware.

Now look away
Into the valley and deep into the unregarded
Sweat that has made it fertile. That curve of ploughland see
As a graph of history, and hear what the young corn tries to say.
Read between those furrows a desperate appeal
Of men who had no other voice.

Now look beyond, this way.
Behold a different growth: set in ancient wood,
Grafted on to the valley stock, a new life – the Town.
Consider the uniform foliage of roofs, hiding decay
And rain-fearing pests and all the diversities of loving:
Wind-screens dazzled by the sun: strip-built roads that stray
Out like suckers to drain the country; and routes familiar
To night-expresses, the fire-crest flyers, migrating south.

Now come away
From these self-flattering heights, and like a diver plunging
Into his own image, enter the Town. You pass

L   163

Nurseries that splash crude colour over war's pale griefs,
Nurturing seed for a soil shallow as soldiers' graves:
Huts, the butt-ends of a war, Honour's sloven retreat;
And ashamed asphalt where the naked put on indifference – to-
day
Willowherb grows in the cracks, the idiot flower of exhaustion.

Now closer look this way.
Do not be deceived by the two-faced traffic signs, the expensive
Flood-lit smile of civic beauties, the fountains that play
In limelight like spoilt children. See rather how the old
Their wintering ghosts creep out on gusts of warm nostalgia:
The young, their run-ahead hope barred by Death's one-way
Approach: and the good like madmen preaching to locked faces.

Look not away –
Though ugly this, it is your foundation and your predicament.
Behind the image of glass, the mirage of brick, you await
A judgment and a choice. But listen for that which is still
Less than the whisper of clouds assembling, of arrows falling.
But look to him we will call Noah, figure of your fate,
Him understand, him obey.

SECOND CHORUS

Since you have come thus far,
Your visible past a steamer's wake continually fading
Among the receding hours tumbled, and yet you carry
Souvenirs of dead ports, a freight of passion and fear,
Remembrance of loves and landfalls and much deep-sea predica-
ment
Active upon the heart: – consider by what star
Your reckoning is, and whether conscious a course you steer
Or whether you rudderless yaw, self-mutinied, all at sea.

You have come far
To the brink of this tableland where the next step treads air,
Your thoughts like antennæ feeling doubtfully towards the
                                                    future,
Your will swerving all ways to evade that unstable void;
High stakes, hard falls, comfortless contacts lie before,
But to sidestep these is to die upon a waterless plateau;
You must uncase and fly, for ahead is your thoroughfare.

   Consider Noah's fate,
Chosen to choose between two claims irreconcilable,
Alive on this island, old friends at his elbow, the floods at his feet.
Whether the final sleep, fingers curled about
The hollow comfort of a day worn smooth as holy relics;
Or trusting to walk the waters, to see when they abate
A future solid for sons and for him the annealing rainbow.

   It is your fate
Also to choose. On the one hand all that habit endears:
The lawn is where bishops have walked; the walled garden is
                                                    private
Though your bindweed lust overruns it; the roses are sweet
                                                    dying;
Soil so familiar to your roots you cannot feel it effete.
On the other hand what dearth engenders and what death
Makes flourish: the need and dignity of bearing fruit, the fight
For resurrection, the exquisite grafting on stranger stock.

   Stand with us here and now
Consider the force of these waters, the mobile face of the flood
Trusting and terrible as a giant who turns from sleep. Think
                                                    how
You called them symbols of purity and yet you daily defiled
                                                    them:

They failed you never; for that they were always the disregarded.
Ubiquitous to your need they made the barley grow
Or bore you to new homes; they kept you hale and handsome.
Of all flesh they were the sign and substance. All things flow.

    Stand with us now
Looking back on a time you have spent, a land that you know.
Ask what formed the dew and dressed the evening in awe;
What hands made buoyant your ships, what shaped the im-
                        patient prow,
Turned sea-shells and dynamos and wheels on river and railroad:
Truth's bed and earth's refreshment – one everywhere element
In the tissue of man, the tears of his anger, the sweat of his brow.

    Then look with Noah's eyes
On the waters that wait his choice. Not only are they insurgent
Over the banks and shallows of their birthplace, but they rise
Also in Noah's heart: their rippling fingers erase
The ill-favoured façade of his present, the weird ancestral folly,
The maze of mirrors, the corrupting admirers, the silted lies.
Now must he lay his naked virtue upon their knees.

    Then turn your eyes
Upon that unbounded prospect and your dwindling island of ease,
Measuring your virtue against its challenger, measuring well
Your leap across the gulf, as the swallow-flock that flies
In autumn gathers its strength on some far-sighted headland.
Learn the migrant's trust, the intuition of longer
Sunlight: be certain as they you have only winter to lose,
And believe that beyond this flood a kinder country lies.

OVERTURES TO DEATH

To E. M. Forster

Maple and Sumach

Maple and sumach down this autumn ride –
Look, in what scarlet character they speak!
For this their russet and rejoicing week
Trees spend a year of sunsets on their pride.
You leaves drenched with the lifeblood of the year –
What flamingo dawns have wavered from the east,
What eves have crimsoned to their toppling crest
To give the fame and transience that you wear!
Leaf-low he shall lie soon: but no such blaze
Briefly can cheer man's ashen, harsh decline;
His fall is short of pride, he bleeds within
And paler creeps to the dead end of his days.
O light's abandon and the fire-crest sky
Speak in me now for all who are to die!

February 1936

Infirm and grey
This leaden-hearted day
Drags its lank hours, wishing itself away.

Grey as the skin
Of long-imprisoned men
The sky, and holds a poisoned thought within.

Whether to die,
Or live beneath fear's eye –
Heavily hangs the sentence of this sky.

The unshed tears
Of frost on boughs and briers
Gathering wait discharge like our swoln fears.

Servant and host
Of this fog-bitter frost,
A carrion-crow flaps, shadowing the lost.

Now to the fire
From killing fells we bear
This new-born lamb, our premature desire.

We cannot meet
Our children's mirth, at night
Who dream their blood upon a darkening street.

Stay away, Spring!
Since death is on the wing
To blast our seed and poison every thing.

Bombers

Through the vague morning, the heart preoccupied,
A deep in air buried grain of sound
Starts and grows, as yet unwarning –
The tremor of baited deepsea line.

Swells the seed, and now tight sound-buds
Vibrate, upholding their paean flowers
To the sun. There are bees in sky-bells droning,
Flares of crimson at the heart unfold.

Children look up, and the elms spring-garlanded
Tossing their heads and marked for the axe.
Gallant or woebegone, alike unlucky –
Earth shakes beneath us: we imagine loss.

Black as vermin, crawling in echelon
Beneath the cloud-floor, the bombers come:
The heavy angels, carrying harm in
Their wombs that ache to be rid of death.

This is the seed that grows for ruin,
The iron embryo conceived in fear.
Soon or late its need must be answered
In fear delivered and screeching fire.

Choose between your child and this fatal embryo.
Shall your guilt bear arms, and the children you want
Be condemned to die by the powers you paid for
And haunt the houses you never built?

A Parting Shot

He said, 'Do not point your gun
At the dove in the judas tree:
It might go off, you see.'

So I fired, and the tree came down
Limed leaf, branch and stock,
And the fantail swerving flew
Up like a shuttlecock
Released into the blue.

And he said, 'I told you so'.

Newsreel

Enter the dream-house, brothers and sisters, leaving
Your debts asleep, your history at the door:
This is the home for heroes, and this loving
Darkness a fur you can afford.

Fish in their tank electrically heated
Nose without envy the glass wall: for them
Clerk, spy, nurse, killer, prince, the great and the defeated,
Move in a mute day-dream.

Bathed in this common source, you gape incurious
At what your active hours have willed –
Sleep-walking on that silver wall, the furious
Sick shapes and pregnant fancies of your world.

There is the mayor opening the oyster season:
A society wedding: the autumn hats look swell:
An old crocks' race, and a politician
In fishing-waders to prove that all is well.

Oh, look at the warplanes! Screaming hysteric treble
In the long power-dive, like gannets they fall steep.
But what are they to trouble –
These silver shadows to trouble your watery, womb-deep sleep?

See the big guns, rising, groping, erected
To plant death in your world's soft womb.
Fire-bud, smoke-blossom, iron seed projected –
Are these exotics? They will grow nearer home:

Grow nearer home – and out of the dream-house stumbling
One night into a strangling air and the flung
Rags of children and thunder of stone niagaras tumbling,
You'll know you slept too long.

Regency Houses

In the abandoned heaven
Light shrinks like pools on sand –
One in a million days
That dying where they stand
Image our last and leave an
Adored light behind.

Autumn is soon. We gaze
At a Regency terrace, curved
Like the ritual smile, resigned
And formidable, that's carved
On the stone face of the dead.
Shallow a breath divides us
From the formal-smiling dead.
Light leaves this shore, these shells,
The windows glazed in death,
And soon on us beneath
A first leaf falls,
And then the next night hides us.

We who in younger days,
Hoping too much, tried on
The habit of perfection,
Have learnt how it betrays
Our shrinking flesh: we have seen
The praised transparent will
Living now by reflection.
The panes darken: but still
We have seen peering out
The mad, too mobile face
Under the floral hat.
Are we living – we too,
Living extravagant farce
In the finery of spent passions?
Is all we do and shall do
But the glib, habitual breathing
Of clocks where time means nothing,
In a condemned mansion?

Landscapes

1

This autumn park, the sequin glitter of leaves
Upon its withering bosom, the lake a moonstone –
O light mellifluous, glossing the stone-blind mansion,
October light, a godsend to these groves!

These unkempt groves, blind vistas, mark the defeat
Of men who imposed on Nature a private elegance
And died of dropsy. Let still the gay ghosts dance,
They are heartless ones we should wish nor fear to meet.

A ruin now, but here the Folly grinned –
The mad memento that one joker built:
Mocking their reasoned crops, a fabulous guilt
Towered up and cursed them fruitless from the ground.

Light drops, the hush of fallen ash, submission
Of a dying face now muted for the grave:
Through mansion, lake and the lacklustre groves
We see the landscape of their dissolution.

2

A landscape, now, with no remorse
Or symmetry, hacked out by those
Whom versatile history later chose –
Her ugliest, cash Conquistadors.

An inflamed sky reflects the wrath
Of babes from whom they hid the sun:
Disease and slag-tip smoulder on
With rancour round their narrowing path.

Towns there are choked with desperate men,
Scrap-iron gluts the sidings here:
Iron and men they mould for war,
But in their death that war will end.

From the gashed hills of desolation
Our life-blood springs to liberty,
And in the callous eyes we see
The landscape of their dissolution.

Sex-Crime

For one, the sudden fantastic grimace
Above, the red clown's-grin ripping the chalk sad sky,
Hailstones hatched out of midsummer, a face
Blanched with love's vile reversal.

                                   The spirit died
First – such blank amazement took away its breath,
And let the body cry
Through the short scuffle and infamy of death.
For the other, who knows what nice proportion of loathing
And lust conjured the deep devil, created
That chance of incandescence? Figures here prove nothing.
One step took him through the roaring waterfall
That closed like a bead-curtain, left him alone with the writhing
Of what he loved or hated.
His hands leapt out: they took vengeance for all
Denials and soft answers. There was one who said
Long since, 'rough play will end in tears'. There was Cain
In the picture-book. Forgotten. Here is one dead,
And one could never be whole again.

                                   The news
Broke a Sunday inertia: ring after ring
Across that smug mirror went echoing
And fainting out to the dim margins of incredulity.
A few raw souls accuse
Themselves of this felony and find not guilty –
Acquitted on a mere alibi or technical point.

175

Most see it as an island eruption, viewed
From the safe continent; not dreaming the same fire pent
Within their clay that warps
The night with fluent alarm, their own wrath spewed
Through the red craters of that undistinguished corpse.
All that has reached them is the seismic thrill:
The ornaments vibrate on the shelf; then they are still.
Snugly we settle down
Into our velvet and legitimate bed,
While news-sheets are yet falling all over the town
Like a white ash. Falling on one dead
And one can never be whole again.

                                           You watch him
Pulpited in the dock, preaching repentance
While the two professionals in fancy dress
Manœuvre formally to score off him or catch him.
But grief has her conventions –
The opaque mask of misery will confess
Nothing, nor plead moving extenuations.
But you who crowd the court-room, will you never be called
To witness for the defence?

                                         Accomplices,
All of you, now – though now is still too late –
Bring on the missing evidence! Reveal the coiled
Venom, the curse that needs
Only a touch to be articulate.
You, Judge, strip off! Show us the abscess boiling
Beneath your scarlet. Oh point, someone, to where it spreads
On every hand – the red, collusive stain . . .
All too well you have done your work: for one is dead,
And the other will not be whole again.

The Bells that Signed

The bells that signed a conqueror in
Or franked the lovers' bed, now mean
Nothing more heavenly than their
Own impulse and recoil of air.

But still at eve, when the wind swells
Out of the west, those rocking bells
Buoy up the sunken light, or mark
What rots unfathomed in the dark.

Broods the stone-lipped conqueror still
Abject upon his iron hill,
And lovers in the naked beds
Cry for more than maidenheads.

A Happy View

. . . So take a happy view —
This lawn graced with the candle-flames of crocus,
Frail-handed girls under the flowering chestnut,
Or anything will do
That time takes back before it seems untrue:

And, if the truth were told,
You'd count it luck, perceiving in what shallow
Crevices and few crumbling grains of comfort
Man's joy will seed, his cold
And hardy fingers find an eagle's hold.

Overtures to Death

For us, born into a world
Of fledged, instinctive trees,
Of lengthening days, snowfall at Christmas
And sentried palaces,

You were the one our parents
Could not forget or forgive –
A remittance man, a very very
Distant relative.

We read your name in the family
Bible. It was tabu
At meals and lessons, but in church sometimes
They seemed to be praying for you.

You lived overseas, we gathered:
And often lying safe
In bed we thought of you, hearing the indrawn
Breath of the outcast surf.

Later we heard them saying
You had done well in the War.
And, though you never came home to us,
We saw your name everywhere.

When home grew unsympathetic,
You were all the rage for a while –
The favourite uncle with the blank-cheque-book
And the understanding smile.

Some of us went to look for you
In aeroplanes and fast cars:
Some tried the hospitals, some took to vice,
Others consulted the stars.

But now, sir, that you may be going
To visit us any night,
We watch the french windows, picturing you
In rather a different light.

The house, we perceive, is shabby,
There's dry-rot in the wood:
It's a poor welcome and it won't keep you out
And we wish we had been good.

But there's no time now for spring-cleaning
Or mending the broken lock.
We are here in the shrouded drawing-room till
Your first, your final knock.

2

When all the sky is skimming
And lovers frisk in the hay,
When it's easy forgiving the dead or the living,
He is not so far away.

When love's hands are too hot, too cold,
And justice turns a deaf ear,
When springs congeal and the skies are sealed,
We know that he is near.

Now here was a property, on all sides
Considered quite imposing:
Take a good look round at house and grounds –
The mortgage is foreclosing.

Now Death he is the bailiff
And he sits in our best room
Appraising chintz and ornaments
And the child in the womb.

M   179

We were not shysters or loonies,
Our spirit was up to proof:
Simpler far is the reason for our
Notice to quit this roof.

We paid for our lease and rule of life
In hard cash; and one day
The news got through to you-know-who
That we'd ceased to pay our way.

Oh what will happen to our dear sons,
Our dreams of pensioned ease?
They are downed and shredded, for the wind
                  we dreaded
Worries the blossom trees.

Oh Death he is the bailiff
And his men wait outside:
We shall sleep well in our handsome shell
While he auctions away our pride.

3

Sir, I'd not make so bold as to lack all
Respect for one whose prowess in the bed and the battlefield
Have excited (and justly) universal comment.
Nor could I, if I wished –
Who, in the small hours and the talkative
Reception, have felt you ticking within my belly –
Pretend there's any worse ordeal to come.
You and I, my friend, are antagonists
And the fight's framed: for this I blame not you
But the absentee promoter. If I seem to treat
Your titles, stamina, skill with levity,
Call it the rat's bad-loser snarl, the madman
Humouring the two doctors, the point declaring
War on the calm circumference. . . .
    You have appeared to us in many guises –

Pale priest, black camel, the bemedalled sergeant
Of general conscription, a bugbear to affright
Second childhood, or the curtain drawn so deftly
To show that diamond-tiered tree
Evergreen with bliss for all good boys and girls.
You have been called the Leveller: but little
That meant to the aristos you transferred
Straight from one rotten borough to another;
Nor can our state, hollow and cold as theirs,
Much envy the drab democrats of the grave.
Happiest, in our nervous time, who name you
Peace. You are the peace that millions die for.
    If there's a moment's solace, laid like the bloom
Of dew upon our meadows; if honeysuckle
Clings to its sweetened hour, and the appealing
Beauty of flesh makes time falter in his stride;
If anywhere love-lips, flower-flaunt, crimson of cloud-crest
With flames impassioned hold off the pacing shadows –
You can rest indulgent: soon enough
They shall be all, all of your complexion.
    I grant you the last word. But what of these –
The criminal agents of a dying will
Who, frantic with defeat, conspire to force your
Earlier intervention?
It is they, your damned auxiliaries, must answer
For the self-slain in the foodless, fireless room,
For stunted hearts that droop by our olive-green
Canals, the blossom of children untimely shattered
By their crazed, random fire, and the fear like a black frost
Foreshortening our prospect, metallic on our tongues.
If I am too familiar with you, sir,
It is that these have brought you into contempt.
You are in nature. These are most unnatural.
We shall desire your peace in our own time:
But with those, your free-lance and officious gunmen,
Our war is life itself and shall not fail.

4

Forgive us, that we ever thought
You could with innocence be bought,
Or, puffed with queasy power, have tried
Your register to override.

Such diamond-faced and equal laws
Allow no chink or saving clause:
Besotted may-fly, bobbish wren
Count in your books as much as men.

No North-West Passage can be found
To sail those freezing capes around,
Nor no smooth by-pass ever laid
Shall that metropolis evade.

The tampering hand, the jealous eye
That overlooked our infancy –
Forgiven soon, they sank their trust
And our reproach into the dust.

We also, whom a bawdy spring
Tempted to order everything,
Shall shrink beneath your first caress
Into a modest nothingness.

The meshes of the imperious blood,
The wind-flown tower, the poet's word
Can catch no more than a weak sigh
And ghost of immortality.

O lord of leisure, since we know
Your image we shall ne'er outgrow,
Teach us the value of our stay
Lest we insult the living clay.

This clay that binds the roots of man
And firmly foots his flying span —
Only this clay can voice, invest,
Measure and frame our mortal best.

O lord of night, bid us beware
The wistful ghost that speaks us fair:
Once let him in — he clots the veins
And makes a still-birth of our pains.

Now we at last have crossed the line
Where earth's exuberant fields begin,
That green illusion in the sky
Born of our desert years can die.

No longer let predestined need
Cramp our design, or hunger breed
Its windy dreams, or life distil
Rare personal good from common ill.

Lord of us all, now it is true
That we are lords of all but you,
Teach us the order of our day
Lest we deface the honoured clay.

5

The sun came out in April,
The hawthorn in May:
We thought the year, like other years,
Would go the Christmas way.

In June we picked the clover,
And sea-shells in July:
There was no silence at the door,
No word from the sky.

A hand came out of August
And flicked his life away:
We had not time to bargain, mope,
Moralize, or pray.

Where he had been, was only
An effigy on a bed
To ask us searching questions or
Hear what we'd left unsaid.

Only that stained parchment
Set out what he had been –
A face we might have learned better,
But now must read unseen.

Thus he resigned his interest
And claims, all in a breath,
Leaving us the long office work
And winding-up of death:

The ordinary anguish,
The stairs, the awkward turn,
The bearers' hats like black mushrooms
Placed upon the lawn.

As a migrant remembers
The sting and warmth of home,
As the fruit bears out the blossom's word,
We remember him.

He loved the sun in April,
The hawthorn in May:
Our tree will not light up for him
Another Christmas Day.

6

It is not you I fear, but the humiliations
You mercifully use to deaden grief –
The downward graph of natural joys,
Imagination's slump, the blunted ear.

I hate this cold and politic self-defence
Of hardening arteries and nerves
Grown dull with time-serving. I see that the heart lives
By self-betrayal, by circumspection is killed.

That boy, whose glance makes heaven open and edges
Each dawning pain with gold, must learn to disbelieve:
The wildfire lust of the eyes will gutter down
To age's dim recalcitrance.

Have we not seen how quick this young girl's thoughts,
Wayward and burning as a charm of goldfinches
Alarmed from thistle-tops, turn into
Spite or a cupboard love or clipped routine?

Nearing the watershed and the difficult passes,
Man wraps up closer against the chill
In his familiar habits; and at the top
Pauses, seeing your kingdom like a net beneath him spread.

Some climbed to this momentous peak of the world
And facing the horizon – that notorious pure woman
Who lures to cheat the last embrace,
Hurled themselves down upon an easier doom.

One the rare air made dizzy renounced
Earth, and the avalanche took him at his word:
One wooed perfection – he's bedded deep in the glacier, perfect
And null, the prince and image of despair.

The best, neither hoarding nor squandering
The radiant flesh and the receptive
Spirit, stepped on together in the rhythm of comrades who
Have found a route on earth's true reckoning based.

They have not known the false humility,
The shamming-dead of the senses beneath your hunter's hand;
But life's green standards they've advanced
To the limit of your salt unyielding zone.

7

For us, born into a still
Unsweetened world, of sparse
Breathing-room, alleys brackish as hell's pit
And heaven-accusing spires,

You were never far nor fable,
Judgement nor happy end:
We have come to think of you, mister, as
Almost the family friend.

Our kiddies play tag with you often
Among the tornado wheels;
Through fevered nights you sit up with them,
You serve their little meals.

You lean with us at street-corners,
We have met you in the mine;
Your eyes are the foundry's glare, you beckon
From the snake-tooth, sly machine.

Low in the flooded engine room,
High on the yawing steeple –
Wherever we are, we begin to fancy
That we're your chosen people.

They came to us with charity,
They came to us with whips,
They came with chains behind their back
And freedom on their lips:

Castle and field and city –
Ours is a noble land,
Let us work for its fame together, they said;
But we don't quite understand.

For they took the land and the credit,
Took virtue and double-crossed her;
They left us the scrag-end of the luck
And the brunt of their disaster.

And now like horses they fidget
Smelling death in the air:
But we are your chosen people, and
We've little to lose or fear.

When the time comes for a clearance,
When light brims over the hill,
Mister, you can rely on us
To execute your will.

When they have Lost

When they have lost the little that they looked for,
The poor allotment of ease, custom, fame:
When the consuming star their fathers worked for
Has guttered into death, a fatuous flame:
When love's a cripple, faith a bed-time story,
Hope eats her heart out and peace walks on knives,
And suffering men cry an end to this sorry
World of whose children want alone still thrives:

187

Then shall the mounting stages of oppression
Like mazed and makeshift scaffolding torn down
Reveal his unexampled, best creation –
The shape of man's necessity full-grown.
Built from their bone, I see a power-house stand
To warm men's hearts again and light the land.

In the Heart of Contemplation

In the heart of contemplation –
Admiring, say, the frost-flowers of the white lilac,
Or lark's song busily sifting like sand-crystals
Through the pleased hourglass an afternoon of summer,
Or your beauty, dearer to me than these –
Discreetly a whisper in the ear,
The glance of one passing my window recall me
From lark, lilac, you, grown suddenly strangers.

In the plump and pastoral valley
Of a leisure time, among the trees like seabirds
Asleep on a glass calm, one shadow moves –
The sly reminder of the forgotten appointment.
All the shining pleasures, born to be innocent,
Grow dark with a truant's guilt:
The day's high heart falls flat, the oaks tremble,
And the shadow sliding over your face divides us.

In the act of decision only,
In the hearts cleared for action like lovers naked
For love, this shadow vanishes: there alone
There is nothing between our lives for it to thrive on.
You and I with lilac, lark and oak-leafed
Valley are bound together
As in the astounded clarity before death.
Nothing is innocent now but to act for life's sake.

188

Sonnet for a Political Worker

Is this what wears you out – having to weigh
One mote against another, the time spent
Fitting each thumbed and jig-saw argument
Into a pattern clear to you as day?
Boredom, the dull repetitive delay,
Opponents' tricky call, the discontent
Of friends, seem to deny what history meant
When first she showed her hand for you to play.

Do you not see that history's high tension
Must so be broken down to each man's need
And his frail filaments, that it may feed
Not blast all patience, love and warm invention?
On lines beyond your single comprehension
The circuit and full day of power proceed.

Questions

How long will you keep this pose of self-confessed
And aspen hesitation
Dithering on the brink, obsessed
Immobilized by the feminine fascination
Of an image all your own,
Or doubting which is shadow, which is bone?

Will you wait womanish, while the flattering stream
Glosses your faults away?
Or would you find within that dream
Courage to break the dream, wisdom to say
That wisdom is not there?
Or is it simply the first shock you fear?

189

Do you need the horn in your ear, the hounds at your heel,
Gadflies to sting you sore,
The lightning's angry feint, and all
The horizon clouds boiling like lead, before
You'll risk your javelin dive
And pierce reflection's heart, and come alive?

The Volunteer

Tell them in England, if they ask
What brought us to these wars,
To this plateau beneath the night's
Grave manifold of stars —

It was not fraud or foolishness,
Glory, revenge, or pay:
We came because our open eyes
Could see no other way.

There was no other way to keep
Man's flickering truth alight:
These stars will witness that our course
Burned briefer, not less bright.

Beyond the wasted olive-groves,
The furthest lift of land,
There calls a country that was ours
And here shall be regained.

Shine to us, memoried and real,
Green-water-silken meads:
Rivers of home, refresh our path
Whom here your influence leads.

Here in a parched and stranger place
We fight for England free,
The good our fathers won for her,
The land they hoped to see.

The Nabara[1]

*They preferred, because of the rudeness of their heart,
to die rather than to surrender.*

PHASE ONE

Freedom is more than a word, more than the base coinage
Of statesmen, the tyrant's dishonoured cheque, or the dreamer's
                                                              mad
Inflated currency. She is mortal, we know, and made
In the image of simple men who have no taste for carnage
But sooner kill and are killed than see that image betrayed.
Mortal she is, yet rising always refreshed from her ashes:
She is bound to earth, yet she flies as high as a passage bird
To home wherever man's heart with seasonal warmth is stirred:
Innocent is her touch as the dawn's, but still it unleashes
The ravisher shades of envy. Freedom is more than a word.

I see man's heart two-edged, keen both for death and creation.
As a sculptor rejoices, stabbing and mutilating the stone
Into a shapelier life, and the two joys make one –
So man is wrought in his hour of agony and elation
To efface the flesh to reveal the crying need of his bone.
Burning the issue was beyond their mild forecasting
For those I tell of – men used to the tolerable joy and hurt
Of simple lives: they coveted never an epic part;
But history's hand was upon them and hewed an everlasting
Image of freedom out of their rude and stubborn heart.

[1] The episode upon which this poem is based is related in G. L. Steer's *The Tree of Gernika.*

The year, Nineteen-thirty-seven: month, March: the men,
                                                 descendants
Of those Iberian fathers, the inquiring ones who would go
Wherever the sea-ways led: a pacific people, slow
To feel ambition, loving their laws and their independence –
Men of the Basque country, the Mar Cantabrico.
Fishermen, with no guile outside their craft, they had weathered
Often the sierra-ranked Biscayan surges, the wet
Fog of the Newfoundland Banks: they were fond of *pelota*: they
                                                 met
No game beyond their skill as they swept the sea together,
Until the morning they found the leviathan in their net.

Government trawlers *Nabara, Guipuzkoa, Bizkaya,*
Donostia, escorting across blockaded seas
Galdames with her cargo of nickel and refugees
From Bayonne to Bilbao, while the crest of war curled higher
Inland over the glacial valleys, the ancient ease.
On the morning of March the fifth, a chill North-Wester fanned
                                                 them,
Fogging the glassy waves: what uncharted doom lay low
There in the fog athwart their course, they could not know:
Stout were the armed trawlers, redoubtable those who manned
                                                 them –
Men of the Basque country, the Mar Cantabrico.

Slowly they nosed ahead, while under the chill North-Wester
Nervous the sea crawled and twitched like the skin of a beast
That dreams of the chase, the kill, the blood-beslavered feast:
They too, the light-hearted sailors, dreamed of a fine fiesta,
Flags and their children waving, when they won home from the
                                                 east.
Vague as images seen in a misted glass or the vision
Of crystal-gazer, the ships huddled, receded, neared,
Threading the weird fog-maze that coiled their funnels and
                                                 bleared

Day's eye. They were glad of the fog till *Galdames* lost position
– Their convoy, precious in life and metal – and disappeared.

But still they held their course, the confident ear-ringed captains,
Unerring towards the landfall, nor guessed how the land lay,
How the guardian fog was a guide to lead them all astray.
For now, at a wink, the mist rolled up like the film that curtains
A saurian's eye; and into the glare of an evil day
Bizkaya, Guipuzkoa, Nabara, and the little
Donostia stepped at intervals; and sighted, alas,
Blocking the sea and sky a mountain they might not pass,
An isle thrown up volcanic and smoking, a giant in metal
Astride their path – the rebel cruiser, *Canarias.*

A ship of ten thousand tons she was, a heavyweight fighter
To the cocky bantam trawlers: and under her armament
Of eight- and four-inch guns there followed obedient
Towards Pasajes a prize just seized, an Estonian freighter
Laden with arms the exporters of death to Spain had sent.
A hush, the first qualm of conflict, falls on the cruiser's burnished
Turrets, the trawlers' grimy decks: fiercer the lime-
Light falls, and out of the solemn ring the late mists climb,
And ship to ship the antagonists gaze at each other astonished
Across the quaking gulf of the sea for a moment's time.

The trawlers' men had no chance or wish to elude the fated
Encounter. Freedom to these was natural pride that runs
Hot as the blood, their climate and heritage, dearer than sons.
Bizkaya, Guipuzkoa, knowing themselves outweighted,
Drew closer to draw first blood with their pairs of four-inch
                                                    guns.
Aboard *Canarias* the German gun-layers stationed
Brisk at their intricate batteries – guns and men both trained
To a hair in accuracy, aimed at a pitiless end –
Fired, and the smoke rolled forth over the unimpassioned
Face of a day where nothing certain but death remained.

PHASE TWO

The sound of the first salvo skimmed the ocean and thumped
Cape Machichaco's granite ribs: it rebounded where
The salt-sprayed trees grow tough from wrestling the wind: it
jumped
From isle to rocky isle: it was heard by women while
They walked to shrine or market, a warning they must fear.
But, beyond their alarm, as
Though that sound were also a signal for fate to strip
Luck's last green shoot from the falling stock of the Basques,
Galdames

Emerged out of the mist that lingered to the west
Under the reeking muzzles of the rebel battleship:

Which instantly threw five shells over her funnel, and threw
Her hundred women and children into a slaughter-yard panic
On the deck they imagined smoking with worse than the foggy
dew,
So that *Galdames* rolled as they slipped, clawed, trampled,
reeled
Away from the gape of the cruiser's guns. A spasm galvanic,
Fear's chemistry, shocked the women's bodies, a moment
before
Huddled like sheep in a mist, inert as bales of rag,
A mere deck-cargo; but more
Than furies now, for they stormed *Galdames'* bridge and
swarmed
Over her captain and forced him to run up the white flag.

Signalling the Estonian, 'Heave-to', *Canarias* steamed
Leisurely over to make sure of this other prize:
Over-leisurely was her reckoning – she never dreamed
The Estonian in that pause could be snatched from her shark-
shape jaws
By ships of minnow size.
Meanwhile *Nabara* and *Guipuzkoa*, not reluctant

For closer grips while their guns and crews were still entire,
Thrust forward: twice *Guipuzkoa* with a deadly jolt was rocked,
                                                              and
The sea spat up in geysers of boiling foam, as the cruiser's
Heavier guns boxed them in a torrid zone of fire.

And now the little *Donostia* who lay with her 75's
Dumb in the offing – her weapons against that leviathan
Impotent as pen-knives –
Witnessed a bold manœuvre, a move of genius, never
In naval history told. She saw *Bizkaya* run
Ahead of her consorts, a berserk atom of steel, audacious,
Her signal-flags soon to flutter like banderillas, straight
Towards the Estonian speeding, a young bull over the spacious
And foam-distraught arena, till the sides of the freight-ship
                                                        screen her
From *Canarias* that will see the point of her charge too late.

'Who are you and where are you going?' the flags of *Bizkaya*
                                                        questioned.
'Carrying arms and forced to go to Pasajes,' replied
The Estonian. 'Follow me to harbour.' 'Cannot, am threatened.'
Bizkaya's last word – 'Turn at once!' – and she points her
                                                  peremptory guns
Against the freighter's mountainous flanks that blankly hide
This fluttering language and flaunt of signal insolence
From the eyes of *Canarias*. At last the rebels can see
That the two ships' talk meant a practical joke at their expense:
They see the Estonian veering away, to Bermeo steering,
Bizkaya under her lee.

(To the Basques that ship was a tonic, for she carried some
                                                    million rounds
Of ammunition: to hearts grown sick with hope deferred
And the drain of their country's wounds
She brought what most they needed in face of the aid evaded

N   195

And the cold delay of those to whom freedom was only a word.)[1]
Owlish upon the water sat the *Canarias*
Mobbed by those darting trawlers, and her signals blinked in
vain
After the freighter, that still she believed too large to pass
Into Bermeo's port – a prize she fondly thought,
When she'd blown the trawlers out of the water, she'd take
again.

Brisk at their intricate batteries the German gun-layers go
About death's business, knowing their longer reach must foil
The impetus, break the heart of the government ships: each
blow
Deliberately they aim, and tiger-striped with flame
Is the jungle mirk of the smoke as their guns leap and recoil.
The Newfoundland trawlers feel
A hail and hurricane the like they have never known
In all their deep-sea life: they wince at the squalls of steel
That burst on their open decks, rake them and leave them
wrecks,
But still they fight on long into the sunless afternoon.

– Fought on, four guns against the best of the rebel navy,
Until *Guipuzkoa*'s crew could stanch the fires no more
That gushed from her gashes and seeped nearer the magazine.
Heavy
At heart they turned away for the Nervion that day:
Their ship, *Guipuzkoa*, wore
Flame's rose on her heart like a decoration of highest honour
As listing she reeled into Las Arenas; and in a row

[1] Cf. Byron's comments upon 'Non-Intervention' in *The Age of Bronze*:
Lone, lost, abandoned in their utmost need
By Christians, unto whom they gave their creed,
The desolated lands, the ravaged isle,
The fostered feud encouraged to beguile,
The aid evaded, and the cold delay
Prolonged but in the hope to make a prey: –
These, these shall tell the tale, and Greece can show
The false friend worse than the infuriate foe.

On her deck there lay, smoke-palled, that oriflamme's crackling
        banner
Above them, her dead – a quarter of the fishermen who had
        fought her –
Men of the Basque country, the Mar Cantabrico.

PHASE THREE

And now the gallant *Nabara* was left in the ring alone,
The sky hollow around her, the fawning sea at her side:
But the ear-ringed crew in their berets stood to the guns, and
        cried
A fresh defiance down
The ebb of the afternoon, the battle's darkening tide.
Honour was satisfied long since; they had held and harried
A ship ten times their size; they well could have called it a day.
But they hoped, if a little longer they kept the cruiser in play,
Galdames with the wealth of life and metal she carried
Might make her getaway.

Canarias, though easily she outpaced and out-gunned her,
Finding this midge could sting
Edged off, and beneath a wedge of smoke steamed in a ring
On the rim of the trawler's range, a circular storm of thunder.
But always *Nabara* turned her broadside, manœuvring
To keep both guns on the target, scorning safety devices.
Slower now battle's tempo, irregular the beat
Of gunfire in the heart
Of the afternoon, the distempered sky sank to the crisis,
Shell-shocked the sea tossed and hissed in delirious heat.

The battle's tempo slowed, for the cruiser could take her time,
And the guns of *Nabara* grew
Red-hot, and of fifty-two Basque seamen had been her crew
Many were dead already, the rest filthy with grime
And their comrades' blood, weary with wounds all but a few.
Between two fires they fought, for the sparks that flashing spoke

197

From the cruiser's thunder-bulk were answered on their own
craft
By traitor flames that crawled out of every cranny and rift
Blinding them all with smoke.
At half-past four *Nabara* was burning fore and aft.

What buoyancy of will
Was theirs to keep her afloat, no vessel now but a sieve –
So jarred and scarred, the rivets starting, no inch of her safe
From the guns of the foe that wrapped her in a cyclone of
shrieking steel!
Southward the sheltering havens showed clear, the cliffs and
the surf
Familiar to them from childhood, the shapes of a life still dear:
But dearer still to see
Those shores insured for life from the shadow of tyranny.
Freedom was not on their lips; it was what made them endure,
A steel spring in the yielding flesh, a thirst to be free.

And now from the little *Donostia* that lay with her 75's
Dumb in the offing, they saw *Nabara* painfully lower
A boat, which crawled like a shattered crab slower and slower
Towards them. They cheered the survivors, thankful to save
these lives
At least. They saw each rower,
As the boat dragged alongside, was wounded – the oars they held
Dripping with blood, a bloody skein reeled out in their wake:
And they swarmed down the rope-ladders to rescue these men so
weak
From wounds they must be hauled
Aboard like babies. And then they saw they had made a mistake.

For, standing up in the boat,
A man of that grimy boat's-crew hailed them: 'Our officer asks
You give us your bandages and all your water-casks,
Then run for Bermeo. We're going to finish this game of *pelota*.'

Donostia's captain begged them with tears to escape: but the
Basques
Would play their game to the end.
They took the bandages, and cursing at his delay
They took the casks that might keep the fires on their ship at bay;
And they rowed back to *Nabara*, trailing their blood behind
Over the water, the sunset and crimson ebb of their day.

For two hours more they fought, while *Nabara* beneath their feet
Was turned to a heap of smouldering scrap-iron. Once again
The flames they had checked a while broke out. When the
forward gun
Was hit, they turned about
Bringing the after gun to bear. They fought in pain
And the instant knowledge of death: but the waters filling their
riven
Ship could not quench the love that fired them. As each man fell
To the deck, his body took fire as if death made visible
That burning spirit. For two more hours they fought, and at
seven
They fired their last shell.

Of her officers all but one were dead. Of her engineers
All but one were dead. Of the fifty-two that had sailed
In her, all were dead but fourteen – and each of these half killed
With wounds. And the night-dew fell in a hush of ashen tears,
And *Nabara*'s tongue was stilled.
Southward the sheltering havens grew dark, the cliffs and the
green
Shallows they knew; where their friends had watched them as
evening wore
To a glowing end, who swore
Nabara must show a white flag now, but saw instead the fourteen
Climb into their matchwood boat and fainting pull for the shore.

Canarias lowered a launch that swept in a greyhound's curve
Pitiless to pursue

And cut them off. But that bloodless and all-but-phantom crew
Still gave no soft concessions to fate: they strung their nerve
For one last fling of defiance, they shipped their oars and threw
Hand-grenades at the launch as it circled about to board them.
But the strength of the hands that had carved them a hold on
history
Failed them at last: the grenades fell short of the enemy,
Who grappled and overpowered them,
While *Nabara* sank by the stern in the hushed Cantabrian sea.

*   *   *   *   *

They bore not a charmed life. They went into battle foreseeing
Probable loss, and they lost. The tides of Biscay flow
Over the obstinate bones of many, the winds are sighing
Round prison walls where the rest are doomed like their ship to
rust —
Men of the Basque country, the Mar Cantabrico.
Simple men who asked of their life no mythical splendour,
They loved its familiar ways so well that they preferred
In the rudeness of their heart to die rather than to surrender . . .
Mortal these words and the deed they remember, but cast a seed
Shall flower for an age when freedom is man's creative word.

Freedom was more than a word, more than the base coinage
Of politicians who hiding behind the skirts of peace
They had defiled, gave up that country to rack and carnage:
For whom, indelibly stamped with history's contempt,
Remains but to haunt the blackened shell of their policies.
For these I have told of, freedom was flesh and blood — a mortal
Body, the gun-breech hot to its touch: yet the battle's height
Raised it to love's meridian and held it awhile immortal;
And its light through time still flashes like a star's that has
turned to ashes,
Long after *Nabara*'s passion was quenched in the sea's heart.

Spring Song

Floods and the voluble winds
Have warned the dead away:
In swaying copse the willows
Wave their magic wands.

The sun is here to deal
With the dull decay we felt:
In field and square he orders
The vague shadows to heel.

The licence is renewed
And all roads lead to summer:
Good girls come to grief,
Fish to the springy rod.

Our thoughts like sailplanes go
To and fro sauntering
Along fantastic cloud-streets
On warmer currents' flow.

A larger appetite,
A tautening of the will,
The wild pony tamed,
The common gorse alight.

Now the bee finds the pollen,
The pale boy a cure:
Who cares if in the sequel
Cocky shall be crestfallen?

Night Piece

Down the night-scented borders of sleep
They walk hand in hand, the lovers
Whom day abashed like the cross
Eye of the rheumatic keeper.
They are laid in the grass, and above
Their limbs a syringa blossoms
In brief and bridal white,
Under whose arch of moonshine
The impotent is made straight,
The ice-queen delighted,
And the virgin loves to moan,
And the schoolboy finds the equator.

Here too the dark plays tricks
On some of accredited glory.
The chairman's forgot his speech:
The general meets his victims,
And the pale wounds weep once more:
The archbishop is preaching
Stark naked: standing alone
Among his people, the dictator
Glares round for a bodyguard.
All the fears cold-shouldered at noonday
Flock to these shades, and await
In displeasure those who ignored them.

The Three Cloud-Maidens

Says winding Trent
Among the low pastures –
In my crystal read
Your real wish and features:
May no accident

Of flood or mist be flawing
The chaste, prophetic reed,
The child-face stream's flowing –
Says winding Trent
Among the low pastures.

Say the three cloud-maidens
Over the soiled valley –
To reproach you we rise
Wind-flushed and early:
The mist that maddens,
The clumsy floods that hurt
Innocence, all arise
Out of your shallow heart –
Say the three cloud-maidens
Over the soiled valley.

Behold the Swan

Behold the swan
Riding at her image, anchored there
Complacent, a water-lily upon
The ornamental water:
Queen of the mute October air,
She broods in that unbroken
Reverie of reed and water.

Now from the stricken
Pool she hoists and flurries,
And passes overhead
In hoarse, expressive flight:
Her wings bear hard

On the vibrant air: unhurried
The threat and pulse of wings, the throat
Levelled towards the horizon, see –
They are prophecy.

Song

It was not far through the pinewoods
That day to the lodge gate,
But far enough for the wind to phrase
My ten-year-long regret.

It was not far by the cornfield,
The tall ears looked alive:
But my heart, like corn, was broken for
A harvest I could not have.

From husk of words unspoken
I'll winnow a ripe seed:
From woods where love was shy to trespass
I'll learn the airs I need.

Oh here and unlamenting
Her graceful ghost shall shine –
In the heart mature as fruited fields,
The singing words of pine.

The Escapist

Before a rumour stirred, he fled the country
Preferring blank disgrace to any gesture
That could wipe out his failure with himself.
A warmer man no doubt had realized
His assets in our buoyant love, and taken
Some bonds to gild an unromantic exile.

Before their first reproach could reach his ears,
He had set up a private court, accepted
Full responsibility, and passed judgement.
The man whom later they reviled because
He would not face their music, was already
Self-flayed and branded in his heart for ever.

Before the story broke, he had sat down
To write it out, determined that no vestige
Of guilt be missed, no tiniest false inflection
Of heroism creep in to justify
The ugly tale. They said he was too proud to
Trust other hands even with his dishonour.

Before you heap quick-lime upon that felon
Memory, think how nothing you can do
Could touch his self-vindictiveness, and nothing
You did to cure the cowardice it avenged for.
Say, if you like, escape was in his blood –
Escape's as good a word as any other.

Passage from Childhood

His earliest memory, the mood
Fingered and frail as maidenhair,
Was this – a china cup somewhere
In a green, deep wood.
He lives to find again somewhere
That wood, that homely cup; to taste all
Its chill, imagined dews; to dare
The dangerous crystal.

Who can say what misfeatured elf
First led him into that lifelong
Passage of mirrors where, so young,
He saw himself

Balanced as Blondin, more headstrong
Than baby Hercules, rare as a one-
Cent British Guiana, above the wrong
And common run?

He knew the secrecy of squirrels,
The foolish doves' antiphony,
And what wrens fear. He was gun-shy,
Hating all quarrels.
Life was a hostile land to spy,
Full of questions he dared not ask
Lest the answer in mockery
Or worse unmask.

Quick to injustice, quick he grew
This hermit and contorted shell.
Self-pity like a thin rain fell,
Fouling the view:
Then tree-trunks seemed wet roots of hell,
Wren or catkin might turn vicious,
The dandelion clock could tell
Nothing auspicious.

No exile has ever looked so glum
With the pines fretful overhead,
Yet he felt at home in the gothic glade –
More than at home.
You will forgive him that he played
Bumble-puppy on the small mossed lawn
All by himself for hours, afraid
Of being born.

Lying awake one night, he saw
Eternity stretched like a howl of pain:
He was tiny and terrible, a new pin
On a glacier's floor.

Very few they are who have lain
With eternity and lived to tell it:
There's a secret process in his brain
And he cannot sell it.

Now, beyond reach of sense or reason,
His life walks in a glacial sleep
For ever, since he drank that cup
And found it poison.
He's one more ghost, engaged to keep
Eternity's long hours and mewed
Up in live flesh with no escape
From solitude.

Self-Criticism and Answer

It was always so, always —
My too meticulous words
Mocked by the unhinged cries
Of playground, mouse or gull,
By throats of nestling birds
Like bells upturned in a peal —
All that has innocence
To praise and far to fall.

I fear this careful art
Would never storm the sense:
Its agonies are but the eager
Retching of an empty heart;
It never was possessed
By divine incontinence,
And for him whom that eygre
Sweeps not, silence were best.

Your politicians pray silence
For the ribald trumpeter,
The falsetto crook, the twitching
Unappeasable dictator.
For any else you should be pleased
To hold your tongue: but Satan
Himself would disown his teaching
And turn to spit on these.

When madmen play the piper
And knaves call the tune,
Honesty's a right passion –
She must call to her own.
Let yours be the start and stir
Of a flooding indignation
That channels the dry heart deeper
And sings through the dry bone.

WORD OVER ALL

Word over all, beautiful as the sky,
Beautiful that war and all its deeds of carnage must in time
    be utterly lost,
That the hands of the sisters Death and Night incessantly
    softly wash again, and ever again, this soiled world.

WALT WHITMAN

To Rosamond Lehmann

The Lighted House

One night they saw the big house, some time untenanted
But for its hand-to-mouth recluse, room after room
Light up, as when Primavera herself has spirited
A procession of crocuses out of their winter tomb.

Revels unearthly are going forward, one did remark –
He has conjured a thing of air or fire for his crazed delight:
Another said, It is only a traveller lost in the dark
He welcomes for mercy's sake. Each, in a way, was right.

You were the magic answer, the sprite fire-fingered who came
To lighten my heart, my house, my heirlooms; you are the wax
That melts at my touch and still supports my prodigal flame:

But you were also the dead-beat traveller out of the storm
Returned to yourself by almost obliterated tracks,
Peeling off fear after fear, revealing love's true form.

The Album

I see you, a child
In a garden sheltered for buds and playtime,
Listening as if beguiled
By a fancy beyond your years and the flowering maytime.
The print is faded: soon there will be
No trace of that pose enthralling,
Nor visible echo of my voice distantly calling
'Wait! Wait for me!'

o

Then I turn the page
To a girl who stands like a questioning iris
By the waterside, at an age
That asks every mirror to tell what the heart's desire is.
The answer she finds in that oracle stream
Only time could affirm or disprove,
Yet I wish I was there to venture a warning, 'Love
Is not what you dream.'

Next you appear
As if garlands of wild felicity crowned you –
Courted, caressed, you wear
Like immortelles the lovers and friends around you.
'They will not last you, rain or shine,
They are but straws and shadows,'
I cry: 'Give not to those charming desperadoes
What was made to be mine.'

One picture is missing –
The last. It would show me a tree stripped bare
By intemperate gales, her amazing
Noonday of blossom spoilt which promised so fair.
Yet, scanning those scenes at your heyday taken,
I tremble, as one who must view
In the crystal a doom he could never deflect – yes, I too
Am fruitlessly shaken.

I close the book;
But the past slides out of its leaves to haunt me
And it seems, wherever I look,
Phantoms of irreclaimable happiness taunt me.
Then I see her, petalled in new-blown hours,
Beside me – 'All you love most there
Has blossomed again,' she murmurs, 'all that you missed there
Has grown to be yours.'

The Hunter's Game

I am an arrow, I am a bow –
The bow sings fierce and deep,
The arrow's tipped with cruel flame,
Feathered with passionate sleep.
When you play the hunter's game,
I am your arrow and your bow.

Only my love can bend the bow:
When the bow leaps to kill
And darkly as a nerve of night
The string throbs out, you are the skill
That drew the impulsive bowstring tight,
The hand that bent the bow.

What is the air that floats my arrow
Smoothly aloft and bears
It up to the sun, down to the dark?
You are the wanton airs
Which shape and hold its shining arc,
The innocent air that flights the arrow.

What is the victim of this arrow
That flies so fast and true?
Deep in the close, fawn-dappled glade,
Pierced by a shaft of light are you
The huntress, white and smiling, laid –
The victim of your arrow.

Departure in the Dark

Nothing so sharply reminds a man he is mortal
As leaving a place
In a winter morning's dark, the air on his face
Unkind as the touch of sweating metal:

Simple goodbyes to children or friends become
A felon's numb
Farewell, and love that was a warm, a meeting place –
Love is the suicide's grave under the nettles.

Gloomed and clemmed as if by an imminent ice-age
Lies the dear world
Of your street-strolling, field-faring. The senses, curled
At the dead end of a shrinking passage,
Care not if close the inveterate hunters creep,
And memories sleep
Like mammoths in lost caves. Drear, extinct is the world,
And has no voice for consolation or presage.

There is always something at such times of the passover,
When the dazed heart
Beats for it knows not what, whether you part
From home or prison, acquaintance or lover –
Something wrong with the time-table, something unreal
In the scrambled meal
And the bag ready packed by the door, as though the heart
Has gone ahead, or is staying here for ever.

No doubt for the Israelites that early morning
It was hard to be sure
If home were prison or prison home: the desire
Going forth meets the desire returning.
This land, that had cut their pride down to the bone
Was now their own
By ancient deeds of sorrow. Beyond, there was nothing sure
But a desert of freedom to quench their fugitive yearnings.

At this blind hour the heart is informed of nature's
Ruling that man
Should be nowhere a more tenacious settler than
Among wry thorns and ruins, yet nurture

A seed of discontent in his ripest ease.
There's a kind of release
And a kind of torment in every goodbye for every man
And will be, even to the last of his dark departures.

Cornet Solo

Thirty years ago lying awake,
Lying awake
In London at night when childhood barred me
From livelier pastimes, I'd hear a street-band break
Into old favourites – 'The Ash Grove', 'Killarney'
Or 'Angels Guard Thee'.

That was the music for such an hour –
A deciduous hour
Of leaf-wan drizzle, of solitude
And gaslight bronzing the gloom like an autumn flower –
The time and music for a boy imbrued
With the pensive mood.

I could have lain for hours together,
Sweet hours together,
Listening to the cornet's cry
Down wet streets gleaming like patent leather
Where beauties jaunted in cabs to their revelry,
Jewelled and spry.

Plaintive its melody rose or waned
Like an autumn wind
Blowing the rain on beds of aster,
On man's last bed: mournful and proud it complained
As a woman who dreams of the charms that graced her,
In young days graced her.

Strange how those yearning airs could sweeten
And still enlighten
The hours when solitude gave me her breast.
Strange they could tell a mere child how hearts may beat in
The self-same tune for the once-possessed
And the unpossessed.

Last night, when I heard a cornet's strain,
It seemed a refrain
Wafted from thirty years back – so remote an
Echo it bore: but I felt again
The prophetic mood of a child, too long forgotten,
Too lightly forgotten.

O Dreams, O Destinations

1

For infants time is like a humming shell
Heard between sleep and sleep, wherein the shores
Foam-fringed, wind-fluted of the strange earth dwell
And the sea's cavernous hunger faintly roars.
It is the humming pole of summer lanes
Whose sound quivers like heat-haze endlessly
Over the corn, over the poppied plains –
An emanation from the earth or sky.
Faintly they hear, through the womb's lingering haze,
A rumour of that sea to which they are born:
They hear the ringing pole of summer days,
But need not know what hungers for the corn.
They are the lisping rushes in a stream –
Grace-notes of a profound, legato dream.

2

Children look down upon the morning-grey
Tissue of mist that veils a valley's lap:
Their fingers itch to tear it and unwrap
The flags, the roundabouts, the gala day.
They watch the spring rise inexhaustibly –
A breathing thread out of the eddied sand,
Sufficient to their day: but half their mind
Is on the sailed and glittering estuary.
Fondly we wish their mist might never break,
Knowing it hides so much that best were hidden:
We'd chain them by the spring, lest it should broaden
For them into a quicksand and a wreck.
But they slip through our fingers like the source,
Like mist, like time that has flagged out their course.

3

That was the fatal move, the ruination
Of innocence so innocently begun,
When in the lawless orchard of creation
The child left this fruit for that rosier one.
Reaching towards the far thing, we begin it;
Looking beyond, or backward, more and more
We grow unfaithful to the unique minute
Till, from neglect, its features stale and blur.
Fish, bird or beast was never thus unfaithful –
Man only casts the image of his joys
Beyond his senses' reach; and by this fateful
Act, he confirms the ambiguous power of choice.
Innocence made that first choice. It is she
Who weeps, a child chained to the outraged tree.

4

Our youthtime passes down a colonnade
Shafted with alternating light and shade.
All's dark or dazzle there. Half in a dream

217

Rapturously we move, yet half afraid
Never to wake. That diamond-point, extreme
Brilliance engraved on us a classic theme:
The shaft of darkness had its lustre too,
Rising where earth's concentric mysteries gleam.
Oh youth-charmed hours, that made an avenue
Of fountains playing us on to love's full view,
A cypress walk to some romantic grave –
Waking, how false in outline and in hue
We find the dreams that flickered on our cave:
Only your fire, which cast them, still seems true.

5

All that time there was thunder in the air:
Our nerves branched and flickered with summer lightning.
The taut crab-apple, the pampas quivering, the glare
On the roses seemed irrelevant, or a heightening
At most of the sealed-up hour wherein we awaited
What? – some explosive oracle to abash
The platitudes on the lawn? heaven's delegated
Angel – the golden rod, our burning bush?
No storm broke. Yet in retrospect the rose
Mounting vermilion, fading, glowing again
Like a fire's heart, that breathless inspiration
Of pampas grass, crab-tree's attentive pose
Never were so divinely charged as then –
The veiled Word's flesh, a near annunciation.

6

Symbols of gross experience! – our grief
Flowed, like a sacred river, underground:
Desire bred fierce abstractions on the mind,
Then like an eagle soared beyond belief.
Often we tried our breast against the thorn,
Our paces on the turf: whither we flew,
Why we should agonize, we hardly knew –

Nor what ached in us, asking to be born.
Ennui of youth! – thin air above the clouds,
Vain divination of the sunless stream
Mirror that impotence, till we redeem
Our birthright, and the shadowplay concludes.
Ah, not in dreams, but when our souls engage
With the common mesh and moil, we come of age.

7

Older, we build a road where once our active
Heat threw up mountains and the deep dales veined:
We're glad to gain the limited objective,
Knowing the war we fight in has no end.
The road must needs follow each contour moulded
By that fire in its losing fight with earth:
We march over our past, we may behold it
Dreaming a slave's dream on our bivouac hearth.
Lost the archaic dawn wherein we started,
The appetite for wholeness: now we prize
Half-loaves, half-truths – enough for the half-hearted,
The gleam snatched from corruption satisfies.
Dead youth, forgive us if, all but defeated,
We raise a trophy where your honour lies.

8

But look, the old illusion still returns,
Walking a field-path where the succory burns
Like summer's eye, blue lustre-drops of noon,
And the heart follows it and freshly yearns:
Yearns to the sighing distances beyond
Each height of happiness, the vista drowned
In gold-dust haze, and dreams itself immune
From change and night to which all else is bound.
Love, we have caught perfection for a day
As succory holds a gem of halcyon ray:

219

Summer burns out, its flower will tarnish soon –
Deathless illusion, that could so relay
The truth of flesh and spirit, sun and clay
Singing for once together all in tune!

9

To travel like a bird, lightly to view
Deserts where stone gods founder in the sand,
Ocean embraced in a white sleep with land;
To escape time, always to start anew.
To settle like a bird, make one devoted
Gesture of permanence upon the spray
Of shaken stars and autumns; in a bay
Beyond the crestfallen surges to have floated.
Each is our wish. Alas, the bird flies blind,
Hooded by a dark sense of destination:
Her weight on the glass calm leaves no impression,
Her home is soon a basketful of wind.
Travellers, we're fabric of the road we go;
We settle, but like feathers on time's flow.

Part Two

Word Over All

Now when drowning imagination clutches
At old loves drifting away,
Splintered highlights, hope capsized – a wrecked world's
Flotsam, what can I say
To cheer the abysmal gulfs, the crests that lift not
To any land in sight?
How shall the sea-waif, who lives from surge to surge, chart
Current and reef aright?

Always our time's ghost-guise of impermanence
Daunts me: whoever I meet,
Wherever I stand, a shade of parting lengthens
And laps around my feet.
But now, the heart-sunderings, the real migrations –
Millions fated to flock
Down weeping roads to mere oblivion – strike me
Dumb as a rooted rock.

I watch when searchlights set the low cloud smoking
Like acid on metal: I start
At sirens, sweat to feel a whole town wince
And thump, a terrified heart,
Under the bomb-strokes. These, to look back on, are
A few hours' unrepose:
But the roofless old, the child beneath the debris –
How can I speak for those?

Busy the preachers, the politicians weaving
Voluble charms around
This ordeal, conjuring a harvest that shall spring from
Our hearts' all-harrowed ground.
I, who chose to be caged with the devouring
Present, must hold its eye
Where blaze ten thousand farms and fields unharvested,
And hearts, steel-broken, die.

Yet words there must be, wept on the cratered present,
To gleam beyond it:
Never was cup so mortal but poets with mild
Everlastings have crowned it.
See wavelets and wind-blown shadows of leaves on a stream
How they ripple together,
As life and death intermarried – you cannot tell
One from another.

Our words like poppies love the maturing field,
But form no harvest:
May lighten the innocent's pang, or paint the dreams
Where guilt is unharnessed.
Dark over all, absolving all, is hung
Death's vaulted patience:
Words are to set man's joy and suffering there
In constellations.

We speak of what we know, but what we have spoken
Truly we know not –
Whether our good may tarnish, our grief to far
Centuries glow not.
The Cause shales off, the Humankind stands forth
A mightier presence,
Flooded by dawn's pale courage, rapt in eve's
Rich acquiescence.

The Image

From far, she seemed to lie like a stone on the sick horizon:
Too soon that face, intolerably near,
Writhed like a furious ant-hill. Whoever, they say, set eyes on
Her face became a monument to fear.

But Perseus, lifting his shield, beheld as in a view-finder
A miniature monster, darkly illustrious.
Absorbed, pitying perhaps, he struck. And the sky behind her
Woke with a healthier colour, purified thus.

Now, in a day of monsters, a desert of abject stone
Whose outward terrors paralyse the will,
Look to that gleaming circle until it has revealed you

The glare of death transmuted to your own
Measure, scaled-down to a possible figure the sum of ill.
Let the shield take that image, the image shield you.

The Poet

For me there is no dismay
Though ills enough impend.
I have learned to count each day
Minute by breathing minute –
Birds that lightly begin it,
Shadows muting its end –
As lovers count for luck
Their own heart-beats and believe
In the forest of time they pluck
Eternity's single leaf.

Tonight the moon's at the full.
Full moon's the time for murder.
But I look to the clouds that hide her –
The bay below me is dull,
An unreflecting glass –
And chafe for the clouds to pass,
And wish she suddenly might
Blaze down at me so I shiver
Into a twelve-branched river
Of visionary light.

For now imagination,
My royal, impulsive swan,
With raking flight – I can see her –
Comes down as it were upon
A lake in whirled snow-floss
And flurry of spray like a skier
Checking. Again I feel
The wounded waters heal.
Never before did she cross
My heart with such exaltation.

Oh, on this striding edge,
This hare-bell height of calm
Where intuitions swarm
Like nesting gulls and knowledge
Is free as the winds that blow,
A little while sustain me,
Love, till my answer is heard!
Oblivion roars below,
Death's cordon narrows: but vainly,
If I've slipped the carrier word.

Dying, any man may
Feel wisdom harmonious, fateful
At the tip of his dry tongue.
All I have felt or sung
Seems now but the moon's fitful
Sleep on a clouded bay,
Swan's maiden flight, or the climb
To a tremulous, hare-bell crest.
Love, tear the song from my breast!
Short, short is the time.

It Would Be Strange

It would be strange
If at a crucial question, in wild-beast dens
Or cellars sweating with pain the stammerers
Should find their confidence.

It would be strange
If the haphazard starling learned a neat
Construction from the goldcrest, and the blackcap's
Seamless song in a night.

It would be strange
If from the consternation of the ant-hill
Arose some order angelic, ranked for loving,
Equal to good or ill.

It would be more than strange
If the devil we raised to avenge our envy, grief,
Weakness, should take our hand like a prince and raise us
And say, 'I forgive'.

The Assertion

Now, in the face of destruction,
In the face of the woman knifed out of all recognition
By flying glass, the fighter spinning like vertigo
On the axis of the trapped pilot and crowds applauding,
Famine that bores like a death-watch deep below,
Notice of agony splashed on headline and hoarding,
In the face of the infant burned
To death, and the shattered ship's-boat low in the trough –
Oars weakly waving like a beetle overturned –
Now, as never before, when man seems born to hurt
And a whole wincing earth not wide enough
For his ill will, now is the time we assert
To their face that men are love.

For love's no laughing matter,
Never was a free gift, an angel, a fixed equator.
Love's the big boss at whose side for ever slouches
The shadow of the gunman: he's mortar and dynamite;
Antelope, drinking pool, but the tiger too that crouches.
Therefore be wise in the dark hour to admit
The logic of the gunman's trigger,
Embrace the explosive element, learn the need
Of tiger for antelope and antelope for tiger.

O love, so honest of face, so unjust in action,
Never so dangerous as when denied,
Let your kindness tell us how false we are, your bloody correction
Our purpose and our pride.

Watching Post

A hill flank overlooking the Axe valley.
Among the stubble a farmer and I keep watch
For whatever may come to injure our countryside –
Light-signals, parachutes, bombs, or sea-invaders.
The moon looks over the hill's shoulder, and hope
Mans the old ramparts of an English night.

In a house down there was Marlborough born. One night
Monmouth marched to his ruin out of that valley.
Beneath our castled hill, where Britons kept watch,
Is a church where the Drakes, old lords of this countryside,
Sleep under their painted effigies. No invaders
Can dispute their legacy of toughness and hope.

Two counties away, over Bristol, the searchlights hope
To find what danger is in the air tonight.
Presently gunfire from Portland reaches our valley
Tapping like an ill-hung door in a draught. My watch
Says nearly twelve. All over the countryside
Moon-dazzled men are peering out for invaders.

The farmer and I talk for a while of invaders:
But soon we turn to crops – the annual hope,
Making of cider, prizes for ewes. Tonight
How many hearts along this war-mazed valley
Dream of a day when at peace they may work and watch
The small sufficient wonders of the countryside.

Image or fact, we both in the countryside
Have found our natural law, and until invaders
Come will answer its need: for both of us, hope
Means a harvest from small beginnings, who this night
While the moon sorts out into shadow and shape our valley,
A farmer and a poet, are keeping watch.

July, 1940

The Stand-To

Autumn met me today as I walked over Castle Hill.
The wind that had set our corn by the ears was blowing still:
Autumn, who takes the leaves and the long days, crisped the air
With a tang of action, a taste of death; and the wind blew fair

From the east for men and barges massed on the other side –
Men maddened by numbers or stolid by nature, they have their
pride
As we in work and children, but now a contracting will
Crumples their meek petitions and holds them poised to kill.

Last night a Stand-To was ordered. Thirty men of us here
Came out to guard the star-lit village – my men who wear
Unwitting the season's beauty, the received truth of the spade –
Roadmen, farm labourers, masons, turned to another trade.

A dog barked over the fields, the candle stars put a sheen
On the rifles ready, the sandbags fronded with evergreen:
The dawn wind blew, the stars winked out on the posts where we
lay,
The order came, Stand Down, and thirty went away.

Since a cold wind from Europe blows back the words in my teeth,
Since autumn shortens the days and the odds against our death,

And the harvest moon is waxing and high tides threaten harm,
Since last night may be the last night all thirty men go home,

I write this verse to record the men who have watched with me –
Spot who is good at darts, Squibby at repartee,
Mark and Cyril, the dead shots, Ralph with a ploughman's gait,
Gibson, Harris and Long, old hands for the barricade,

Whiller the lorry-driver, Francis and Rattlesnake,
Fred and Charl and Stan – these nights I have lain awake
And thought of my thirty men and the autumn wind that blows
The apples down too early and shatters the autumn rose.

Destiny, History, Duty, Fortitude, Honour – all
The words of the politicians seem too big or too small
For the ragtag fighters of lane and shadow, the love that has grown
Familiar as working-clothes, faithful as bone to bone.

Blow, autumn wind, upon orchard and rose! Blow leaves along
Our lanes, but sing through me for the lives that are worth a song!
Narrowing days have darkened the vistas that hurt my eyes,
But pinned to the heart of darkness a tattered fire-flag flies.

September, 1940

Where are the War Poets?

They who in folly or mere greed
Enslaved religion, markets, laws,
Borrow our language now and bid
Us to speak up in freedom's cause.

It is the logic of our times,
No subject for immortal verse –
That we who lived by honest dreams
Defend the bad against the worse.

Angel

We thought the angel of death would come
As a thundering judge to impeach us,
So we practised an attitude of calm or indignation
And prepared the most eloquent speeches.

But when the angel of death stepped down,
She was like a spoilt girl in ermine:
She tipped a negligent wing to some
And treated the rest as vermin.

Now we have seen the way she goes on,
Our self-possession wavers:
We'd fear a hanging judge far less than
That bitch's casual favours.

Airmen Broadcast

Speak for the air, your element, you hunters
Who range across the ribbed and shifting sky:
Speak for whatever gives you mastery —
Wings that bear out your purpose, quick-responsive
Fingers, a fighting heart, a kestrel's eye.

Speak of the rough and tumble in the blue,
The mast-high run, the flak, the battering gales:
You that, until the life you love prevails,
Must follow death's impersonal vocation —
Speak from the air, and tell your hunters' tales.

Lidice

Not a grave of the murdered for freedom but grows seed for freedom. WALT WHITMAN

Cry to us, murdered village. While your grave
Aches raw on history, make us understand
What freedom asks of us. Strengthen our hand
Against the arrogant dogmas that deprave
And have no proof but death at their command.

Must the innocent bleed for ever to remedy
These fanatic fits that tear mankind apart?
The pangs we felt from your atrocious hurt
Promise a time when even the killer shall see
His sword is aimed at his own naked heart.

Ode to Fear

The lustre bowl of the sky
Sounds and sustains
A throbbing cello-drone of planes.
Entombed beneath this caving liberty,
We note how doom endorses
Our devious fraud and folly where skeins
Of wild geese flew direct on visionary courses.

Now Fear has come again
To live with us
In poisoned intimacy like pus,
Hourly extending the area of our pain,
It seems I must make the most
Of fever's pulsing dreams and thus
Live to allay this evil or dying lay its ghost.

Fear has so many symptoms –
Planes throbbing above
Like headache, rumours that glibly move
Along the bloodstream, sleep's prophetic phantoms
Condemning what we have built,
Heartburn anxiety for those we love –
And all, yes all, are proof of an endemic guilt.

The bones, the stalwart spine,
The legs like bastions,
The nerves, the heart's natural combustions,
The head that hives our active thoughts – all pine,
Are quenched or paralysed
When Fear puts unexpected questions
And makes the heroic body freeze like a beast surprised.

The sap will rise anew in
Both man and brute:
Wild virtues even now can shoot
From the reviled interstices of ruin.
But oh, what drug, what knife
Can wither up our guilt at the root,
Cure our discoloured days and cleanse the blood of life?

Today, I can but record
In truth and patience
This high delirium of nations
And hold to it the reflecting, fragile word.
Come to my heart then, Fear,
With all your linked humiliations,
As wild geese flight and settle on a submissive mere.

The Dead

They lie in the sunday street
Like effigies thrown down after a fête
Among the bare-faced houses frankly yawning revulsion,
Fag-ends of fires, litter of rubble, stale
Confetti-sprinkle of blood. Was it defeat
With them, or triumph? Purification
Or All Fools' Day? On this they remain silent.
Their eyes are closed to honour and hate.

We cannot blame the great
Alone – the mad, the calculating or effete
Rulers. Whatever grotesque scuffle and piercing
Indignant orgasm of pain took them,
All that enforced activity of death
Did answer and compensate
Some voluntary inaction, soft option, dream retreat.
Each man died for the sins of a whole world:
For the ant's self-abdication, the fat-stock's patience
Are sweet goodbye to human nations.

Still, they have made us eat
Our knowing words, who rose and paid
The bill for the whole party with their uncounted courage.
And if they chose the dearer consolations
Of living – the bar, the dog race, the discreet
Establishment – and let Karl Marx and Freud go hang,
Now they are dead, who can dispute their choice?
Not I, nor even Fate.

Reconciliation

All day beside the shattered tank he'd lain
Like a limp creature hacked out of its shell,
Now shrivelling on the desert's grid,
Now floating above a sharp-set ridge of pain.

There came a roar, like water, in his ear.
The mortal dust was laid. He seemed to be lying
In a cool coffin of stone walls,
While memory slid towards a plunging weir.

The time that was, the time that might have been
Find in this shell of stone a chance to kiss
Before they part eternally:
He feels a world without, a world within

Wrestle like old antagonists, until each is
Balancing each. Then, in a heavenly calm,
The lock gates open, and beyond
Appear the argent, swan-assemblied reaches.

Will it be so again?

Will it be so again
That the brave, the gifted are lost from view,
And empty, scheming men
Are left in peace their lunatic age to renew?
Will it be so again?

Must it be always so
That the best are chosen to fall and sleep
Like seeds, and we too slow
In claiming the earth they quicken, and the old usurpers reap
What they could not sow?

Will it be so again —
The jungle code and the hypocrite gesture?
A poppy wreath for the slain
And a cut-throat world for the living? that stale imposture
Played on us once again?

Will it be as before —
Peace, with no heart or mind to ensue it,
Guttering down to war
Like a libertine to his grave? We should not be surprised: we
                                                knew it
Happen before.

Shall it be so again?
Call not upon the glorious dead
To be your witnesses then.
The living alone can nail to their promise the ones who said
It shall not be so again.

Part Three

The Innocent

A forward child, a sullen boy,
My living image in the pool,
The glass that made me look a fool —
He was my judgement and my joy.

The bells that chimed above the lake,
The swans asleep in evening's eye,
Bright transfers pressed on memory
From him their gloss and anguish take.

When I was desolate, he came
A wizard way to charm my toys:
But when he heard a stranger's voice
He broke the toys, I bore the shame.

I built a house of crystal tears
Amid the myrtles for my friend:
He said, no man has ever feigned
Or kept the lustre of my years.

Later, a girl and I descried
His shadow on the fern-flecked hill,
His double near our bed: and still
The more I lived, the more he died.

Now a revenant slips between
The fine-meshed minutes of the clock
To weep the time we lost and mock
All that my desperate ditties mean.

One and One

I remember, as if it were yesterday,
Watching that girl from the village lay
The fire in a room where sunlight poured,
And seeing, in the annexe beyond, M. play
A prelude of Bach on his harpsichord.

I can see his face now, heavy and numb
With resignation to the powers that come
At his touch meticulous, smooth as satin,
Firm as hammers: I can hear the air thrum
With notes like sun-motes in a twinkling pattern.

Her task there fetched from the girl the innate
Tingling response of glass to a note:
She fitted the moment, too, like a glove,
Who deft and submissive knelt by the grate
Bowed as if in the labour of love.

Their orbits touched not: but the pure submission
Of each gave value and definition
To a snapshot printed in that morning's sun.
From any odd corner we may start a vision
Proving that one and one make One.

Windy Day in August

Over the vale, the sunburnt fields
A wind from the sea like a streamer unreels:
Dust leaps up, apples thud down,
The river's caught between a smile and a frown.

An inn-sign swinging, swinging to the wind,
Whines and whinges like a dog confined,
Round his paddock gallops the colt,
Dinghies at moorings curvet and jolt.

Sunlight and shadow in the copse play tig,
While the wallowing clouds talk big
About their travels, and thistledown blows
Ghosting above the rank hedgerows.

Cornfield, orchard and fernland hail
Each other, waving from hill to hill:
They change their colours from morn to night
In play with the lissom, engaging light.

The wind roars endlessly past my ears,
Racing my heart as in earlier years.
Here and everywhere, then and now
Earth moves like a wanton, breathes like a vow.

After the Storm

Have you seen clouds drifting across a night sky
After storm's blown out, when the wind that urged them
Lies asleep elsewhere and the earth is buoyed in
Moon-locked oblivion?

Slow the clouds march: only the moon is wakeful,
Watching them trail past in their brown battalions
Spent as storm-troops after defeat or triumph
Deeply indifferent.

No, not storm-troops now, but as crowds that wander
Vague and sluggish down the disordered boulevardes
After a football match or a coronation,
Riot or lynching.

Done the act which tied them together, all its
Ebbing excitement leaves the heart a quicksand:
So betrayed by passion they move, remembering
Each his aloneness.

Clouds are not men. Yet, if I saw men move like
Clouds the wind inspires and abandons, I should
Feel that wakeful sympathy, feel the moon's wild
Ache for oblivion.

Fame

Spurred towards horizons
Beyond the common round,
Trained in ambition's cruellest ring,
Their powers grew muscle-bound

Like those equestrian public statues
Pawing the sky, that rear
And snort with furious nostrils
Nobly, and get nowhere:

A target for birds, a suntrap
For the elderly or infirm,
Children bowl hoops around them, a plaque
Nails them to their fame,

Whose strenuous flanks the sunlight grooms
While sculptured hyacinths
Breathe an odour of worship
Bedded below their plinths.

Fine for the public statues amid
Those noonday crowds: but when
Night falls and the park is emptied,
What do they think of then?

Does expectation still cast
Its overweening shadow
Onwards? Or do they look back in grief
To a foal of the green meadow? —

That foal with its mane like a carpet-fringe
And its hobbledehoy hooves;
That colt of the restive eye
Whose breast in amazement heaves —

Or, clamped to the sky in a tortured
Pose of the *haute école*,
Have they lost all kinship, horse and rider,
With the dead, the impatient foal?

The Singing Match

(Translated from the Third Eclogue of Virgil)

(*Air:* 'O waly, waly')

DAMOETAS From Juppiter the Muse begins, and Juppiter is everywhere:
He makes the earth all fruitful to be, he doth unto my ditties give ear.

MENALCAS But I'm the man that Phoebus loves. My garden is Apollo's seat.
I give him gifts, the bay-tree and the hyacinth do blush so sweet.

D. Now Galatea throws at me an apple, she's a wanton maid:
Off to the sally-trees she do run, wishing I spy where to she's fled.

M. But dear Amyntas is my flame. He is my flame, and never coy:
My little dog knows Delia well, far better doth he know that boy.

D. I have a present for my Venus, I've a present for my love,
Since I myself did notice a spot where nesties high have builded the doves.

M. Ten golden apples did I pluck, ten golden apples a wild tree bore:
All that I could I sent to my boy, tomorrow he shall have ten more.

D. O many times, O charming words she's spoke to me – my Galatea!
Whisper a little part of them, you breezes, into heaven's ear!

M. Oh what avails, Amyntas dear, that after me your heart's inclined,
If while you hunt the ravening boar, you leave me the nets to mind?

D. Send Phyllis here, send Phyllis now, Iollas, since it is my birthday:
Until I sacrifice a heifer for the crops, you keep away!

M. Phyllis I love before the rest, and Phyllis wept when she saw
me go:
Long did she say farewell to me, farewell, farewell, my
handsome beau.

D. The wolf is cruel to the sheep, and rain to cornfields that
ripened be,
Cruel the wind to orchard trees, Amaryllis' rage is cruel to me.

M. Sweet is a shower to crops, and arbute boughs to kids that
weaned be,
Sallies are sweet to breeding herds, none but Amyntas sweet
to me.

D. My Muse is but a country girl, yet Pollio this girl adores:
Fatten a heifer, Pierian maids, for him who reads the song
that is yours.

M. Fatten a bull, I'd liefer say, for Pollio new songs doth write:
Fatten a bull with venturesome horn and hooves that kick
the dust about.

D. Let him who loves thee, Pollio, come thither where thy
enjoyment lies:
Let honey flow for him in streams and brambles bear the
cardamum spice.

M. Let one who hates not Bavius, let him admire e'en Maevius'
ditties –
Aye, let him yoke a fox to his plough and milk he-goats that
have no titties.

D. O children dear who gather flowers, who gather flowers and
wild strawberries,
Run away fast, dear children, Oh run! A cold cold snake do
lurk on the leaze.

M. O sheep, beware, stray not too far, and never trust the river
bank:
Look at the ram your master, O sheep, drying his fleece that
still is dank.

D. Now Tityrus, keep you the kids from grazing nigh to the
river brim:
I mean to dip them all myself into the spring when it be time.

M. Now fold the flock, my shepherd boys: for if the heat turn the
milk again
As it has done these latter days, then we shall squeeze their
dugs all in vain.

D. Ah welladay, my little bull he peaks and pines where thick
vetches grow:
Love is the same for man or beast, 'tis death to herd and
herdsman also.

M. My flock are naught but skin and bone – and 'tis not love, I
tell thee true
An evil eye hath overlooked my pretty lambs, I know not
who.

D. I have a riddle – where on earth do space of Sky measure but
three yard?
Answer my riddle, and I'll say Apollo's not a greater bard.

M. I have a riddle – where on earth are flowers signed with a
king's name grown?
Answer my riddle, and I'll say that Phyllis you shall keep for
your own.

Jig

That winter love spoke and we raised no objection, at
Easter 'twas daisies all light and affectionate,
June sent us crazy for natural selection – not
Four traction-engines could tear us apart.
Autumn then coloured the map of our land,
Oaks shuddered and apples came ripe to the hand,
In the gap of the hills we played happily, happily,
Even the moon couldn't tell us apart.

Grave winter drew near and said, 'This will not do at all –
If you continue, I fear you will rue it all.'
So at the New Year we vowed to eschew it
Although we both knew it would break our heart.

But spring made hay of our good resolutions –
Lovers, you may be as wise as Confucians,
Yet once love betrays you he plays you and plays you
Like fishes for ever, so take it to heart.

Hornpipe

Now the peak of summer's past, the sky is overcast
And the love we swore would last for an age seems deceit:
Paler is the guelder since the day we first beheld her
In blush beside the elder drifting sweet, drifting sweet.

Oh quickly they fade – the sunny esplanade,
Speed-boats, wooden spades, and the dunes where we've lain:
Others will be lying amid the sea-pinks sighing
For love to be undying, and they'll sigh in vain.

It's hurrah for each night we have spent our love so lightly
And never dreamed there might be no more to spend at all.
It's goodbye to every lover who thinks he'll live in clover
All his life, for noon is over soon and night-dews fall.

If I could keep you there with the berries in your hair
And your lacy fingers fair as the may, sweet may,
I'd have no heart to do it, for to stay love is to rue it
And the harder we pursue it, the faster it's away.

The Fault

After the light decision
Made by the blood in a moon-blanched lane,
Whatever weariness or contrition
May come, I could never see you plain;
No, never again

See you whose body I'm wed to
Distinct, but always dappled, enhanced
By a montage of all that moment led to –
Dunes where heat-haze and sea-pinks glanced,
The roads that danced

Ahead of our aimless car,
Scandal biting the dust behind us,
The feel of being on a luckier star,
Each quarrel that came like a night to blind us
And closer to bind us.

Others will journey over
Our hill up along this lane like a rift
Loaded with moon-gold, many a lover
Sleepwalking through the moon's white drift,
Loved or bereft.

But for me it is love's volcanic
Too fertile fault, and will mark always
The first shock of that yielding mood, where satanic
Bryony twines and frail flowers blaze
Through our tangled days.

The Rebuke

Down in the lost and April days
What lies we told, what lies we told!
Nakedness seemed the one disgrace,
And there'd be time enough to praise
The truth when we were old.

The irresponsible poets sung
What came into their head:
Time to pick and choose among
The bold profusions of our tongue
When we were dead, when we were dead.

Oh wild the words we uttered then
In woman's ear, in woman's ear,
Believing all we promised when
Each kiss created earth again
And every far was near.

Little we guessed, who spoke the word
Of hope and freedom high
Spontaneously as wind or bird
To crowds like cornfields still or stirred,
It was a lie, a heart-felt lie.

Now the years advance into
A calmer stream, a colder stream,
We doubt the flame that once we knew,
Heroic words sound all untrue
As love-lies in a dream.

Yet fools are the old who won't be taught
Modesty by their youth:
That pandemonium of the heart,
That sensual arrogance did impart
A kind of truth, a kindling truth.

Where are the sparks at random sown,
The spendthrift fire, the holy fire?
Who cares a damn for truth that's grown
Exhausted haggling for its own
And speaks without desire?

POEMS 1943-1947

I seem but a dead man held on end
To sink down soon . . .

THOMAS HARDY

Le vent se lève . . . il faut tenter de vivre!

PAUL VALÉRY

To Laurie Lee

The Double Vision

The river this November afternoon
Rests in an equipoise of sun and cloud:
A glooming light, a gleaming darkness shroud
Its passage. All seems tranquil, all in tune.

Image and real are joined like Siamese twins:
Their doubles draw the willows, a brown mare
Drinks her reflection. There's no margin where
Substance leaves off, the illusory begins.

You and I by the river contemplate
Our ideal selves, glossed here, crystal-divined:
We yearn to them, knowing one sigh of wind
Will rub these precious figures from the slate.

It is not of their transience I'm afraid,
But thinking how most human loves protract
Themselves to unreality – the fact
Drained of its virtue by the image it made.

O double vision of the autumnal stream,
Teach me to bear love's fusion or diffusion!
O gems of purest water, pure illusion,
Answer my rays and cluster to a theme!

Juvenilia

So this is you
That was an I twenty-five years ago –
One I may neither disown nor renew.
Youth of the smouldering heart, the seamless brow,
What affinity between you and me?
You are a skin I have long since cast,
A ghost I carry now:
I am the form you blindly, fitfully glassed,
And the finish of your bright vow.

When I seek to peer
Through the fancy-dress words wherein you are woodenly posed
And to feel the ardours quivering there,
I am as one eavesdropping upon a captive past
Of which nothing remains but echoes and chains.
Yet, could I lay bare that primitive mural
Whereon I am superimposed,
What boldness of line and colour, what pure quaint moral
Emblems might be disclosed!

Youth of the seamless brow, the smouldering heart,
You are my twin,
Yet we seem worlds apart.
More than mere time-grains pile this desert between:
The sands that efface each instant trace
Of my passage – I think they proceed
From my own nature, their origin
Some inexhaustible need
For oblivion, and reservoir of it, deep within.

Were it not so, surely I could remember
The lyric light,
The primrose-and-violet ember
Which was your soul, my soul, when we came to write
These poems. But gone is the breath of dawn,
Clinker the dreams it fanned:
These bones, anonymous now and trite,
Are a message scrawled on the sand
That only in dying could a self indite.

What links the real to the wraith?
My self repudiates myself of yesterday;
But the words it lived in and cast like a shell keep faith
With that dead self always.
And if aught holds true between me and you,
It is the heart whose prism can break

Life's primal rays
Into a spectrum of passionate tones, and awake
Fresh blossom for truth to swell and sway.

Speak to me, then, from the haunted
Hollow of fears and yearnings lost to view,
The instrument my youth, your truth, first sounded –
This heart of impassioned hue!
Speak through the crystal, tell me the gist
Of the shadowy sequence that now is I –
What unseen clue
Threads my pearl-sliding hours, what symmetry
My deaths and metaphors pursue!

When a phoenix opens her rainbow span,
The ashes she rose from warmly speak,
'Your flight, which ends in fire as it began,
Is fuelled by all you seek.'
O beacon bird, I too am fired
To bring some message home
Whose meaning I know not. So from peak to peak
I run – my life, maybe, a palindrome,
But each lap unique.

And since at every stage I need
A death, a new self to reveal me,
And only through oblivion's veil can read
The signs of what befell me,
May not the grave of rigored love
Be but one more abyss
Between two peaks, appointed to compel me
Along the chain of light? . . . Dead youth, is this
What you have to tell me?

Sketches for a Self-Portrait

Consider the boy that you were, although you would hardly
Recognize him if you met him, even in his old haunts –
The well-shaved lawn or the Rip Van Winkle forest,
With the slag-tip reek acrid as youth's resentments
Tainting their green, or the mellow South West town
That spoke to him words unheeded but unforgotten –
Even in the haunts where he was most himself,
If a chaos can be a self: there perhaps least of all,
So deceptive are youth's environs, so quick to promise
What is not in your power, to fall in with caving moods.
But question the boy that you were, for you have no other
Clue to the man you are, to the heart divided.

Green boy, green boy, who walk through the furzes
Unsinged, and undevoured through the dandelions,
Tell me your secret.

                 I am one who peered
In every stranger's face for my identity,
In every mirror for a family likeness,
In lakes and dewdrops for the antiself.
I stunned myself upon their shallow eyes
Like a chaffinch slamming against a windowpane,
Until at last I learned to use my blindness.
I hung upon their words, and they always broke
Like the old rope they were, letting me down
Into a pit where lidless poisoners coiled:
So was I trained to climb on my own thread.
Love I desired, but the father I loved and hated
Lived too much in me, and his images of me
Fretted a frame always outgrowing them:
I went into the wilderness bearing all
My faults and his ambitions on my head.

Solitude then was my métier. I wore it
As an invisible cloak, or a glass cloche
To save from nibbling teeth and clodhopper boots
And focus the sun's eye on my sullen growth.
I kept my solitude as a young girl guards
Virginity yet wishes it away,
Impatient of the blossom cloud that endears her.
The bee forces the blossom. I knew the weak
Involuntary spasms of consent –
Ah, *coitus interruptus* with a cheating world!
I wished to commit myself to the irretrievable
As a bee is committed to the bell, or a suicide
Already half way from the parapet, to the river:
But the river whisked away and the flower turned nasty.
Or perhaps I was a coward.

Green boy, green boy,
What did the lawn teach, what did the Rip Van Winkle
Forest say, and the mellow South West town?

Resilience first, release perhaps, the lawn.
Morning brought tears and daisies, afternoon
A tennis party. Athletic clergymen. Flannels –
The uniform of a class, of a way of thinking,
Or of not thinking: as I looked for a lost ball
In the laurels, they smirched with pit-grime. It was good –
The sensual leap, the stinging drive and return
Of the blood, conflict without relationship.
I preferred singles – the world, such as it was,
Where I wanted it, on the run, with a net between us.
Winters, I walked much alone, rubbing my thoughts
Together, and prayed for a spark and imagined a forest
My tinderbox. Around me, sodden bracken:
Overhead, interlocked branches snickering.
A roar from a distant pithead as the cage dropped
Like a stone into the well of an orphic mystery.
Otherwise the forest was silent: birdless; nymphless;

Oaks hollow as history; morose and regimented
Conifers; birches with the hauteur of fashion-plates.
    And the silence said something, something about a wish
To be rooted, a wish profounder than roots, more insidious:
But the whirring wheels at the pithead, 'Stay on the surface,
You were not made to dip your hand in darkness
Or hew at the mystery's face': and the lawn replied,
'There is coal beneath us, everywhere coal, the dream
Of the deep sleep of forests, so sleep and dream':
And the oaks, 'We are hollow with unfulfilled desire –
Hurry, all is not the same in a thousand years.'
    So I returned to school, a kaleidoscope
Of shaken images, arguments jangling like glass.
And the wise grey South West town claimed me, calmed me
With the sedatives of routine, the balm of multitude.
Snatches of wisdom borne on a wet wind
Like bells or wood smoke or ancestral memories –
Borne from the high, dry plateaux of reason, weathered
To a romantic tone: and the god was reborn
In the echo. Words unheeded but unforgotten.
Call no man happy . . . Our actions burst like spray
Upon a reef, nevertheless we must act . . .
Know yourself . . . But knowing, do not presume
To swerve or sweeten what is foreordained . . .
For the heart, magnanimity; for the mind, good sense;
For the soul, a natural piety; for fate,
A stoic's bending steel . . . Nothing too much.
Pinnacles of a drowned, four-square age broke surface
Between the waking bell and the afternoon wicket –
Temperate isles in a distempered sea,
Isles of the blessed, a landfall for my tossed dreams.

Green boy, green boy, tell me your dreams.

                                                        Sit here
On the harbour wall with me. Look down at the water
Swaying, impassive, transparent, evasive:

Motiveless swaying, vibrantly motionless,
Rumpling the olive-green and slate-blue boulders
Fathomed below, and glossing the seaweed
To hair hyacinthine of marble statuary.
Look at the seabrow, puckered in sunlight,
Jigged over by millions of sparklers for ever
Quenched, re-illumined: and beyond the fireworks
A swell, a haze, a forever encroaching
Receding question. Such were my daydreams.
Dare you interpret them? Had we not better
Turn round to the castles of sand and the starfish
Sunbathers? return to our spade and bucket?
  Sleepwalking with the tides, unskilled to dive
Into the heart of my images, I practised
Words like a secret vice: words perpetually
Flung up, encroached on, crumbling, superseded,
Real to me as wet sand to a child's fingers,
More real than the quaking asphalt of the sea front
Or the rook-babble of bathers. Oh, innocent vice –
Could everything be reduced to a form of words!
But they were only a guesswork map of the terrain
Where soon I should have to fight; or else a petition
To be exempted. The love I feared and longed for
Would come in out of the sea, a terrible sun
Thrusting aside my screen of words, and pin me
To the sand like a starfish, and pick my dreams
And bleach my fears and make my dry words live.

  So, when he met a girl in the forest, he knew her
A nymph. His random casts had found a quarry.
The dead wood woke with her, she dappled the night wood
With carillons of noon, siftings elusive
Of light from the fountain of all truth and legend.
Pursuing then, he quickened his solitude
With a thousand images of her – images
More real to him than the fugitive flesh that awoke them.

Charmed life of a green boy, threading the maze
But alone no longer! The eyes and claws drew back
Deeper into the shade, biding their time.
Was he hunter or hunted? He cared not.

                                        The pursuit led
Out of the forest, over the lawn, past pitheads
Where steam puffed out in a squall of imprecation,
Through smoke-rings in college rooms and the blackened circles
Of picnic fires, across the common and
The garden, and over the moon, with a coursed hare's
Demented doublings and the closed circuit
Of the electric hare – a thousand repetitions
Of a routine immemorial, each unique,
While the horn hummed like autumn in the blood
Always a field before him, or behind him.
Till at last they came to the verge of the sea, where hunter
And hunted face the effacing and are one.

Marriage of Two

So they were married, and lived
Happily for ever?
Such extravagant claims are not in heaven's gift –
Much less earth's, where love is chanceful as weather:
Say they were married, and lived.

Tell me his marriage vow.
Not the church responses,
But alone at a window one night saying, 'Now
Let me be good to her, all my heart owns or wants is
Staked on this hazardous vow.'

When was the marriage sealed?
One day the strange creature
He loved was missing; he found her, concealed
In a coign of, wearing the secret stamp of his nature.
So matings, if ever, are sealed.

How did the marriage end?
Some marriages die not.
The government goes into exile; then
The underground struggle is on, whose fighters fly not
Even at the bitter end.

What is the marriage of two?
The loss of one
By wounds or abdication; a true
Surrender mocked, an unwished victory won:
Rose, desert – mirage too.

Married Dialogue

HE   It is out at last–
The truth that fevered my cheek and frostily glassed
My eyes against you: a creeping
Incurable disease, it passed
Into your heart from mine while we were sleeping.

SHE   I dreamt of the past,
The primrose and prairie of youth that so contrast
With this unvernal time.
Autumn is here too soon, the blast
Perplexed with waftings of our violet prime.

HE   Autumn is here. But see
With what august forgiveness the rose burns
Her faithful torch away, and the leaf turns
Her cheek to winter, and the tree
Turns the wind's edge with rags of old felicity.

SHE   There was a time when we
Were all in all, one to another. Then
I lived not by this ghostly regimen,
Breathing old summers' pot-pourri,
Rustling the faded hours we glowed in formerly.

HE   There was a time. But time piles flake on flake
Lapping the traveller asleep:
And in that sleep the heart grows numb. So we awake
To severance. Oh deep
The drifts between, treacherous the frozen lake!

SHE   Once I watched a young ocean laugh and shake
With spillikins of aspen light.
I was your sail, your keel. Nothing could overtake
Love trimmed and stiffened aright.
But now I drown, a white reef in your wake.

HE   No reef I saw. If we were shoaled,
It was the ebbing of some tide within.
But aching I behold
Fingers upon a gunwale blue with cold,
And one too weak to draw you in.

SHE   Oh crooked tide, what lies it told
So to get round me. Then, cut off, I lay
Weeping. And then I doled
My scraps of you, with hopes of you consoled
Myself, like any castaway.

HE   Love's ruin came in love's impenetrable disguise.
Ivy-shoots will prise
Apart the house they grew to adorn;
Lulling poppies snare the corn:
The lies bred up on truth are the worst lies.

SHE   I must live on where love first homed, though the wind cries
Through all its crumbling eyes;
Must walk alone the field-path where
Our linked illusions trod on air
And honeybeams of moonshine brushed our thighs.

HE   Where shall he roam
Who bears old trothings like a chain abroad
And wears a new love like a knotted cord
Over his brow at home,
But in some echoing limbo of the self-outlawed?

SHE   Let a new lover
Exploit the solitudes I first explored,
Feed on the grain I grew. Is he not scored
And signed with me? Yes, rough or
Smooth be his ways, my touch the contours still record.

HE   Oh perverse heart, that can forgive
All error and misuse
But show yourself no mercy – must you grieve
As for a fault when love-knots lose
Their angel hues?

SHE   Oh piteous heart, how could I blame
You that your sighs accuse
My lack? But would that we two were the same
As when we thought love aye renews
Our dawns and dews!

The Woman Alone

1

Take any place – this garden plot will do
Where he with mower, scythe or hook goes out
To fight the grass and lay a growing fever,
Volcanic for another, dead to me;
Meek is the ghost, a banked furnace the man.

Take any time – this autumn day will serve,
Ripe with grassed fruit, raw with departing wings,
When I, whom in my youth the season tempted
To oceanic amplitudes, bend down
And pick a rotting apple from the grass.

From every here and now a thread leads back
Through faithless seasons and devouring seas:
New blooms, dead leaves bury it not, nor combers
Break it – my life line and my clue: the same
That brought him safe out of a labyrinth.

So I, the consort of an absent mind,
The emerald lost in a green waste of time,
The castaway for whom all space is island –
To follow, find, escape, this thread in hand,
Warp myself out upon the swelling past.

2

Take any joy – the thread leads always on
To here and now: snow, silence, vertigo;
His frozen face, a woman who bewails not
Only because she fears one echoing word
May bring the avalanche about her ears.

Take any joy that was – here it remains,
Corruptless, irrecoverable, cold
As a dead smile, beneath the cruel glacier
That moved upon our kisses, lambs and leaves,
Stilled them, but will not let their forms dissolve.

O tomb transparent of my waxen joys!
O lifelike dead under the skin of ice!
O frozen face of love where my one treasure
Is locked, and the key lost! May I not share
Even the bare oblivion of your fate?

But dare I throw the past into one fire,
One burning cry to break the silence, break
The cataleptic snows, the dream of falling?
Last night I thought he stood beside my bed
And said, 'Wake up! You were dreaming. I am here.'

3

Take any grief – the maggot at the nerve,
The words that bore the skull like waterdrops,
The castaway's upon the foam-racked island,
The lurching figures of a mind's eclipse –
I have felt each and all as love decayed.

Yet every grief revives a fainting love.
They are love's children too; I live again
In them; my breast yearns to their innocent cruelty.
If only tears can float a stranded heart,
If only sighs can move it, I will grieve.

The pleasured nerve, the small-talk in the night,
The voyaging when isles were daisy-chains,
The dance of mere routine – if I could reach them
Again through this sick labyrinth of grief,
I would rejoice in it, to reach them so.

R 259

Alas, hull-down upon hope's ashen verge
Hastens the vessel that our joined hands launched,
Stretching my heart-strings out beyond endurance.
Ah, will they never snap? Can I not climb
The signal hill, and wave, and *mean* goodbye?

Ending

That it should end so! –
Not with mingling tears
Nor one long backward look of woe
Towards a sinking trust,
A heyday's afterglow;
Not even in the lash and lightning
Cautery of rage!
But by this slow
Fissure, this blind numb grinding severance
Of floe from floe.
Merciless god, to mock your failures so!

Heart and Mind

Said Heart to Mind at the close of day,
I was older than you, yet I led you astray
Fancying I knew each twist and turn of our way,
Said Heart to Mind.
The blind would still have been leading the blind
Whichever of us had held the sway,
Answered the pensive Mind.

I was younger than you, the Mind went on,
Yet you carried me through the fire of noon
And the chilling shades: of all I encountered, none
Was stronger than you.
Said Heart, I could feed upon dust or rue,
But you, the daintiest eater, have shown
What a rational diet can do.

So queer a partnership never was sealed –
A sceptic hungry for truth revealed,
A fool to his rule-of-thumb vision unreconciled
From the very start:
No wonder we almost pulled apart,
Envious each of his comrade's field,
Pursued the plaintive Heart.

No marriage is proof against travail or bliss,
Spoke Mind. How uniting can be the abyss,
How chafing the bond between all earth's denizens – this
Is what marriages prove.
And this we have learnt from our seasoned love –
When heart and mind agree, they kiss
Over an opening grave.

A Failure

The soil was deep and the field well-sited,
    The seed was sound.
Average luck with the weather, one thought,
    And the crop would abound.

If harrowing were all that is needed for
    Harvest, his field
Had been harrowed enough, God knows, to warrant
    A record yield.

He gazed from a hill in the breezy springtime:
    That field was aflow
With wave upon wave like a sea's green shallows
    Breathing below.

He looked from a gate one summer morning
    When the mists uprolled:
Headland to headland those fortunate acres
    Seemed solid gold.

He stood by the field as the day of harvest
    Dawned. But, oh,
The fruit of a year's work, a lifetime's lore,
    Had ceased to grow.

No wickedest weather could thus have turned,
    As it were overnight,
His field to so wan and weedy a showing:
    Some galloping blight

From earth's metabolism must have sprung
    To ruin all;
Or perhaps his own high hopes had made
    The wizened look tall.

But it's useless to argue the why and wherefore.
    When a crop is so thin,
There's nothing to do but to set the teeth
    And plough it in.

The Unwanted

On a day when the breath of roses
    Plumpened a swooning breeze
And all the silken combes of summer
    Opened wide their knees,
Between two sighs they planted one –
A willed one, a wanted one –
And he will be the sign, they said, of our felicities.

Eager the loins he sprang from,
    Happy the sheltering heart:
Seldom had the seed of man
    So charmed, so clear a start.
And he was born as frail a one,
As ailing, freakish, pale a one
As ever the wry planets knotted their beams to thwart.

Sun locked up for winter;
    Earth an empty rind:
Two strangers harshly flung together
    As by a flail of wind.
Oh was it not a furtive thing,
A loveless, damned, abortive thing –
This flurry of the groaning dust, and what it left behind!

Sure, from such warped beginnings
    Nothing debonair
Can come? But neither shame nor panic,
    Drugs nor sharp despair
Could uproot that untoward thing,
That all too fierce and froward thing:
Willy-nilly born it was, divinely formed and fair.

263

The Sitting

(*for Laurence Gowing*)

So like a god I sit here,
One of those stone dreamers quarried from solitude,
A genius – if ever there was one – of the place:
The mountain's only child, lips aloof as a snow-line,
Forearms impassive along the cloud-base of aeons,
Eyes heavy on distance –
Graven eyes that flinch not, flash not, if eagles
Clap their wings in my face.

With hieratic gestures
He the suppliant, priest, interpreter, subtly
Wooing my virtue, officiates by the throne.
I know the curious hands are shaping, reshaping the image
Of what is only an image of things impalpable.
I feel how the eyes strain
To catch a truth behind the oracular presence –
Eyes that augur through stone.

And the god asks, 'What have I for you
But the lichenous shadow of thought veiling my temple,
The runnels a million time-drops have chased on my cheek?'
And the man replies, 'I will show you the creed of your bone,
                                             I'll draw you
The shape of solitude to which you were born.'
And the god cries, 'I am meek,
Brushed by an eagle's wing; and a voice bids me
Speak. But I cannot speak.'

The god thinks, Let him project, if
He must, his passionate shapings on my stone heart,
Wrestle over my body with his sprite,
Through these blind eyes imagine a skin-deep world in per-
spective:
Let him make, if he will, the crypt of my holy mountain
His own: let even the light
That bathes my temple become as it were an active
Property of his sight.

O man, O innocent artist
Who paint me with green of your fields, with amber or yellow
Of love's hair, red of the heart's blood, eyebright blue,
Conjuring forms and rainbows out of an empty mist –
Your hand is upon me, as even now you follow
Along the immortal clue
Threading my veins of emerald, topaz, amethyst,
And know not it ends in you.

Statuette: Late Minoan

Girl of the musing mouth,
The mild archaic air,
For whom do you subtly smile?
Yield to what power or prayer
Breasts vernally bare?

I seem to be peering at you
Through the wrong end of time
That shrinks to a bright, far image –
Great Mother of earth's prime –
A stature sublime.

So many golden ages
Of sunshine steeped your clay,
So dear did the maker cherish
In you life's fostering ray,
That you warm us today.

Goddess or girl, you are earth.
The smile, the offered breast –
They were the dream of one
Thirsting as I for rest,
As I, unblest.

The Revenant

Out of the famous canyon
Deeper than sleep,
From the nerveless tarn of oblivion
She climbed. Dark was the slope,
And her companion
Gave not one love-glance back to brighten it.
Only the wind-chafed rope
Of melody held her
To him that haled her
Lifeward, praising the fire and delight in it.

On the gist of that lay or its burden
Legend is dumb.
How else, though, with love-looks forbidden
Could he say, 'Come back to me, come' –
Could he touch the long-hidden
Spring of a shade unfleshed, unfertilized
Than by singing, oh, crust and crumb,
Bark, sap, flesh, marrow –
Life's all, in the narrow
Ambit of sense flowering, immortalized?

Glimmering tall through the gloom
In her phantom garment,
Like a daffodil when its stem
Feels trembling the first endearment
Of amorous bloom,
She palely paused, on the verge of light again.
One step to break from her cerement,
Yes, daffodil-rayed
From the mould of the shade –
No revenant now, a golden wife again.

Had death become then, already,
A habit too strong
For her to break? The steady
Pulsing of Orpheus' song
– Though lightwards led he –
Grew faint in her. She wept for astonishment,
Feared she could never belong
To life, be at home there,
Find aught but harm there,
Till that last step seemed less a birth than a banishment.

What strand of his love was the weak one,
Or how it befell
That a song which could melt the Dark One,
Death's granite lord, with its spell
Saved not his meek one,
Moved not his meek one to step from the last of her
Terrors, no man may tell.
He felt the cord parting,
The death-wound smarting:
He turned his head but to glimpse the ghost of her.

So, as a pebble thrown
From a cliff face, soaring
Swerves back, less like a stone
Than a bird, ere it falls to the snoring

Surf, she was gone.
Reluctant her going: but the more bitterly
Mocked were his love, his imploring –
That the gods spoke
As seldom they speak
On matters of life and death, non-committally.

The House-Warming

Did you notice at all as you entered the house,
    Your dove-treed house,
Traces of one who was there before you
Imagining roseate company for you,
    While the locked rooms lay in a drowse?

One there was who paced to and fro,
    To and fro
Through the empty house with an occupied air,
Veiled in the passage, soft on the stair,
    And kept its heart aglow.

Did you feel, when first you stepped in the hall,
    Stepped in the hall,
A note of warmth like a weir's deep humming?
A message marked 'To await her coming'
    Written on hearth and wall?

One had been there for better or worse,
    Better or worse,
Curtaining, carpeting, lighting all
Your rooms with a love ineffaceable;
    And still in the night he stirs.

Fear him not. He is but a shade,
    A homely shade
For no dread signs or haunting cast:
Not a phantom risen like spray from the past,
    But a ghost by the future made.

Love enmeshed in his own folly –
    Mischance or folly –
Expiates a deed for ever undone,
Weeps for all that it could have won
    Of living together wholly.

Such is the tenant you'll have beside you,
    Often beside you
Through the spoilt Junes when a gusty rain
Strums fitful arpeggios on the pane,
    The dawns when light is denied you.

But here may you find, for all his fretting
    And gaunt regretting,
Between the dove-tops and the weir's
Undying fall, how broken years
    Can sing to a new setting.

Meeting

Did I meet you again?
Did I meet you again in the flesh we have come to know,
That evening of chorusing colours a week ago?
Or was it delusion wrung from a faulted brain
When we seemed enveloped in love like naked dunes
Effaced by a seventh wave's onrush and undertow?
Did I meet you again?

Though I meet you again,
Though I meet you a thousand times, surely the crest
Of our quickening, breaking love can never be blessed
With so generous a reach and radiance as fired it then.
Since meetings must have their peak, and the luckiest matings
Fade from golden to drab, perhaps it is best
Not to meet you again.

If I met you again,
Met you again after years of extinct days,
Oh, from dry air such a dance of aureate sprays
Would break and freshly figure the lost refrain
That a tremor would wring my heart's rock, and I'd sigh,
'Two loves which might have bloomed at the zenith always
Are meeting again.'

The Heartsease

Do you remember that hour
In a nook of the flowing uplands
When you found for me, at the cornfield's edge,
A golden and purple flower?
Heartsease, you said. I thought it might be
A token that love meant well by you and me.

I shall not find it again
With you no more to guide me.
I could not bear to find it now
With anyone else beside me.
And the heartsease is far less rare
Than what it is named for, what I can feel nowhere.

Once again it is summer:
Wildflowers beflag the lane
That takes me away from our golden uplands,
Heart-wrung and alone.
The best I can look for, by vale or hill,
A herb they tell me is common enough – self-heal.

Is it far to go?

Is it far to go?
   A step – no further.
Is it hard to go?
   Ask the melting snow,
   The eddying feather.

What can I take there?
   Not a hank, not a hair.
What shall I leave behind?
   Ask the hastening wind,
   The fainting star.

Shall I be gone long?
   For ever and a day.
To whom there belong?
   Ask the stone to say,
   Ask my song.

Who will say farewell?
   The beating bell.
Will anyone miss me?
   That I dare not tell –
   Quick, Rose, and kiss me.

New Year's Eve

ODE

The moon slides through a whey of cloud; the running
Cloud thins over the moon, and again curdles.
Milk of the word, flow!
Shine forth, my shadowed clay!

A five-bell peal stumbles up from the valley;
The midnight constellations mass their fire.
Aspire, my blindworm heart!
Arrogant heart, be humble!

The midnight constellations hold their fire,
The bells ring up to volley a new year in.
Now comes the zero between
Desire and resignation,

Between cast-iron past and plastic future;
But equally, haunters of this unnatural pause,
Remorse for what is to be,
Doubt of all that has passed.

Moon-floods heighten the valley with glimmerings like
The feel of a memory before it is born:
The stars burn to deliver
Their pregnant souls of the dying.

We are caught, all of us, in time's fine net,
Walled up in time: yet still we seek a secret
Spring, a weak mesh, where we may
Break out and be immortal.

So conscience, need, imagination pierce
An arbitrary point between two years:
The fabric tears; but in truth
It is we, not time, who bleed.

We lament not one year only
Gone with its chance and change
Disavowed, its range of blessings unbought or unpaid for,
But all our time lost, profitless, misspent.

Through this pinprick, like life-blood,
The ghosts of time we killed
Spill out – an age coarse custom has buried alive,
And sightless hours, and pallor of weeks unquickened.

Cuckoophrase of children
In their green enchantment
Where slanting beams fall warm and cool as larksong –
A woodnote rill unheard through afterdays.

Unseen the sunburst Aprils
And the bloomed Octobers –
Oh, tremulous rivers danced by primula light!
Oh, blaze of marigold where love has been!

The holly fire unfelt,
The snowmaid left asleep,
The cheap, the rare joy thrown away half-eaten,
The nimbus round each truth-pang unacknowledged.

Unfelt, unseen, unheard
So much that would have ripened
An open heart, and left a sweet taste there
After its blossomy aura was dispelled.

But, if the fluent senses
So often are benumbed,
What has our fumbling virtue to look back on?
How much has it passed up, mishandled, ruined!

Tonight, as flyers stranded
On a mountain, the battery fading, we tap out
Into a snow-capped void our weakening
Vocations and desires.

Bound by the curse of man –
To live in his future, which is to live surely
In his own death – we endure the embrace of the present
But yearn for a being beyond us;

Beyond our powers and our time,
Behind the pinnacle stars, the horizon sleep,
Beneath the deepest kiss of heaven's azure
And the roots of Atlantis flowers.

Into the blue we project
Our dreaming shadows. And is the hope forlorn
That in them we may be reborn, that our images
More masterful are, more true

Than we? The bells upclamouring
Like hungry beaks from a nest, the eyes that strain
To read the stars – vainly still they implore
Eternity to reveal

The virgin truths it is sworn
By its own laws to guard . . . Then turn away
Before the star-scape blinds or the moon maddens.
Earth is your talent. Use it.

Ring bells for here and now.
Time's your condition; and in time alone
May man, full grown, reach out over the void
A rapt, creator's wing.

MEDITATION

At a junction of years I stand, with the stars palsied
And the bells stumbling o'er me;
My life a pinprick in time, and half a lifetime
At the very most before me.
The trembling stars, the cracked bells tongue in chorus,
'Begone! It is better to go
Not when the going but the staying is good.'
I have suspected so
Often enough, looking down from a height of love
On the flats it momently crowned,
Looking up from the workaday, golden, orthodox level
To the bluffs and the terrors beyond.
But living becomes a habit, like any other
No easier to break than to sanction;
It numbs the sense and dissembles the earth's raw features
With action drifted on action:
Till at last, as a child picking flowers near home, from flower to
Flower enticed, will find
Himself the next moment lost in another country;
As, when a hill's undermined,
A windowframe jammed or a door flying open tell one
The hill has invisibly moved: –
So we look up one day and see we are dying
From the difference in all we have loved.

If I balance the year's account, in the right-hand column
What new assets are shown?
One cloud left behind in a cloudless sky, like a plume
From a white May-day long flown:
One elm ash-budded with starlings which brassily jingled
Like a sack of curtain-rings shaken:
Some nights when thought of my love was sweet as a child's
Birthday to dream of, to wake on.
What can a few such casual entries amount to

S   275

Against the perpetual drain
Of the real into abstractions – life just jetting
And falling in a fountain's rain?
And then, the expansive follies, the petty withdrawals
Swelling an overdraft
I must carry forward to next year, not to be cancelled
By any godsend or graft.
Look at this left-hand column! Does it read like
A soul whose credit is good? –
This mind wasting on wildcat speculation
Half it has understood;
This man for ever trimming, tacking and wearing
His truth to keep the capricious
Wind of a woman's favour; this heart by turns
Too gullible, too suspicious?

Lost, profitless, misspent – how can last year's self
Gratify or engross,
Unless you believe that, by spiritual accountings,
The profit is in the loss?
Turn to the future, you say: plan to improve:
Tonight we make good resolutions.
But I would plan for the present, and this involves
Such a whirl of lightning decisions
And intuitions, that for the nearest distance
I'd have not a glance to spare.
Let them take their turn, I say – the unborn roses,
The morrows foul or fair;
Let them wait their turn, those siren hills exhaling
A violet fluorescence,
The one-eyed cannibals and the horned dilemmas –
All, all that is not Presence.
Our fear makes myths of the future, even as our love does
Of the past: and, I ask myself, how
Can I face a mythical future unless I am armed
Cap-à-pie in a magical Now?

Invulnerable Now, my saviour, always
Dying, but never dead!
My winged shoes, my clairvoyant shield, my cap of
Darkness upon the head!

Yet the Now is a ghost too, fleetingly glimpsed at the turn
Of an agony, or in the lee of
A joy, for ever vanishing through some secret
Door that I have not the key of –
An unborn thing, a ghost of the real miscarried
By accident or neglect –
Unless it is free to drink my living blood
And in my flesh to be decked:
My flesh and blood, themselves a web of experience
Discarded, renewed, amassed.
Ah no, the present is nothing unless it is spun from
A live thread out of the past,
As the clarinet airs of the early morn are echoed
By eve's full-hearted strings,
As the stars and the bells in April grass foreshadow
Winter's pure crystallings.
There are September mornings when every shrub
Sparkles an hour and dances
Spangled with diamond parures, for a heavy dew
Makes visible and enhances
The spider webs. Oh fleeting, magical Presence!
Oh time-drops caught in a few
Workaday filaments! Nevertheless, the spider
Spins not to catch the dew.

To live the present, then, not to live for it –
Let this be one of today's
Resolutions; and the other, its corollary,
To court the commonplace.
Whatever is common to life's diversity must,
For me, be the one eternal

Truth, or if naught is for ever, at least the medium
Wherein I may best discern all
The products of time, embalmed, alive, or prefigured.
Let me brood on the face of a field,
The faces in streets, until each hero is honoured,
Each unique blade revealed.
Alluring the past, the future, their bright eyes veiled
Or enlarged in a mist of fable:
But he who can look with the naked eye of the Now –
He is the true seer, able,
To witness the rare in the common, and read the common
Theme for all time appointed
To link our variations . . . And though my todays are
Repetitive, dull, disjointed,
I must continue to practise them over and over
Like a five-finger exercise,
Hoping my hands at last will suddenly flower with
Passion, and harmonize.

Emily Brontë

All is the same still. Earth and heaven locked in
A wrestling dream the seasons cannot break:
Shrill the wind tormenting my obdurate thorn trees,
Moss-rose and stone-chat silent in its wake.
Time has not altered here the rhythms I was rocked in,
Creation's throb and ache.

All is yet the same, for mine was a country
Stoic, unregenerate, beyond the power
Of man to mollify or God to disburden –
An ingrown landscape none might long endure
But one who could meet with a passion wilder-wintry
The scalding breath of the moor.

All is yet the same as when I roved the heather
Chained to a demon through the shrieking night,
Took him by the throat while he flailed my sibylline
Assenting breast, and won him to delight.
O truth and pain immortally bound together!
O lamp the storm made bright!

Still on those heights prophetic winds are raving,
Heath and harebell intone a plainsong grief:
'Shrink, soul of man, shrink into your valleys —
Too sharp that agony, that spring too brief!
Love, though your love is but the forged engraving
Of hope on a stricken leaf!'

Is there one whom blizzards warm and rains enkindle
And the bitterest furnace could no more refine?
Anywhere one too proud for consolation,
Burning for pure freedom so that he will pine,
Yes, to the grave without her? Let him mingle
His barren dust with mine.

But is there one who faithfully has planted
His seed of light in the heart's deepest scar?
When the night is darkest, when the wind is keenest,
He, he shall find upclimbing from afar
Over his pain my chaste, my disenchanted
And death-rebuking star.

Birthday Poem for Thomas Hardy

Is it birthday weather for you, dear soul?
Is it fine your way,
With tall moon-daisies alight, and the mole
Busy, and elegant hares at play
By meadow paths where once you would stroll
In the flush of day?

I fancy the beasts and flowers there beguiled
By a visitation
That casts no shadow, a friend whose mild
Inquisitive glance lights with compassion,
Beyond the tomb, on all of this wild
And humbled creation.

It's hard to believe a spirit could die
Of such generous glow,
Or to doubt that somewhere a bird-sharp eye
Still broods on the capers of men below,
A stern voice asks the Immortals why
They should plague us so.

Dear poet, wherever you are, I greet you.
Much irony, wrong,
Innocence you'd find here to tease or entreat you,
And many the fate-fires have tempered strong,
But none that in ripeness of soul could meet you
Or magic of song.

Great brow, frail frame – gone. Yet you abide
In the shadow and sheen,
All the mellowing traits of a countryside
That nursed your tragi-comical scene;
And in us, warmer-hearted and brisker-eyed
Since you have been.

Who Goes There?

(for Walter de la Mare, on his 75th birthday)

Who goes there?
What sequestered vale at the back of beyond
Do you come from – you with the moonbeam wand,
The innocent air?
And how got you here, spirited on like a bubble of silence past
The quickset ears, the hair-trigger nerves at each post?

> My staff is cut from the knowledge tree.
> My place no infidel eye can see.
> My way is a nonchalant one,
> Wilful as wind yet true as the line of a bee.
> My name is – Anon.

Are you aware
That you're trespassing, sir, on a battleground?
It's hard to see what excuse can be found
For magicians where
All light and airy ways must endanger the men's morale.
What business have you with the sturdy ranks of the real?

> I bring them dew from earth's dayspring.
> Fire from the first wild rose I bring.
> And this – my deepest art –
> I bring them word from their own hungering
> Beleaguered heart.

Pass, friend. You bear
Gifts that, although men commonly flout them
Being hardened, or born, to live without them,
Are none the less rare.
Pass, friend, and fare you well, and may all such travellers be
                                                        speeded
Who bring us news we had almost forgot we needed.

Lines for Edmund Blunden on his Fiftieth Birthday

Your fiftieth birthday. What shall we give you?
    An illuminated address
Would be hard on one who was never at home with
    Pomp or pretentiousness.
Here is a loving-cup made from verse,
    For verse is your favourite of metals:
Imagine its stem like a tulip stalk,
    Its bowl a tulip's petals
And the whole as gracefully formed and charactered
    As a poem of your own.
What shall the toast be? Fifty years more?
    A century? Let it be known
That a true poet's age is truthfully reckoned
    Not in years but in song:
So we drink instead to that happy girl
    Your Muse – may she live long!
But we pledge our love, our love for one
    Who never has burned or bowed
To popular gods, and when fame beckons
    Modestly melts in the crowd.
Into the crowd of your haunting fancies –
    The streams, the airs, the dews,
The soldier shades and the solacing heartbeams –
    You melt, and fame pursues;
And our good wishes follow you, even
    To the fortunate meadows where
Tonight your loving-cup is raised
    By Shelley, Hunt and Clare.

Buzzards Over Castle Hill

A world seems to end at the top of this hill.
Across it, clouds and thistle-clocks fly,
And ragged hedges are running down from the sky,
As though the wild had begun to spill
Over a rampart soon to be drowned
With all it guards of domesticated ground.

It was silent here on the slope of the hill.
But now, now, as if the wild grass
And the wild sky had found their voices at last
And they were one voice, there comes a shrill
Delirious mewing, thin as air,
A wraith-like rumour, nowhere and everywhere.

Over the hill three buzzards are wheeling
On the glass sky their skaters' curves.
Each in its solemn figures-of-nought preserves
Some thread invisible, reeling, unreeling,
Then glides to a stop and with wings outlined
Motionless broods there balancing on the wind.

Often enough ere now I have eyed them –
Those three celestial bodies appear
Cutting their abstract figures year after year –
But never have fathomed what instinct rides them
Round heaven's dome like a frozen pond,
Nor why they are always three, and what is the bond

Between them: although you might well surmise
They are earth-souls doomed in their gyres to unwind
Some tragic love-tangle wherein they had mortally pined,
When you hear those phantom, famishing cries.
But birds are birds. No human key
Of fond frustration unites the haunting three.

Wild natures, kin to all cageless things –
Thistledown, grass and cloud – yet mewing
So ghostly, no prey nor animal need pursuing
In those pure rings and hoverings,
I watch the angelic pastime until
I seem to know what is beyond the hill.

A Hard Frost

A frost came in the night and stole my world
And left this changeling for it – a precocious
Image of spring, too brilliant to be true:
White lilac on the windowpane, each grass-blade
Furred like a catkin, maydrift loading the hedge.
The elms behind the house are elms no longer
But blossomers in crystal, stems of the mist
That hangs yet in the valley below, amorphous
As the blind tissue whence creation formed.
 The sun looks out, and the fields blaze with diamonds.
Mockery spring, to lend this bridal gear
For a few hours to a raw country maid,
Then leave her all disconsolate with old fairings
Of aconite and snowdrop! No, not here
Amid this flounce and filigree of death
Is the real transformation scene in progress,
But deep below where frost
Worrying the stiff clods unclenches their
Grip on the seed and lets our future breathe.

The Christmas Tree

Put out the lights now!
Look at the Tree, the rough tree dazzled
In oriole plumes of flame,
Tinselled with twinkling frost fire, tasselled
With stars and moons – the same
That yesterday hid in the spinney and had no fame
Till we put out the lights now.

Hard are the nights now:
The fields at moonrise turn to agate,
Shadows are cold as jet;
In dyke and furrow, in copse and faggot
The frost's tooth is set;
And stars are the sparks whirled out by the north wind's fret
On the flinty nights now.

So feast your eyes now
On mimic star and moon-cold bauble:
Worlds may wither unseen,
But the Christmas Tree is a tree of fable,
A phoenix in evergreen,
And the world cannot change or chill what its mysteries mean
To your hearts and eyes now.

The vision dies now
Candle by candle: the tree that embraced it
Returns to its own kind,
To be earthed again and weather as best it
May the frost and the wind.
Children, it too had its hour – you will not mind
If it lives or dies now.

The Chrysanthemum Show

Here's Abbey Way: here are the rooms
    Where they held the chrysanthemum show –
Leaves like talons of greenfire, blooms
Of a barbarous frenzy, red, flame, bronze –
And a schoolboy walked in the furnace once,
    Thirty years ago.

You might have thought, had you seen him that day
    Mooching from stall to stall,
It was wasted on him – the prize array
Of flowers with their resinous, caustic tang,
Their colours that royally boomed and rang
    Like gongs in the pitchpine hall.

Any tongue could scorch him; even hope tease
    As if it dissembled a leer:
Like smouldering fuse, anxieties
Blindwormed his breast. How should one feel,
Consuming in youth's slow ordeal,
    What flashes from flower to flower?

Yet something did touch him then, at the quick,
    Like a premature memory prising
Through flesh. Those blooms with the bonfire reek
And the flaming of ruby, copper, gold –
There boyhood's sun foretold, retold
    A full gamut of setting and rising.

Something touched him. Always the scene
    Was to haunt his memory –
Not haunt – come alive there, as if what had been
But a flowery idea took flesh in the womb
Of his solitude, rayed out a rare, real bloom.
    I know, for I was he.

And today, when I see chrysanthemums,
   I half envy that boy
For whom they spoke as muffled drums
Darkly messaging, 'All decays;
   But youth's brief agony can blaze
      Into a posthumous joy.'

Two Songs

Written to Irish Airs

'LOVE WAS ONCE LIGHT AS AIR' (Air: *Dermott*)

   Love was once light as air
   Brushed over all my thoughts and themes;
   Love once seemed kind as air
   When the dewfall gleams.
   Now he's another thing –
   Naked light, oh hard to bear,
   Too much discovering
   With his noonday beams.

   Long had I sought for you,
   Long, long by subtle masks delayed:
   Fair shapes I thought were you
   On my green heart played.
   Now love at his height informs
   All that was so vague to view,
   Shall not those slighter forms
   In his noon hour fade?

Fade they then fast as snow
When April brings the earth to light,
One shape – alas 'tis so –
Still lingers white:
One heart-wrung phantom still,
One I would not tell to go,
Shadows my noontime still
And haunts my night.

'OH LIGHT WAS MY HEAD' (Air: *St. Patrick's Day*)

Oh light was my head as the seed of a thistle
And light as the mistletoe mooning an oak,
I spoke with the triton, I skimmed with the nautilus,
Dawn was immortal as love awoke.
  But when a storm began to blow
  My thistle was dashed, my tree laid low,
  My folk of the wave went down to their deep, so I
Frown on a thistledown floating capriciously,
Scorn as mere fishes the folk of the sea,
Agree the renowned golden bough is a parasite,
Love but a gallous-eyed ghost for me.

Ah, fooled by the cock at the cool of the morning
And fooled by the fawning mirage of the day,
I say that I'm truly well rid of this featherwit –
Reason has tethered it down in clay.
  But when the light begins to go,
  When shadows are marching heel and toe,
  When day is a heap of ashes, I know that I'll
Ride to love's beam like a barque at her anchorage,
Glide on the languorous airs of the past,
For fast as the pride of our reason is waning,
Old follies returning grow wise at last.

Minor Tragedy

Hundreds went down to the ocean bed,
Hundreds fell from the sky,
The shades in the street thickened,
Blood stood in every eye.
Oh kiss me or I'll die, she said,
Kiss me or I'll die!

He took a shadow into the bed
Where she had drained him dry:
With words that buzzed like bullets
She pinned him to a lie.
Don't kiss me or I'll die, she said,
Don't kiss me or I'll die!

Thousands twined on the ocean bed,
Thousands burned in the sky:
Nursing a spent bullet
He let the world go by,
And I'll kiss it till I die, he said,
Kiss it till I die!

On the Sea Wall

As I came to the sea wall that August day,
One out of all the bathers there
Beckoned my eye, a girl at play
With the surf-flowers. Was it the dark, dark hair
Falling Egyptian-wise, or the way
Her body curved to the spray? —

I know not. Only my heart was shaking
Within me, and then it stopped; as though
You were dead and your shape had returned to haunt me
On the very same spot where, five years ago,
You slipped from my arms and played in the breaking
Surges to tease and enchant me.

I could not call out. Had there been no more
Than those thickets of rusty wire to pen us
Apart, I'd have gone to that girl by the shore
Hoping she might be you. But between us
Lie tangled, severing, stronger far,
Barbed relics of love's old war.

Ewig

Multitudes of corn
Shock-still in July heat,
Year upon foaming year
Of may and meadowsweet –
Soon, soon they fleet.

So many words to unsay,
So much hue and cry
After a wisp of flame,
So many deaths to die
Ere the heart runs dry.

All Gone

The sea drained off, my poverty's uncovered –
Sand, sand, a rusted anchor, broken glass,
The listless sediment of sparkling days
When through a paradise of weed joy wavered.

The sea rolled up like a blind, oh pitiless light
Revealing, shrivelling all! Lacklustre weeds
My hours, my truth a salt-lick. Love recedes
From rippled flesh bared without appetite.

A stranded time, neap and annihilation
Of spirit. Gasping on the inglorious rock,
I pray the sea return, even though its calm
Be treachery, its virtue a delusion.

Put forth upon my sands, whether to mock,
Revive or drown, a liberating arm!

The Neurotic

The spring came round, and still he was not dead.
Skin of the earth deliciously powdered
With buttercups and daisies – oh, Proserpina
Refreshed by sleep, wild-cherry-garlanded
And laughing in the sallies of the willow-wren!
With lambs and lilies spring came round again.

Who would suppose, seeing him walk the meadows,
He walks a treadmill there, grinding himself
To powder, dust to greyer dust, or treads
An invisible causeway lipped by chuckling shadows?
Take his arm if you like, you'll not come near him.
His mouth is an ill-stitched wound opening: hear him.

'I will not lift mine eyes unto the hills
For there white lambs nuzzle and creep like maggots.
I will not breathe the lilies of the valley
For through their scent a chambered corpse exhales.
If a petal floats to earth, I am oppressed.
The grassblades twist, twist deep in my breast.'

The night came on, and he was still alive.
Lighted tanks of streets a-swarm with denizens
Darting to trysts, sauntering to parties.
How all the heart-fires twinkle! Yes, they thrive
In the large illusion of freedom, in love's net
Where even the murderer can act and the judge regret.

This man who turns a phrase and twiddles a glass
Seems far from that pale muttering magician
Pent in a vicious circle of dilemmas.
But could you lift his blue, thick gaze and pass
Behind, you would walk a stage where endlessly
Phantoms rehearse unactable tragedy.

'In free air captive, in full day benighted,
I am as one for ever out of his element
Transparently enwombed, who from a bathysphere
Observes, wistful, amazed, but more affrighted,
Gay fluent forms of life weaving around,
And dares not break the bubble and be drowned.'

His doomsdays crawled like lava, till at length
All impulse clogged, the last green lung consumed,
Each onward step required the sweat of nightmare,
Each human act a superhuman strength . . .
And the guillemot, clotted with oil, droops her head.
And the mouse between the elastic paws shams dead.

Death mask of a genius unborn:
Tragic prince of a rejected play:
Soul of suffering that bequeathed no myth:
A dark tower and a never-sounded horn. –
Call him what we will, words cannot ennoble
This Atlas who fell down under a bubble.

Two Travellers

One of us in the compartment stares
Out of his window the whole day long
With attentive mien, as if he knows
There is hid in the journeying scene a song
To recall or compose
From snatches of vision, hints of vanishing airs.

He'll mark the couched hares
In grass whereover the lapwing reel and twist:
He notes how the shockheaded sunflowers climb
Like boys on the wire by the railway line;
And for him those morning rivers are love-in-a-mist,
And the chimneystacks prayers.

The other is plainly a man of affairs,
A seasoned commuter. His looks assert,
As he opens a brief-case intent on perusing
Facts and figures, he'd never divert
With profitless musing
The longest journey, or notice the dress it wears.

Little he cares
For the coloured drift of his passage: no, not a thing
Values in all that is hurrying past,
Though dimly he senses from first to last
How flaps and waves the smoke of his travelling
At the window-squares.

One is preoccupied, one just stares,
While the whale-ribbed terminus nears apace
Where passengers all must change, and under
Its arch triumphal quickly disperse.
So you may wonder,
Watching these two whom the train indifferently bears,

What each of them shares
With his fellow-traveller, and which is making the best of it,
And whether this or the other one
Will be justified when the journey's done,
And if either may carry on some reward or regret for it
Whither he fares.

Seen From The Train

Somewhere between Crewkerne
And Yeovil it was. On the left of the line
Just as the crinkled hills unroll
To the plain. A church on a small green knoll –
A limestone church,
And above the church
Cedar boughs stretched like hands that yearn
To protect or to bless. The whole

Stood up, antique and clear
As a cameo, from the vale. I swear
It was not a dream. Twice, thrice had I found it
Chancing to look as my train wheeled round it.
But this time I passed,
Though I gazed as I passed
All the way down the valley, that knoll was not there,
Nor the church, nor the trees it mounded.

What came between to unsight me? . . .
But suppose, only suppose there might be
A secret look in a landscape's eye
Following you as you hasten by,
And you have your chance –
Two or three chances
At most – to hold and interpret it rightly,
Or it is gone for aye.

There was a time when men
Would have called it a vision, said that sin
Had blinded me since to a heavenly fact.
Well, I have neither invoked nor faked
Any church in the air,
And little I care
Whether or no I shall see it again.
But blindly my heart is racked

When I think how, not twice or thrice,
But year after year in another's eyes
I have caught the look that I missed today
Of the church, the knoll, the cedars – a ray
Of the faith, too, they stood for,
The hope they were food for,
The love they prayed for, facts beyond price –
And turned my eyes away.

Outside and In

How pretty it looks, thought a passer-by –
That cyclamen on her windowsill:
Flowers flushed like the butterfly kisses of sleep that illumine
A child's alabaster cheek.
She who set it there must have warm hopes to bloom in,
So happy it looks, thought the passer-by,
On the newcomer's windowsill.

O passer-by, can you not feel my glances
Beating against the pane,
Fluttering like a moth shut off from the glades of musk
And the moonlit dances?
O passer-by, can you not see it plain?

She comes not to meet us, muttered the neighbours
Peering in from the stony street:
But look at her parlour, all lighted and spider-spruce!
How saucily wink the brasses!
So garnished a room never tokens a pure recluse.
Let us hope she'll bring, said the gossiping neighbours,
No scandal upon our street.

Ah, what do you know of the crippled heart, my neighbours,
That shrinks from the light and the press?
My winking brass, all the fine repetitive web
Of my house-proud labours –
Even I dare not know them for signals of distress.

A happy release, murmured the living
As they carried at last out into the world
Her body, light as a bird's that has died of hunger
Beneath some warped hedgerow:
Though it was her own doing if all humanity shunned her,
Yet a happy release to be done with living
An outcast from the world.

O living hearts, you are wrong once more. Unassuaged
Even now are my pangs, my fears.
I starved amid plenty. Death seemed no deliverance
To flesh that was caged,
O living hearts, in a ghost these fifty years.

The Misfit

At the training depot that first morning
When the west-country draft came forth on parade –
Mechanics, labourers, men of trade
Herded with shouts like boneheaded cattle –
One stood out from the maul
Who least of them all
Looked metal for killing or meat for the butchery blade.

He wore a long black cutaway coat
Which should have been walking by blackthorn-fleeced
Hedges to church; and good as a feast
Was the spare, wild face much weather had flavoured.
A shepherd or ploughman
I thought, or a cowman –
One with a velvet hand for all manner of beast.

I cannot forget how he stood, bemused,
With the meek eye of a driven thing:
But a solitude old as a cromlech ring
Was around him; a freeborn air of the downland,
A peace of deep combes
No world-anger consumes
Marked him off from the herd to be branded for soldiering.

I saw him not after. Is he now buried
Far from pastures buttercup-strewed,
Or tending his beasts again with the same rude
Rightness of instinct which then had brought him
So quaintly dressed
In his Sunday best
For the first step along the Calvary road?

In the Shelter

In a shelter one night, when death was taking the air
Outside, I saw her, seated apart – a child
Nursing her doll, to one man's vision enisled
With radiance which might have shamed even death to its lair.

Then I thought of our Christmas roses at home – the dark
Lanterns comforting us a winter through
With the same dusky flush, the same bold spark
Of confidence, O sheltering child, as you.

Genius could never paint the maternal pose
More deftly than accident had roughed it there,
Setting amidst our terrors, against the glare
Of unshaded bulb and whitewashed brick, that rose.

Instinct was hers, and an earthquake hour revealed it
In flesh – the meek-laid lashes, the glint in the eye
Defying wrath and reason, the arms that shielded
A plaster doll from an erupting sky.

No argument for living could long sustain
These ills: it needs a faithful eye, to have seen all
Love in the droop of a lash and tell it eternal
By one pure bead of its dew-dissolving chain.

Dear sheltering child, if again misgivings grieve me
That love is only a respite, an opal bloom
Upon our snow-set fields, come back to revive me
Cradling your spark through blizzard, drift and tomb.

Two Translations

THE FOOTSTEPS

(from Paul Valéry)

Born of my voiceless time, your steps
Slowly, ecstatically advance:
Toward my expectation's bed
They moved in a hushed, ice-clear trance.

Pure being, shadow-shape divine –
Your step deliberate, how sweet!
God! – every gift I have imagined
Comes to me on those naked feet.

If so it be your offered mouth
Is shaped already to appease
That which occupies my thought
With the live substance of a kiss,

Oh hasten not this loving act,
Rapture where self and not-self meet:
My life has been the awaiting you,
Your footfall was my own heart's beat.

THE GRAVEYARD BY THE SEA

(from Paul Valéry)

This quiet roof, where dove-sails saunter by,
Between the pines, the tombs, throbs visibly.
Impartial noon patterns the sea in flame –
That sea for ever starting and re-starting.
When thought has had its hour, oh how rewarding
Are the long vistas of celestial calm!

What grace of light, what pure toil goes to form
The manifold diamond of the elusive foam!
What peace I feel begotten at that source!
When sunlight rests upon a profound sea,
Time's air is sparkling, dream is certainty –
Pure artifice both of an eternal Cause.

Sure treasure, simple shrine to intelligence,
Palpable calm, visible reticence,
Proud-lidded water, Eye wherein there wells
Under a film of fire such depth of sleep –
O silence! . . . Mansion in my soul, you slope
Of gold, roof of a myriad golden tiles.

Temple of time, within a brief sigh bounded,
To this rare height inured I climb, surrounded
By the horizons of a sea-girt eye.
And, like my supreme offering to the gods,
That peaceful coruscation only breeds
A loftier indifference on the sky.

Even as a fruit's absorbed in the enjoying,
Even as within the mouth its body dying
Changes into delight through dissolution,
So to my melted soul the heavens declare
All bounds transfigured into a boundless air,
And I breathe now my future's emanation.

Beautiful heaven, true heaven, look how I change!
After such arrogance, after so much strange
Idleness – strange, yet full of potency –
I am all open to these shining spaces;
Over the homes of the dead my shadow passes,
Ghosting along – a ghost subduing me.

My soul laid bare to your midsummer fire,
O just, impartial light whom I admire,
Whose arms are merciless, you have I stayed
And give back, pure, to your original place.
Look at yourself . . . But to give light implies
No less a sombre moiety of shade.

Oh, for myself alone, mine, deep within
At the heart's quick, the poem's fount, between
The void and its pure issue, I beseech
The intimations of my secret power.
O bitter, dark and echoing reservoir
Speaking of depths always beyond my reach.

But know you – feigning prisoner of the boughs,
Gulf which eats up their slender prison-bars,
Secret which dazzles though mine eyes are closed –
What body drags me to its lingering end,
What mind draws *it* to this bone-peopled ground?
A star broods there on all that I have lost.

Closed, hallowed, full of insubstantial fire,
Morsel of earth to heaven's light given o'er –
This plot, ruled by its flambeaux, pleases me –
A place all gold, stone and dark wood, where shudders
So much marble above so many shadows:
And on my tombs, asleep, the faithful sea.

Keep off the idolaters, bright watch-dog, while –
A solitary with the shepherd's smile –
I pasture long my sheep, my mysteries,
My snow-white flock of undisturbéd graves!
Drive far away from here the careful doves,
The vain daydreams, the angels' questioning eyes!

Now present here, the future takes its time.
The brittle insect scrapes at the dry loam;
All is burnt up, used up, drawn up in air
To some ineffably rarefied solution . . .
Life is enlarged, drunk with annihilation,
And bitterness is sweet, and the spirit clear.

The dead lie easy, hidden in earth where they
Are warmed and have their mysteries burnt away.
Motionless noon, noon aloft in the blue
Broods on itself – a self-sufficient theme.
O rounded dome and perfect diadem,
I am what's changing secretly in you.

I am the only medium for your fears.
My penitence, my doubts, my baulked desires –
These are the flaw within your diamond pride . . .
But in their heavy night, cumbered with marble,
Under the roots of trees a shadow people
Has slowly now come over to your side.

To an impervious nothingness they're thinned,
For the red clay has swallowed the white kind;
Into the flowers that gift of life has passed.
Where are the dead? – their homely turns of speech,
The personal grace, the soul informing each?
Grubs thread their way where tears were once composed.

The bird-sharp cries of girls whom love is teasing,
The eyes, the teeth, the eyelids moistly closing,
The pretty breast that gambles with the flame,
The crimson blood shining when lips are yielded,
The last gift, and the fingers that would shield it –
All go to earth, go back into the game.

And you, great soul, is there yet hope in you
To find some dream without the lying hue
That gold or wave offers to fleshly eyes?
Will you be singing still when you're thin air?
All perishes. A thing of flesh and pore
Am I. Divine impatience also dies.

Lean immortality, all crêpe and gold,
Laurelled consoler frightening to behold,
Death is a womb, a mother's breast, you feign –
The fine illusion, oh the pious trick!
Who does not know them, and is not made sick –
That empty skull, that everlasting grin?

Ancestors deep down there, O derelict heads
Whom such a weight of spaded earth o'erspreads,
Who *are* the earth, in whom our steps are lost,
The real flesh-eater, worm unanswerable
Is not for you that sleep under the table:
Life is his meat, and I am still his host.

'Love', shall we call him? 'Hatred of self', maybe?
His secret tooth is so intimate with me
That any name would suit him well enough,
Enough that he can see, will, daydream, touch –
My flesh delights him, even upon my couch
I live but as a morsel of his life.

Zeno, Zeno, cruel philosopher Zeno,
Have you then pierced me with your feathered arrow
That hums and flies, yet does not fly! The sounding
Shaft gives me life, the arrow kills. Oh, sun! –
Oh, what a tortoise-shadow to outrun
My soul, Achilles' giant stride left standing!

No, no! Arise! The future years unfold.
Shatter, O body, meditation's mould!
And, O my breast, drink in the wind's reviving!
A freshness, exhalation of the sea,
Restores my soul . . . Salt-breathing potency!
Let's run at the waves and be hurled back to living!

Yes, mighty sea with such wild frenzies gifted
(The panther skin and the rent chlamys), sifted
All over with sun-images that glisten,
Creature supreme, drunk on your own blue flesh,
Who in a tumult like the deepest hush
Bite at your sequin-glittering tail – yes, listen!

The wind is rising! . . . We must try to live!
The huge air opens and shuts my book: the wave
Dares to explode out of the rocks in reeking
Spray. Fly away, my sun-bewildered pages!
Break, waves! Break up with your rejoicing surges
This quiet roof where sails like doves were pecking.

AN ITALIAN VISIT

... an Italian visit is a voyage of discovery, not only of scenes and cities, but also of the latent faculties of the traveller's heart and mind.

JASPER MORE: *The Land of Italy*

To Henry Reed

Dialogue at the Airport

TOM So here we are, we three, bound on a new experience.

DICK Three persons in one man, bound for the Eternal City.

HARRY We're not as young as we were, but Italy's some years
older.

TOM Listen, I don't much fancy antiques myself; we've had
some.
Ruins fetch nothing today. The Forum, the Farringdon Market,
The Colosseum, Hiroshima – death's death, however you look at
it,
However composed the remains. Time enough for such bric-à-
brac when
My silver cord is loosed, my arches are fallen. Oh no, if
It's ruins you're after, we'll soon be parting company.

DICK   Wait!
There are ruins and ruins. Some mature their memories, feed
them
On seeding love-spores blown from age to age; or it may be
Their ghosts fly back like a silver skein of doves when the crash
Of the fall that tumbled them out has died away. It is these
ghosts
I'm going to look for.

HARRY You think so. But I don't think you will find them.
The only ghosts I believe in are the dangerous self-detachments
We leave behind in places captured or captivating:
Garrisons, call them, or hostages – wiped out soon enough, most
of them,
Yet here and there a hardier self lives on to haunt us
With the old riddle, what is the phantom, what the real.
Temple, aqueduct, belvedere, projects fulfilled or abandoned –
Multiform are the ruins, but the ghosts are always the same
ghost.

TOM We'd better leave you behind, then, to the desk, the
queue and the rush-hour,
Men and women straphanging like clusters of bats, the bodies
That jostle and never touch, the eyes without speculation
But for tomorrow's headline or deadline; leave you behind
With all the white-faced addicts of a patent, cellophaned future.
London's the place for ghosts, if ghosts are invalid monads.
And for God's sake, Harry, don't tell us a crowd is always the
same crowd.

DICK What are we leaving behind, though? The identity
cards that inform us
Not who we are or might be, but how we are interchangeable;
The season tickets that rattle us back and forth in a groove from
Centre to circumference, from dust to dust; the ration books
Entitling each to his cut of the communal mess and heartburn.
The fog, the slush, the slogans.

HARRY   Italy will provide
The same slogans, no doubt, but at least in another language.

TOM No doubt in another language escapism may sound more
attractive.

DICK Well, it's a holiday, isn't it? Even Harry can take a
holiday.

HARRY I have omitted to pack my Kierkegaard, Marx and
Groddeck.
My *angst* I can only hope they will confiscate at the Customs.

TOM I am too old to suppose new facts give new sensations.
Still, like shadows, our senses revive on a shot of sunshine.
One would go far to feel their primitive dance again

DICK Far from the heart's last ditch, the stand on private re-
lationships

HARRY Far from the mind's closed shop and the intellectual
weeklies

TOM So here we are, we three, off for a fortnight's holiday,
Our fingers already reaching out to the treat before us

DICK Like a child's on Christmas Eve who, visioning the dear
morrow
Spangled with expectation, would whip time faster and faster,
And at last whips himself into a humming sleep.

HARRY Travel ought to be sleep – I mean, we should move
oblivious
To the interspace between here and there. We've only a limited
Stock of attention, and this we had better not spend on wayside
Sirens who'd make us break our journey or regret not breaking it.

TOM If he means what I think he means, I am not to look out
of the window.

DICK There's something in what he says, though the motive's
unsound, as usual.
Could the zone between here and there be instead a kind of hiatus
Heart would be spared the throes of departure and anticipation,
The tug-of-war in the tensile flesh between near and far,
The sense of all routes leading to a scheduled anti-climax
Because what they lead away from seems now, too late, the
nonpareil
The truly virgin place.

HARRY   Yes, travel is travail: a witless
Ordeal of self-abasement to an irreversible process.
It would be nice, waking as it were from twilight sleep, to
Find the new bourne beside one.

TOM   But you never can skip the process
And reach a conclusion, the one is woven into the other
Like hues of a shot-silk rainbow: apart from which, your analogy
Falls to the ground – we shall not, I presume, give birth to Italy.

DICK But we should give body to our so tentative viewpoints
of it

HARRY Or rather conceive a self, hitherto inconceivable,
through it.

TOM Both of you ask too much. I'll be quite happy, taking
Snapshots.

309

DICK I shall develop and print them.

HARRY   I shall mount them.
And after a year or two fetching the album out again,
Snapshot or time exposure, in every scene, among each group
Posed before pillars, informally strolling across a piazza,
We'll see, oh yes we shall see them, the usual boring intruders –
Spirits or ectoplasm, who cares? – spoiling the brilliant
Occasion like long-lost cousins or hangovers out of the future,
Whether from Dick's chemicals or Tom's automatic choice
Of the haunted subject.

TOM   I don't deny my photographs would be
More satisfactory if you two could stop interfering.
What with Dick's fancy touches and Harry's insufferable habit
Of scribbling captions across them which later become obsessions–
Spirits or ectoplasm, who cares? – no wonder if
The results are not

DICK There would be no results but for my dark-room,
Where negatives lie steeped in a warm solution, passing
The acid test of Lethe, to emerge with the self-assurance
Of memories; but for this hand that ever so lightly brushes
Over your brash impressions the dove-downed, hallowing haze.
What if I do touch up now and then a defective feature? –
There is no law against putting the best face on experience.

HARRY No law to say we must grind the cornfields into
                                                    vitamins,
Reduce the grape to a formula, express the olive in terms of
Statistics. It is deplorable, yes, and against nature:
Nevertheless, one does it, being of a generation
Whose only faith is the piling of fact on fact, in the hope that
Some day a road may be built of them and may lead somewhere.

TOM In the meanwhile, we go to Italy: Dick, with his
                                              decadent craving
For perfection at any price, who cannot pass by an arc
Without officiously filling in the rest of the circle;

Harry whose conscience bids him take the round world to pieces
And ticket each stone for the use of a possibly grateful posterity;
And I who, with your permission, intend just to enjoy myself.

DICK But even you have been taught the simpler associations –
For example, mouth and famine, lily and corpse, bambino
And bomb – to say nothing of *odi et amo* – which stand in the
light of
Enjoyment pure and simple. Travellers can't be choosers
Any more than the stay-at-homes.

HARRY No, man's gleaming aspirations
Are endlessly batted down as telegraph wire by the poles
When you look from a train window, everywhere and for ever
Abased his soaring creeds by the very proofs which support
them.
Yet still we aspire. Each journey's a bid for the empyrean
Of Absolute freedom, whether we fly to the ends of the earth
Or take a week-end ticket to Clacton; and as certainly
We are twitched back on the thread reeled out from our ruling
passion.

TOM All the more reason for going abroad with a *tabula rasa*
Not trailing clouds of vainglory or the old tin can of conscience
Granted we cannot entirely escape ourselves, and granted
That up to a point we can only see what we're bound to look for,
Still, there is such a thing as simple impressionability,
A sense in which form and colour are more than mere dreams of
our senses,
A moment – though rare – when the lily speaks for itself alone
And the babe's ephemeral laughter chimes with eternity.

DICK And another thing: when the new place, mysteriously
conveying
A promise of maiden surrender and morning glory, invites us,
We are wax in her hands for a little, our former loves effaced,
Ready to take her seal, to believe the rewarding fallacy
That this is it at last, that this time all will be different;

And we really may find the knack of pure freedom, pure sub-
mission,
Whereby a miraculous rebirth is possible – find it
Before the displaced selves crowd back to declare us impotent.

HARRY Since you two appear in agreement on this, the logical
next step
Is to unpack our preconceptions and leave them behind here,
Discarding whatever might come between us and the naked fact.

TOM Myself, I have always travelled light – eyes, ears, nose,
fingers,
And one thing more, I carry. Now Dick, you'll have to jettison
Time, whose ripple prettifies the weed which fouls it, and flaws
The willow it images.

DICK Time, without which there could be no images? –
You might as well go abroad without an interpreter – you, Tom,
Who don't know a word in any tongue but your own. Now
Harry
Has much he should lighten his bag of; props, probes and provisos;
The impressive manner he wears while wooing the heiress,
Truth;
And of course the instruments he will presently use to dissect her.

HARRY Your programmes are too ambitious. I only meant to
suggest
We should expose the Italy faked by our fraudulent vision,
Tear up the glowing prospectus that pictured a heaven on earth

TOM Confess why we are going and what we expect to find
there?

DICK Rub out the shadow our ego projects? Make a clean sheet
of Italy?

HARRY Yes, a cadenza from each on this fantasy movement.
We have
Ten minutes until our flight-number is called. Let Tom begin.

TOM First, a great Elgarian clash and bray of sunshine
Throwing open the day, blaring a paeony fanfare

Through flesh and blood, throwing wide the earth – a fabulous
                                                          mansion
Where every maid is a gift, every moment a pulse in a fun-fair.
None of your fairy gold! The real, royal, vulgar pageant –
Time flung like confetti or twirled in rosettes – was never too
                                                          garish
For me. How much better than your dim flounderings toward
                                                some imagined
Immortal star, to flare like a firework and goldenly perish!
Mornings, I ask a cloudless sky; or if clouds there must be,
Billowy suds that have scoured the sky bluer than corn-flowers:
Acacia and lemon-blossom shall drench me, mimosa dust me,
Violet and rose be banked along my sauntering hours.
Noon shall stand as long as I fancy, and tall as houses –
A fountain pluming itself upon the enchanted air:
Afternoon shall sleep with the goat-flock villages drowsing
Lightly, precipice-high, or deep in shuttered squares.
Ah, but the nights! I see them festooned in a long fiesta –
Mediterranean nights that will send me spinning and flying
With the waltz of a purple Maelstrom, the arrowy glide of a
                                                          Cresta.
Here's to the masks and the music, the dancers ebbing and
                                                          flowing!
Let fairy-lit streets run wine through the veins like a ride on a
                                                          scenic
Railway! and then the ravishing flesh of girls consume me
Flame upon flame to scented ashes, and I a phoenix!
Yes, one thing I know: it's the sting of strangeness renews me.
Listen, the bells tumble from a humming campanile
With a dull pot-and-pan clang: those two at the table – the
                                                          cadence
Is unfamiliar they talk in: banal their gist, but to me they
Are speaking, lover and carillon, with the tongues of angels.
I do not wish to dig down to the sullen roots of existence
Where one clod's the same as the next, or to tangle myself in
                                                humanity's

Fretted heart-strings: not here lies the world of essential
difference,
But above, in the bloom, the spectrum, the transient flavours
and vanities.
Therefore I'd browse on the skin of things, the delicate field of
Diversity, skimming gold from the buttercup, dust from the
nettle.
I, the merely sensual man, have a scope undreamed of
By you whom a larger ambition drives to discard or belittle
Appearance. And so I ask of Italy nothing more than
Mere foreignness, the shock and buoyant feel of the unknown,
And quivering over its surface an irridescent path, an
Arrow to point me, the eternal tripper, away from home.

DICK Different my nature, my needs. I journey as a colonial
Reaching across generations to find the parent stock,
As a child setting out to colour a black-and-white picture book,
A priest entering into the spirit of dead ceremonial . . .
They have been dormant so long, the ghosts that were used to
school us:
Deep-buried as once Pompeii the classroom walls with their jaded
Photos of classical ruin, of statues leprous, abraded.
Did ever those dry bones live? And instantly Ovid, Catullus
Wild for his Lesbia, Virgil, Lucretius – sports of a prosy
Marble-eyed, muscle-bound people – emerge from the shades to
claim one.
Ancestor worship's a form of self-seeking: all the same, one
Is grateful to those who had no immediate hand in our crazy
Present: the Romans at any rate did manage to keep the peace,
Off and on. But that's by the way. Some breathing counterpart
I want for a dead language years ago learnt by heart,
Some vista shaped and haunted by youthful pieties.
Immortal landscape of a day, for ever dreaming
In haze of summers half imagined, half remembered!
Meek-swarded, comely pastoral where nymph and shepherd
Still twine two worlds in a dance! Demesne of phantoms, teeming

With myrtle, vine and olive, pied with fact and fable!
Hero, god, or brute, all hold to the light their antique
Self-sufficiency – a grace which no romantic
Yearnings can discompose nor withering years enfeeble.
Such is the foreground. Behind it vaporously writhes a spectacu-
lar
Region of mounting disquiet, dark meaning, where lie concealed
A lake that shoots down birds with a whiff of the underworld;
Proserpine's trapdoor; a gorge rumbling in tones oracular;
A forest of shadows juddering athwart the golden bough.
Is it I they wait for, the feudal lords of light and mystery
Their kingdoms to unite? Is it they who shall assist me
To define, or abolish, the frontier between my Then and my Now?
There was a time of substance and shadow richly confused,
When a dry Tuscan evelight engraved the cricket-ground
And my study shafted towards the black diamonds and dene
profound
Of Pluto: then the beam went, the pit fell into disuse.
If I could find that place where nymph and shepherd meet
And the distance melts into deity, I would unearth my buried
Heirlooms, my sealed orders. Genius of the place, remarry
These sundered elements, make one circle at last complete!

    HARRY A landscape I also may look for: a town in fiesta would
do
Equally well for the purpose this traveller has in view.
Let me try to explain myself – both artist and analyst; hence
For me the approach that in others would be pure innocence
Were wild irresponsibility. Think! The desirable villa
Haunted by princes, hallowed with cypresses, there on a hillside
Ultimately reduces to a vulgar hop of electrons:
I see the revellers, masked and articulated for faction;
Your language of bells and lovers I hear, but as workable fictions.
Since all strips down to motion, and all's in a state of becoming,
Whoever would master the truth by which your provocative,
charming

315

Strip-tease universe lives, ideally should be at rest
Himself; at any rate disinterested, unimpressed.
And that is why I am far from being a keen traveller.
On the other hand, I admit one cannot hope to unravel
Experience unless one is to a certain degree involved.
Is there a method by which, then, a mutable self may resolve
And fix the ever-changing? Let us try an experiment – briefly
The playing a trick on time. Help me, you two, to achieve it.
To see as it were from the far end of a cypress walk of bereave-
                                                              ment,
Or the eyrie of ten years hence! For look, how the terraced
                                                              garden,
Statues, orange trees, villa, unfocused now by sudden
Tremors – the whole prospect fidgets, vibrates, wavers,
Collapsing always with the present. But if upon that fevered
Hill brow, my brow, should once be laid grief's cooling hand,
Dance and dissolution would come to a dead stand.
Memory needs time before the outraged dwelling, love's centre,
Purified, tear upon tear, shines forth like a shell of candour,
And all around, elegiac in evergreen, new contours
Idealize the old agony. But I have to induce
Years from a moment: therefore I must predicate loss.
Let me take some figure of the dance, so fleetingly fiercely
                                                              exulting
That it quickens the seed of loss, my seed, and itself is halted
And magnified thus, a still from the moving picture, framed
Inparting's hard embrace some beauty, flushed, fleshed, tamed.
Separation's my metier, then, sifting through form the formless:
Creation my end, to subdue and liberate time in the timeless.
I find the whole in elusive fragments: let one be caught
And profoundly known – that way, like a skeleton key, the part
May unlock the intricate whole. What else is the work of art?

PART TWO

Flight to Italy

The winged bull trundles to the wired perimeter.
Cumbrously turns. Shivers, brakes clamped,
Bellowing four times, each engine tested
With routine ritual. Advances to the runway.
Halts again as if gathering heart
Or warily snuffing for picador cross-winds.
Then, then, a roar open-throated
Affronts the arena. Then fast, faster
Drawn by the magnet of his *idée fixe*,
Head down, tail up, he's charging the horizon.
   And the grass of the airfield grows smooth as a fur.
The runway's elastic and we the projectile;
Installations control-tower mechanics parked aeroplanes –
Units all woven to a ribbon unreeling,
Concrete melts and condenses to an abstract
Blur, and our blood thickens to think of
Rending, burning, as suburban terraces
Make for us, wave after wave.
       The moment
Of Truth is here. We can only trust,
Being as wholly committed to other hands
As a babe at birth, Europa to the bull god.
And as when one dies in his sleep, there's no divining
The instant of take-off, so we who were earth-bound
Are air-borne, it seems, in the same breath.
The neutered terraces subside beneath us.

   Bank and turn, bank and turn,
Air-treading bull, my silver Alitalia!
Bank and turn, while the earth below
Swings like a dial on the wing-tip's axis,
Whirls and checks like a wheel of chance!
Now keep your course! On azure currents
Let the wings lift and sidle drowsily –

A halcyon rocked by the ghost of the gale.
To watchers in Kent you appear as a quicksilver
Bead skimming down the tilted sky;
To the mild-eyed aircrew, an everyday office:
To us, immured in motion, you mean
A warm womb pendant between two worlds.
    O trance prenatal and angelic transport!
Like embryos curled in this aluminium belly –
Food and oxygen gratis – again
We taste the pure freedom of the purely submissive,
The passive dominion of the wholly dependent.
Through heaven's transparent mysteries we travel
With a humdrum of engines, the mother's heartbeat:
And our foreshadowed selves begin to take shape, to be
Dimly adapted to their destination.
What migrant fancies this journeying generates! –
Almost we imagine a metempsychosis.

    Over the Channel now, beneath the enchanting
Inane babble of a baby-blue sky,
We soar through cloudland, at the heights of nonsense.
From a distance they might be sifted-sugar-drifts,
Meringues, iced cakes, confections of whipped cream
Lavishly piled for some Olympian party –
A child's idea of heaven. Now radiant
All around the airscrew's boring penumbra
The clouds redouble, as nearer we climb,
Their toppling fantasy. We skirt the fringe of icebergs,
Dive under eiderdowns, disport with snowmen
On fields of melting snow dinted by the wind's feet,
Gleefully brush past atom-bomb cauliflowers,
Frozen fuffs of spray from naval gunfire.
    Wool-gathering we fly through a world of make-believe.
We *are* the aircraft, the humming-bird hawk moth
Hovering and sipping at each cloud corolla;
But also ourselves, to whom these white follies are

Valid as symbols for a tonic reverie
Or as symptoms of febrile flight from the real.
Let us keep, while we can, the holiday illusion,
The heart's altimeter dancing bliss-high,
Forgetting gravity, regardless of earth
Out of sight, out of mind, like a menacing letter
Left at home in a drawer – let the next-of-kin acknowledge it.

    The cloud-floor is fissured suddenly. Clairvoyance
It seems, not sight, when the solid air frays and parts
Unveiling, like some rendezvous remote in a crystal,
Bright, infinitesimal, a fragment of France.
We scan the naked earth as it were through a skylight:
Down there, what life-size encounters, what industrious
Movement and vocations manifold go forward!
But to us, irresponsible, above the battle,
Villages and countryside reveal no more life than
A civilization asleep beneath a glacier,
Toy bricks abandoned on a plain of linoleum . . .
    After a hard winter, on the first warm day
The invalid venturing out into the rock-garden,
Pale as a shaft of December sunshine, pauses,
All at sea among the aubretia, the alyssum
And arabis – halts and moves on how warily,
As if to take soundings where the blossom foams and tumbles:
But what he does sound is the depth of his own weakness
At last, as never when pain-storms lashed him.
So we, convalescent from routine's long fever,
Plummeting our gaze down to river and plain,
Question if indeed that dazzling world beneath us
Be truth or delirium; and finding still so tentative
The answer, can gauge how nearly we were ghosts,
How far we must travel yet to flesh and blood.

    But now the engines have quickened their beat
And the fuselage pulsates, panting like a fugitive.

Below us – oh, look at it! – earth has become
Sky, a thunderscape curdling to indigo,
Veined with valleys of green fork-lightning.
The atrocious Alps are upon us. Their ambush –
A primeval huddle, then a bristling and heaving of
Brutal boulder-shapes, an uprush of Calibans –
Unmasks its white-fanged malice to maul us.
The cabin grows colder. Keep height, my angel!
Where we are, all but terra firma is safe.

    Recall how flyers from a raid returning,
Lightened of one death, were elected for another:
Their homing thoughts too far ahead, a mountain
Stepped from the mist and slapped them down.
We, though trivial the hazard, retract
Our trailing dreams until we have cleared these ranges.
Exalted, numinous, aloof no doubt
To the land-locked vision, for us they invoke
A mood more intimate, a momentary flutter and
Draught of danger – death's fan coquettishly
Tapping the cheek ere she turn to dance elsewhere.
Our mien is the bolder for this mild flirtation,
Our eyes the brighter, since every brush with her
Gives flesh a souvenir, a feel of resurrection.

    Those peaks o'erpassed, we glissade at last to
A gentian pasture, the Genoan sea.
Look south, sky-goers! In flying colours
A map's unrolled there – the Italy
Your schooldays scanned once: the hills are sand-blond,
A pale green stands for the littoral plain:
The sea's bedizened with opening islands
Like iris eyes on a peacock's fan.
How slowly dawns on the drowsy newborn
Whose world's unworn yet – a firelit dress,
An ego's glamorous shell, a womb of rumours –
The first faint glimmering of otherness!

But half awake, we could take this country
For some vague drift from prenatal dreams:
Those hills and headlands, like sleep's projections
Or recollections, mere symbol seem.
 Then hurtling southward along shores of myrtle,
Silverly circle the last lap,
My bull-headed moth! This land is nothing
But a mythical name on an outline map
For us, till we've scaled it to our will's dimensions,
Filled in each wayward, imperious route,
Shaded it in with delays and chagrins,
Traced our selves over it, foot by foot.
Now tighter we circle, as if the vertical
Air is a whirlpool drawing us down;
And the airfield, a candle-bright pinpoint, invites us
To dance ere alighting . . . Hurry! We burn
For Rome so near us, for the phoenix moment
When we have thrown off this traveller's trance,
And mother-naked and ageless-ancient
Wake in her warm nest of renaissance.

PART THREE

A Letter from Rome

We have been here three days, and Rome is really –
I know, I know; it would take three life-times to cover
The glorious junk-heap. Besides, our generation –
Well, you've only to think of James, as one must do here,
Lapping the cream of antiquity, purring over
Each vista that stroked his senses, and in brief
Rubbing himself against Rome like a great tabby,
To see what I mean. We who 'flowered' in the Thirties
Were an odd lot; sceptical yet susceptible,
Dour though enthusiastic, horizon-addicts
And future-fans, terribly apt to ask what
Our all-very-fine sensations were in aid of.
We did not, you will remember, come to coo.
Still, there is hope for us. Rome has absorbed
Other barbarians: yes, and there's nobody quite so
Sensuously rich and reckless as the reformed
Puritan . . . This by the way, to establish a viewpoint.
     You wanted my impressions. If only one were
A simple sieve, be the mesh close or wide,
For Rome to shake (and how it does shake one!), sifting
Some finer stuff from the coarser. But the trouble with me is
– Or perhaps it's the trouble with Rome – to discriminate
Merely between what is here and what has been here,
Between the eye and the mind's eye. The place has had
Over two thousand years of advance publicity
For us, which clouds the taste and saps the judgment.
What are you to do when Catullus buttonholes you
On the way to St. Peter's? When the Colosseum presents
Nero[1] comparing notes with Roderick Hudson
On art and egotism? Sights, sounds, phantoms –
It is all too much for me, it should not be allowed!
     Perhaps, though, it is just here that something emerges.

[1] The Colosseum was built by Vespasian on the site of the Golden House of Nero.

As when, composing a poem, the tangle of images
And jangle of words pressing hard on you, mobbing you, may
Compel you to choose the right moment to disengage
And find the one word, the word of command which makes them
Meekly fall in to their ranks, and the march continues:
So from this Rome, where the past lies weltering
In the blood of the present, and posters of Betty Grable
Affront the ghost of Cato; from all its grandiose
Culs-de-sac – the monumental gateways
That open on nothing, the staircases starting for heaven,
The stone-blind palaces sweltering in the noon;
From the stilled tempest of the Sistine ceiling
To the water exasperated by sirocco
In every fountain basin; from the whole gamut,
Theatrical, vulgar, rhetorical, fractious, sublime,
Of a city young as Tithonus, a city so ancient
That even the shadows here lie thick as dust: –
Emerges from all this, like invisible writing
Drawn out by the heart's warmth, one lucid word.

      Compost. I do not suppose the word original
(Original! Rome is quite beyond that). But think of it –
Century into century rotting down,
Faith piled on faith, Mithra on Jupiter,
Christ upon Mithra, Catholicism on Christ,
Temples imbedded in churches, church-stones in palaces:
Think of the pagan gods, demoted to demons,
Haunting and taunting the Early Fathers; long-dead
Lights of love, immortalized as Madonnas,
Demurely smiling at man's infant idealism.
Superstition, sanctity, cruelty, laws, art, lust –
Layer after layer laid down, course upon course
They renew the soul of this city, a city whose prospects
Are quarried out of its bones, a soul digesting
All foreignness into one rich dark fibre.
Rome, I can tell you, is the very type of
The hugger-mugger of human growth. For here

x   323

You can see the grand design eternally crossed
By the abject means, and its seedy ruin redeemed with
Valerian, arbutus, fennel; a character root-fast
Like a man's in the deposit of all his acts.
          Or say, a woman's; for so she appeared to us
On the first morning when we sauntered out
(The night before, wild strawberries and Frascati
Gold as the Roman May-light, cool as grottoes).
A woman – how shall I put it? – who makes you feel
She has waited two thousand years to meet you, and now
At once she is wholly yours, her liquid tongue,
Her body mantled in the full flush of Ceres,
And Primavera fluttering in her eyes.
She can be tiresome, no doubt, feverish, languid,
Changing her moods like dresses. But today
She has chosen to be divinely acquiescent:
'What shall we do?' the shell-like murmur comes,
'Shall we go shopping? Would you like me to show you the
                                                    sights?

'I will do anything you say, anything.'
. . . So we took, in the end, a carrozza to St. Peter's.
The driver was plainly a phantom; his conveyance
Jarred like old bones and mumbled of better days when
Violet-adorned beauties, sedate or giddy,
Turned all heads on the Corso. Thus we went
Jaunting over the seven hills of Rome
With the streets rocking beneath us as if seven ages
Turned in their grave, while noise upon noise the drift
Of our own – its voices, horns, wheels, bells, loudspeakers –
Washed past us; then it dwindled away to a sea-shell
Cadence, beyond the Tiber, as we came near
Vatican city.
          And now *vates tacete*
Should be the word. Words here can only scrabble
Like insects at the plinth of a colossus,
Scrabble and feebly gesticulate and go elsewhere.

Mere magnitude one might deal with, or pure and simple
Meaning; but both in one, they give no purchase.
A dome superb as heaven's vault, capping a story
Whose hero blessed the meek; a desert of floor
Refracting faith like a mirage; the orchestration
Of gold and marble engulfing the still, small voice: —
You cannot pass over St. Peter's and what it stands for,
Whether you see it as God's vicarious throne
Or the biggest bubble ever yet unpricked.
And here, I have to confess, the old Puritan peeped out;
Not in sour protest against the Scarlet Woman,
Nor quite in the mood of my generation — its volatile
Mixture of hero-worship and disrespect;
But that an early habit of going to church
Prevents me from going to churches, however distinguished
Their provenance, just as a sight-seer. Faith perhaps,
Though unconscious, is not yet dead, its breath still clouding
The glass of aesthetic perception. Apart from which,
I could not do with the guides who spring up like sweat-white
Fungi from every chink, and cling to one, furtively
Offering their curious knowledge; these pimps are not
The type you would choose to lead you to any altar.
So I was lost, ill at ease here, until by chance
In a side chapel we found a woman mourning
Her son: all the *lacrimæ rerum* flowed
To her gesture of grief, all life's blood from his stone.
There is no gap or discord between the divine
And the human in that pieta of Michelangelo.
Then, after a marathon walk through the Vatican galleries,
An endless belt of statues, tapestry, pictures
Glazing the eye, we came out into the streets again.
Better than all the museums, this strolling folk
Who sun themselves in the apricot light of antiquity
And take its prestige for granted. Cameo faces,
Contessa or contadina; bronze boys skylarking
As if they had just wriggled free from a sculptor's hand —

How easily art and nature overlap here!
Another thing you would like about the Romans
Is the way they use their city, not as a warren
Of bolt-holes, nor a machine into which one is fed
Each morning and at evening duly disgorged,
But as an open-air stage. Palazzo, tenement
Seem pure façade – back-cloth for a continuous
Performance of business, love-making, politics, idling,
Conducted with a grand operatic extravagance
At the tempo of family theatricals. That same night
In the Piazza del' Esedra, sipping
Grappa, we watched the people, warm as animals
And voluble as fountains, eddying round
While the floodlit masonry was mere slabs of moonshine.
Rome is a city where flesh and blood can never
Be sacrificed, or mistaken, for abstractions.

      But already (you can imagine how) my mind's
Crisscrossed with figures, memoranda, lightning sketches,
Symbolic doodlings, hour by hour set down
Haphazardly as in Rome era on era.
And time is already shuffling tricks with discards.
Those fountains yesterday at the Villa d'Este
Grouped like patrician spectres in white conclave
Against a drop-scene of terraces and urns –
Did we indeed see them, or have they stepped
From a picture book years ago perused? Last night
We found on a wall of the Pincio a bas-relief,
A wide white calm imperious head suddenly
Surveying us out of the blank wall like some racial
Memory still not deep enough bricked up.

      Yesterday, then, was a day with the dead. We hired
A car, and set out first for the Palatine hill.
The Forum? Well, picture a clearing found
In the depth of a clamorous forest, a low space littered
With bits of temples, arches, altars, mosaics
And God knows what – classical tags, fag ends,

Smatterings and stumps of a once apparently stable
Civilization, which packed up for all that
And left, like a gipsy encampment or picnic party:
And over it all, the silence of sheer exhaustion.
This area, sad as scar-tissue now, was the heart
Of a great republic, the S. P. Q. R.
Here they governed – a people, like the Scots,
Smouldering, pious, intolerant, living hard,
And demon fighters. Warlike was the seed;
But Time has pushed out this crop of decayed teeth.
It was the usual story. Long before
Their aqueducts ran dry and became picturesque,
Their virtue had imperceptibly seeped away
Into the dunes of ambition. They caught
Luxury, like a syphilis, from their conquests.
Then, feeling queer, they appointed one man to cure them
And made a god of him. The disease was arrested
From time to time. But injections grew more frequent,
And the extremities began to rot;
While at home no amount of marble could hide the sick core –
Vestals too free with their flame, tribunes long impotent,
A rabble who had not the wherewithal to redeem its
Too often pledged heirlooms, justice and hardiness.

      So we were glad on the whole to leave this spot
Where glum mementoes of decline and fall
Are cherished like a grievance in Rome's heart,
And drive out towards Tivoli. The name
Had a certain frivolous charm for one oppressed
By dwelling on ruined greatness. The little town,
Modishly perched on an olive-tressed hillside,
Is famous for its sulphur springs (our driver
Stopped the car so that we might inhale it)
And of course, for the Villa d'Este. There at first
In the elaborate Renaissance gardens
Laid out for the lust of the eye, you seem to see
The lineaments of gratified desire.

An illusion though, like the smile on a dead face
Which means nothing but our own wish for peace.
Exquisite, yes: but a sense of the past, to be truly
Felicitous, demands some belief in the present,
Some moral belvedere we have not got.
This villa inhabited only by frescoes,
This garden groomed for sightseers – they mirror
Too clearly our lack of prospect or tenable premise.
The cardinals and princes who adorned them,
Lords of an age when men believed in man,
Are as remote from us as the Colosseum
Where high-tiered beasts howled down professional heroes;
Perhaps – it is a comfortless thought – remoter.

　　　　Back, then, to Rome. At Tivoli our driver
Stopped again like some house-proud, indelicate devil
To remark the smell of sulphur. Presently,
Held in a crook of Rome's old city wall
Close by St. Paul's gate under the pagan shadow
Of Gaius Cestius' pyramid, we found
The English cemetery. An ox-eyed, pregnant,
Slatternly girl opened the gate for us
And showed us round the desirable estate.
Here is one corner of a foreign field
That is for ever garden suburb. See,
In their detached and smug-lawned residences,
Behind a gauze of dusty shrubs, the English
Indulge their life-long taste for privacy.
Garish Campagna knocks at the back door,
Rome calls *en grande tenue*: but 'not at home'
Murmur these tombs, and 'far from home they died,
'The eccentric couple you have come to visit –
'One spitting blood, an outsider and a failure,
'One sailing a boat, his mind on higher things.'
Somewhere close to the pyramid a loud-speaker
Blared jazz while we lingered at Keats' shabby mound,
But the air was drowned by the ghost of a nightingale;

The ground was swimming with anemone tears
Where Shelley lay.
             We could feel at home here, with
This family of exiles. It is our people:
A people from whose reticent, stiff heart
Babble the springtime voices, always such voices
Bubbling out of their clay . . .
                So much for Rome.
Tomorrow we shall take the bus to Florence.

PART FOUR

Bus to Florence

In the white piazza Today is barely awake.
    A well-water breeze freshens
Her nakedness, musky with love, and wafts about
    Her breath of moist carnations.
Oh the beautiful creature, still in a dream pinioned,
    A flutter of meadowsweet thighs!
How she clings to the night, whose fingertips haunt her waxen
    Body! Look at the eyes
Opening – pale, drenched, languid as aquamarines!
    They are open. The mere-smooth light
Starts glancing all over the city in jets and sparklets
    Like a charm of goldfinches in flight.
The tousled alleys stretch. Tall windows blink.
    Hour of alarum clocks and laces.
Sprinklers dust off the streets. The shops hum gently
    As they make up their morning faces.
And today comes out like a bride, a different woman,
    Subtler in hue, hazier,
Until the pensive mist goes, shyly avowing
    Such a zenith of shameless azure.

    This is our day: we mean
To make much of her, tune to her pitch. The enchanting
                                      creature
    Travels with us. For once
There will be no twinge of parting in a departure.
    So eager she is to be off,
Spilling her armful of roses and mignonette,
    Her light feet restlessly echoed
From campanile and wristwatch (will they forget?
    Be late?) What a stir and lustre
Ripple the white square at a lift of her hand!

Look! she has seen us, she points to
That blue bus with the scarab-like trailer behind.

We went the Cassian Way, a route for legions,
    We and the May morning.
Rome flaked off in stucco; blear-eyed villas
    Melancholiac under their awnings.
Rome peeled off like a cataract. Clear beyond us
    A vision good to believe in –
The Campagna with its longdrawn sighs of grass
    Heaving, heaving to heaven.
This young-old terrain of asphodel and tufo
    Opening its heart to the sun,
Was it sighing for death like Tithonus, or still athirst for
    Immortal dews? . . . We run
Towards Tuscany now through a no-man's-land where stilted
    Aqueducts dryly scale
The distance and sport the lizard his antediluvian
    Head and tendril tail.
But soon the road rivers between flowerbanks:
    Such a fume and flamboyance of purple
Vetch, of campions, poppy, wild rose, gladioli,
    Bugloss! The flowery people,
Come out in their best to line our route, how they wave
    At the carnival progress! And higher,
The foothills flush with sanfoin, salutes of broom
    Are setting the rocks on fire.
Sutri, Viterbo, Montefiascone passed:
    Each village, it seemed, was making
A silent bar in the music, the road's hurdy-gurdy
    Winding, the tambourine shaking
Of sunlit leaves. You tatterdemalion townships –
    Elegance freaked with decay –
Your shuttered looks and your black doormouths gaping
    Dumb in the heat of the day
Reject, unanswered, the engine's urgent beat.

But now, groves of acacia
Swing their honeybells peal upon peal to welcome us
   Over the vibrant, azure,
Deep organ chords of Bolsena, the silvery wavelets
   Trilling tranquillamente.
That music followed us for miles, until
   We came to Acquapendente.

Eyes grown used to the light, we were finding our form and
                                                       meeting
   Impressions squarely.
Yet, where all was new, changeful, idyllic, it saddened
   To think how rarely
More than a few snippets remain from the offered fabric,
   And they not always
The ones we'd have chosen. It's sequence I lack, the talent to grasp
   Not a here-and-there phrase
But the music entire, its original stream and logic. I'd better
   Accept this, perhaps,
As nature's way: matter, the physicists tell one, is largely
   A matter of gaps.

Another stage, and a change of key. Listen!
   Rosetted oxen move –
The milky skins, the loose-kneed watersilk gait of
   Priestesses vowed to Love.
A road stubborn with stone pines. Shrines at the roadside.
   A sandsone cliff, where caves
Open divining mouths: in this or that one
   A skeleton sibyl raves.
Signs and omens . . . We approached the haunts of
   The mystery-loving Etruscans.
Earth's face grew rapidly older, ravine-wrinkled,
   Shadowed with brooding dusk on
Temple and cheek. Mountains multiplied round us
   And the flowery guise shredded off as we

Climbed past boulders and gaunt grass high into
    A landscape haggard as prophecy,
Scarred with bone-white riverbeds like veins
    Of inspiration run dry.
Still what a journey away the apocalypse! See it –
    A tower, a town in the sky!
A child from the flowering vale, a youth from the foothills
    May catch glimpses of death
Remote as a star, irrelevant, all of a lifetime
    Ahead, less landmark than myth.
For ages it seems no nearer. But imperceptibly
    The road, twisting and doubling
As if to delay or avoid it, underlines
    That Presence: the man is troubled,
Feeling the road beneath him being hauled in now
    Like slack, the magnetic power
Of what it had always led to over the dreaming
    Hills and the fable of flowers.
So, while the bus toiled upwards and the Apennines
    Swirled like vapours about it,
That town in the sky stayed constant and loomed nearer
    Till we could no more doubt it;
And soon, though still afar off, it darkly foretold us
    We were destined to pass that way.
We passed by the thundercloud castle of Radicofani
    At the pinnacle of our day.

The wrack of cloud, the surly ruinous tower
Stubborn upon the verge of recognition –
    What haunts and weights them so?
    Memory, or premonition?
Why should a mouldering finger in the sky,
An hour of cloud that drifts and passes, mean
    More than the flowering vale,
    The volcanic ravine?
A driven heart, a raven-shadowing mind

Loom above all my pastorals, impend
    My traveller's joy with fears
    That travelling has no end.

But on without pause from that eyrie the bus, swooping,
    Checking and swooping, descends:
The road cascades down the hillface in blonde ringlets
    Looped up with hairpin bends.
The sun rides out. The calcined earth grows mellow
    With place-names sleek as oil –
Montepulciano, Montalcino, Murlo,
    Castiglione. The soil
Acknowledges man again, his hand which husbands
    Each yielding inch and endures
To set the vine amid armies, the olive between
    Death's adamantine spurs.
Presently, on a constellation of three hills,
    We saw crowning the plain
A town from a missal, a huddle of towers and houses,
    Mediaeval Siena.
A gorge of a street, anfractuous, narrow. Our bus
    Crawled up it, stemming a torrent
Of faces – the faces impetuous, proud, intransigent
    Of those who had fought with Florence
For Tuscany. Was it a demonstration they flocked to?
    A miracle? Or some huger
Event? We left the bus stranded amongst them, a monster
    Thrown up from their fathomless future,
And strolled into a far-off present, an age
    Where all is emblematic,
Pure, and without perspective. The twining passages,
    Diagrams of some classic
Doctrinal knot, lap over and under one another.
    The swan-necked Mangia tower
With its ruff stands, clear as Babel, for pride: beneath it,
    Shaped like a scallop, that square

Might be humility's dewpond, or the rose-madder
    Shell from which Aphrodite
Once stepped ashore. And the west front of the Duomo –
    How it images, flight upon flight, the
Ascending torrent, a multitude without number
    Intent on their timeless way
From the world of St. Catherine, Boccaccio and Fiammetta
    Towards the judgment day!

A township cast up high and dry from an age
    When the whole universe
    Of stars lived in man's parish
And the zodiac told his fortune, chapter and verse.
A simple time – salvation or damnation
    One black and white device,
    Eternity foreshortened,
Earth a mere trusting step from Paradise.
O life where mystery grew on every bush,
    Saints, tyrants, thrills and throes
    Were for one end! – the traveller
Dips into your dream and, sighing, goes.

After two hours we went on, for our destination
    Called. The adagio dance
Of olives, their immemorial routine and eccentric
    Variations of stance;
The vines that flourished like semaphore alphabets endlessly
    Flagging from hill to hill:
We knew them by heart now (or never would), seeing them tiny
    And common as tormentil.
Florence invisibly haled us. The intervening
    Grew misted with expectations,
Diminished yet weirdly prolonged, as all the go-between
    World by a lover's impatience.
Through Poggibonsi we glided – a clown's name
    And a history of hard knocks:

But nothing was real till at length we entered the nonpareil
    City . . . A hand unlocks
The traveller's trance. We alight. And the just coming down to
    Earth, the pure sense of arrival,
More than visions or masterpieces, fulfil
    One need for which we travel.

    This day, my bride of a day,
Went with me hand in hand the centuried road:
    I through her charmed eyes gazing,
She hanging on my words, peace overflowed.
    But now, a rose-gold Eve,
With the deep look of one who will unbosom
    Her sweetest to death only,
She opens out, she flames and falls like blossom.
    A spray that lightly trembles
After the warbler's flown. A cloud vibrating
    In the wash of the hull-down sun.
My heart rocks on. Remembering, or awaiting?

PART FIVE

Florence: Works of Art

Florence, father of Michelangelo,
Dante, da Vinci, Fra Angelico,
Cellini, Botticelli, Brunelleschi.
Giotto, Donatello, Masaccio! –

We shall not see their like, or yours, again.
Painters depart, and patrons. You remain,
Your bridges blown, your glory catalogued,
A norm for scholars and for gentlemen.

Reverend city, sober, unperplexed,
Turning your page to genius annexed
I breathe the mint and myrrh of Tuscan hills,
The tart aroma of some classic text.

Shields and medallions; overshadowing eaves
Like studious brows; the light that interleaves
Your past with amber: all's definitive, all
In changeless chiaroscuro one conceives.

I sometimes think the heart is ne'er so dead
As where some vanished era overspread
The soil with titan foliage, scattering down
Eternal rubies when its bloom was shed.

Where rode Lorenzo, panoplied and plumed,
Where Savonarola burned, and Ruskin fumed,
The lady artist sets her easel up,
The tourist with mild wonder is consumed.

Yet still the Arno navigably flows,
And saunterers past the Ponte Vecchio's
Jewel shops cast a shadow: here is still
A taste for life, a market for the rose.

Ah no, it's not the Florentines who fade
Before the statued loggia, the arcade,
The cliffs of floral stone. They live enough
In a pure tongue and a congenial trade.

Should the past overawe them? It's not theirs,
More than a mansion is the caretaker's.
A church by Giotto does as well as any
Other for this day's rendezvous or prayers.

What if along the pot-holed boulevards
Slogans are scrawled, not cantos? if postcards
Stand in for masterpieces, and ice cream
Says more to them than edifying façades?

The past is all-encroaching; and unless
They lopped its tentacles, stemmed its excess
To clear the air for some domestic seed,
They'd soon be strangled by a wilderness.

It's not the Florentine who pales beside
That vast, rank efflorescence. The pop-eyed
Tourist it is who rushes on his doom,
Armed with good taste, a Leica and a guide.

The primitive forest, the renaissance range
So massive are, surely they will estrange
Him from himself, or send him yelping home
To plastic novelties, to art's small change.

Plodding the galleries, we ask how can
That century of the Uncommon Man,
Sovereign here in paint, bronze, marble, suit
The new narcissism of the Also-Ran.

As many men, so many attitudes
Before the artifact. One writhes: one broods:
One preens the ego and one curls the lip:
One turns to stone, one to adjacent nudes.

Each man must seek his own. What do I seek?
Not the sole rights required by snob and freak,
The scholar's or the moralist's reward,
Not even a connoisseur's eye for technique;

But that on me some long-dead master may
Dart the live, intimate, unblinding ray
Which means one more spring of the selfhood tapped,
One tribute more to love wrung from my clay.

And if I miss that radiance where it flies,
Something is gained in the mere exercise
Of strenuous submission, the attempt
To lose and find oneself through others' eyes.

Singing Children: Luca Della Robbia

(T. H.)

I see you, angels with choirboy faces,
 Trilling it from the museum wall
As once, decani or cantoris,
 You sang in a carved oak stall,
Nor deemed any final bar to such time-honoured carollings
 E'er could befall.

I too gave tongue in my piping youth-days,
 Yea, took like a bird to crotchet and clef,
Antheming out with a will the Old Hundredth,
 Salem, or Bunnett in F.,
Unreckoning even as you if the Primal Sapience
 Be deaf, stone-deaf.

Many a matins cheerfully droned I
 To the harmonium's clacking wheeze,
Fidgeted much through prayer and sermon
 While errant bumblebees
Drummed on the ivied window, veering my thoughts to
 Alfresco glees.

But voices break – aye, and more than voices;
 The heart for hymn tune and haytime goes.
Dear Duomo choristers, chirping for ever
 In jaunty, angelic pose,
Would I had sung my last ere joy-throbs dwindled
 Or wan faith froze!

Judith and Holofernes: Donatello
(W. B. Y.)

. . . Next, a rich widow woman comes to mind
Who, when her folk were starving, dined and wined
Alone with Holofernes, until he
Grew rabid for her flesh. And presently,
Matching deceit with bitterer deceit,
She had struck off that tipsy captain's head
Upon the still untousled bed,
And borne it homeward in a bag of meat.

Old Donatello thought it out in bronze –
The wrists trailing, numb as it were from bonds;
The fuddled trunk lugged upright by a loop
Of hair; the falcon-falchion poised to stoop.
Tyrant, and tyrant's man, maybe:
Nevertheless, the sculptural face presents
A victim's irony, the mild innocence
Of passionate men whom passion has set free.

And she, the people's saviour, the patriot?
She towers, mouth brooding, eyes averted, not
In womanly compunction but her need
To chew and savour a vindictive deed;
Or so I construe it. One thing's sure –
Let a man get what issue he has earned,
Where death beds or love tussles are concerned
Woman's the single-minded connoisseur.

A political woman is an atrocious thing.
Come what may, she will have her fling
In flesh and blood. Her heady draughts cajole
A man only to cheat him, body or soul.
Judith took great Holofernes in.
For all the silver lamps that went before,
He made but a remnant on a knacker's floor:
She lives, the brazen kind of heroine.

Annunciation: Leonardo

(R. F.)

There was never a morning quite so tremendous again.
The birth, you think? I'm not for setting great store
By birth. Births aren't beginnings. And anyway
She only wanted to sleep off the pain
Which had made her a beast among beasts on the cow-house
floor.

Shepherds and magnates tiptoeing through the hay
(You get all kinds at an inn, she drowsily thought),
Even the babe – they were part of a snowdrift trance,
Almost unreal. He was to prove a good son
In his way, though his way was beyond her. Whatever he sought
When he left home and led his friends such a dance,
He did not forget her as other boys might have done.

Her morning of mornings was when one flew to bring
Some news that changed her cottage into a queen's
Palace; the table she worked at shone like gold,
And in the orchard it is suddenly spring,
All bird and blossom and fresh-painted green.
What was it the grand visitor foretold
Which made earth heaven for a village Mary?
He was saying something about a Saviour Prince,
But she only heard him say, 'You will bear a child',
And that was why the spring came. Angels carry
Such tidings often enough, but never since
To one who in such blissful ignorance smiled.

Perseus Rescuing Andromeda: Piero di Cosimo

(W. H. A.)

It is all there. The victim broods,
Her friends take up the attitudes
Right for disaster;

The winsome rescuer draws his sword,
While from the svelte, impassive fjord
Breaches terrific, dense and bored
    The usual monster.

When gilt-edged hopes are selling short,
Virtue's devalued, and the swart
    Avenger rises,
We know there'll always be those two
Strolling away without a clue,
Discussing earnestly the view
    Or fat-stock prices.

To either hand the crisis throws
Its human quirks and gestures. Those
    Are not essential.
Look rather at the oafish Dread,
The Cloud-man come to strike it dead,
Armed with a sword and gorgon's head –
    Magic's credentials.

White on the rocks, Andromeda.
Mother had presumed too far.
    The deep lost patience.
The nightmare ground its teeth. The saviour
Went in. A winning hit. All over.
Parents and friends stood round to offer
    Congratulations.

But when the vast delusions break
Upon you from the central lake,
    You'll be less lucky.
I'd not advise you to believe
There's a slick op. to end your grief
Or any nick-of-time reprieve.
    For you, unlikely.

Boy with Dolphin: Verrocchio
(D. T.)

At the crack of spring on the tail of the cold,
When foam whipped over the apple tree aisles
And the grape skin sea swelled and the weltering capes were
bold,
I went to school with a glee of dolphins
Bowling their hoops round the brine tongued isles
And singing their scales were tipped by a sun always revolving.

Oh truant I was and trident and first
Lord of fishes, bearleading all tritons
In the swim of my blood before the foam brewed bubble burst.
And as I was nursling to mermaids, my sun
Cooed through their nestling grottoes a cadence
Of thrummed and choral reefs for the whale sounded gulfs to
hum.

Those were the gambolling days I led
Leviathan a dance in my sea urchin glee
Till the lurching waves shoaled out with a school of wishes. My
head
Was shells and ringing, my shoulders broke
Into a spray of wings. But the sea
Ran dry between two bars of foam, and the fine folk

In the temple of fins were flailed away
And the weed fell flat and the mermilk curdled,
And buoyant no more to bliss are the miles where alone I play
My running games that the waves once aisled,
With a doll of a lithe dead dolphin saddled,
And cold as the back of spring is my tale of the applefroth isles.

PART SIX

Elegy Before Death: At Settignano

(*To R. N. L.*)

> . . . for be it never so derke
> Me thinketh I see hir ever mo.
> CHAUCER

Come to the orangery. Sit down awhile.
The sun is setting: the veranda frames
An illuminated leaf of Italy.
Gold and green and blue, stroke upon stroke,
Seem to tell what nature and man could make of it
If only their marriage were made in heaven. But see,
Even as we hold the picture,
The colours are fading already, the lines collapsing
Fainting into the dream they will soon be.

Again? Again we are baffled who have sought
So long in a melting Now the formula
Of Always. There is no fast dye. Always? –
That is the word the sirens sing
On bone island. Oh stop your ears, and stop
All this vain peering through the haze,
The fortunate haze wherein we change and ripen,
And never mind for what. Let us even embrace
The shadows wheeling away our windfall days.

Again again again, the frogs are screeling
Down by the lilypond. Listen! I'll echo them –
Gain gain gain . . . Could we compel
One grain of one vanishing moment to deliver
Its golden ghost, loss would be gain
And Love step naked from illusion's shell.
Did we but dare to see it,
All things to us, you and I to each other,
Stand in this naked potency of farewell.

The villa was built for permanence. Man laid down
Like wine his heart, planted young trees, young pictures,
Young thoughts to ripen for an heir.
Look how these avenues take the long view
Of things ephemeral! With what aplomb
The statues greet us at the grassy stair!
Time on the sundial was a snail's migration
Over a world of warmth, and each day passing
Left on the fertile heart another layer.

The continuity they took for granted
We wistfully glamourize. So life's devalued:
Worth not a rhyme
These statues, groves, books, bibelots, masterpieces,
If we have used them only to grout a shaken
Confidence or stop up the gaps of time.
We must ride the flood, or go under
With all our works, to emerge, when it recedes,
Derelicts sluggish from the dishonouring slime.

Our sun is setting. Terrestrial planes shift
And slide towards dissolution, the terraced gardens
Quaver like waves, and in the garden urn
Geraniums go ashen. Now are we tempted, each
To yearn that his struggling counterpoint, carried away
Drowned by the flood's finale, shall return
To silence. Why do we trouble
A master theme with cadenzas
That ring out, fade out over its fathomless unconcern?

Love, more than our holidays are numbered.
Not one day but a whole life is drained off
Through this pinprick of doubt into the dark.
Rhadamanthine moment! Shall we be judged
Self-traitors? Now is a chance to make our flux
Stand and deliver its holy spark, –

Now, when the tears rise and the levees crumble,
To tap the potency of farewell.
What ark is there but love? Let us embark.

A weeping firmament, a sac of waters,
A passive chaos – time without wind or tide,
Where on brief motiveless eddy seethe
Lost faces, furniture, animals, oblivion's litter –
Envelop me, just as the incipient poem
Is globed in nescience, and beneath
A heart purged of all but memory, grows.
No landfall yet? No rift in the film? . . . I send you
My dove into the future, to your death.

            *   *   *

A dove went forth: flits back a ghost to me,
Image of her I imagine lost to me,
Up the road through Fiesole we first travelled on –
Was it a week or thirty years ago?
Time vanishes now like a mirage of water,
Touched by her feet returning whence she had gone,
Touched by the tones that darkly appeal to me,
The memories that make her shade as real to me
As all the millions breathing under the upright sun.

We are back at the first time we went abroad together.
Homing to this garden with a love-sure bent
Her phantom has come. Now hand in hand we stray
Through a long-ago morning mounting from a lather
Of azaleas and dizzy with the lemon blossom's scent.
And I seem to hear her murmur in the old romantic way,
'So blissfully, rosily our twin hearts burn here,
'This vernal time, whenever we return here,
'To haunter and haunted will be but yesterday.'

I follow her wraith down the terraced gardens
Through a dawn of nightingales, a murmurous siesta,

By leaf-green frogs on lily leaves screeling again
Towards eve. Is it dark or light? Fireflies glister
Across my noon, and nightlong the cicadas
Whir like a mechanical arm scratching in the brain.
All yesterday's children who fleetingly caressed her
Break ranks, break time, once more to join and part us:
I alone, who possessed her, feel the drag of time's harsh chain.

'Ah, you,' she whispers; 'are you still harping
'On mortal delusion? still the too much hoping
'Who needs only plant an acorn to dream a dryad's kiss?
'Still the doubtful one who, when she came to you
'Out of the rough rind, a naked flame for you,
'Fancied some knot or flaw in love, something amiss?'
Yes, such I am. But since I have found her
A revenant so fleshed in my memories, I wonder
Is she the real one and am I a wisp from the abyss.

Dare I follow her through the wood of obscurity –
This ilex grove where shades are lost in shade?
Not a gleam here, nothing differs, nothing sings, nothing grows,
For the trees are columns which ebonly support
A crypt of hollow silence, a subliminal thought,
A theorem proving the maggot equivalent to the rose.
Undiminished she moves here, shines, and will not fade.
Death, what had she to do with your futile purity,
The dogma of bone that on rare and common you would impose?

Her orbit clasped and enhanced in its diadem
All creatures. Once on a living night
When cypresses jetted like fountains of wine-warm air
Bubbling with fireflies, we going outside
In the palpitating dark to admire them,
One of the fireflies pinned itself to her hair;
And its throbbings, I thought, had a tenderer light
As if some glimmering of love inspired them,
As if her luminous heart was beating there.

Ah, could I make you see this subtle ghost of mine,
Delicate as a whorled shell that whispers to the tide,
Moving with a wavering watersilk grace,
Anemone-fingered, coral-tinted, under whose crystalline
Calm such naiads, angel fish and monsters sleep or slide;
If you could see her as she flows to me apace
Through waves through walls through time's fine mesh magi-
cally drawn,
You would say, this was surely the last daughter of the foam-
born,
One whom no age to come will ever replace.

Eve's last fainting rose cloud; mornings that restored her
With orange tree, lemon tree, lotus, bougainvillea:
The milk-white snake uncoiling and the flute's light-fingered
charm:
Breast of consolation, tongue of tried acquaintance:
A tranquil mien, but under it the nervous marauder
Slithering from covert, a catspaw from a calm:
Heaven's city adored in the palm of a pictured saint:
My vision's *ara coeli*, my lust's familiar,
All hours, moods, shapes, desires that yield, elude, disarm –

All woman she was. Brutalizing, humanizing,
Pure flame, lewd earth was she, imperative as air
And weak as water, yes all women to me.
To the rest, one of many, though they felt how she was rare
In sympathy and tasted in her warm words a sweetness
Of life that has ripened on the sunny side of the tree.
To herself a darker story, as she called her past to witness –
A heart much bruised, how often, how stormily surmising
Some chasmal flaw divided it from whole felicity.

So I bless the villa on the hill above Fiesole,
For here and now was flawless, and the past could not encroach
On its charmed circle to menace or to taunt her.
Oh, time that clung round her in unfading drapery,

Oh, land she wore like an enamelled brooch,
It was for remembrance you thus adorned her!
Now as I look back, how vividly, how gracefully
Ghosting there, she breathes me not the ghost of a reproach.
Happiness, it seems, can be the best haunter.

You later ones, should you see that wraith divulged for a mo-
                                                        ment
Through the sleep-haze of plumbago, glancing out from the
                                                    loggia's
Vain dream of permanence as from a page
Time is already turning again, will you thus comment? –
'She is some dead beauty, no doubt, who queened here awhile
'And clasped her bouquets, and shrinks to leave the lighted
                                                    stage:
'Not quite of the villa's classic period, though –
'Something more wistful, ironic, unstable in act and style,
'A minor masterpiece of a silver age.'

But to me she stands out tall as the Torcello madonna
Against a mosaic of sunlight, for ever upholding
My small, redeeming love. But 'love is all',
She says; and the mortal scene of planets and tides,
Animals, grass and men is transformed, proved, steadied around
                                                        me.
But her I begin to view through a thickening veil,
A gauze of tears, till the figure inscrutably fades –
As every vision must vanish, if we and it keep faith,
Into the racked, unappeasable flesh of the real.

                    *   *   *

But look, the garden storm is stilled, the flood
Blinked away like a tear, earth reconciled to
Her molten birth-bed's long prophetic throes!
Her hills are lizards in their solid trance
Of sun and stone: upon each hill
Vine and olive hold the archaic pose:

Below, the bubble dome looks everlasting
As heaven's womb, and threading the eyes of bridges
Arno endlessly into the loom of oblivion flows.

A ghost, the mere thought of a shade, has done it.
Testing the shifty face of the Now with a dove, I found
Terra firma. Whatever in me was born to praise
Life's heart of blood or stone here reached its zenith,
Conjuring, staying, measuring all by that meek shade . . .
Now, love, you have tried on your phantom dress,
Return to nakedness!
Be breathing again beside me, real, imperfect!
Enmesh, enact my dream till it vanishes!

The oranges are going out? Tomorrow
Will light them up again. Tomorrow will call you
With nightingales; tomorrow will leave
A rose by your plate, and freshen the plumbago's
Blue millinery and open a parasol
Of cedar for you, as it did for the first, ignorant Eve
Before exile or death was thought of. But we know well
On what tenure we have this garden. Each day's a livelier
Paradise when each dawn is a reprieve.

I imagine you really gone for ever. Clocks stop.
Clouds bleed. Flames numb. My world shrunk to an echoing
Memorial skull. (A child playing at hide-
And-seek suddenly feels the whole terrible truth of Absence.)
Too keen the imagined grief, too dearly gained
Its proof of love. I would let all else slide,
Dissolve and perish into the old enigma,
If that could keep you here, if it could keep
Even your sad ghost at my side.

But gold and green and blue still glows before us
This leaf of Italy, the colours fixed

The characters formed by love. It is love's way
To shine most through the slow dusk of adieu.
Long may it glow within us, that timeless, halcyon halt
On our rough journey back to clay.
Oh, may my farewell word, may this your elegy
Written in life blood from a condemned heart
Be quick and haunting even beyond our day.

PART SEVEN

The Homeward Prospect

TOM A word with you, my friends. High summer is scorching
up
Northwards through poplared Umbria to these foothills of
Tuscany.
But I notice a nip in the air, a recession in all around me –
Statues and groves and fountains adopting a cooler attitude,
As if they were already waiving their claims upon us.

DICK I feel – oh look at the stream's face, innocently asleep
But twitching as if a nightmare coursed it! Stagnant as ice,
Bland as silver it seems now: but fast and faster the drift of
Objects inexorably drawn onward unmasks it. I feel
Time's force. It is a last reach. I know the tug of the weir.

HARRY You should not take it to heart so, Dick. It is merely
one more
Holiday ending. Now is a chance to count the change,
To check the income against the outgoings, and find our balance.
We shall come back some day – if only to demonstrate
Upon our person the law of diminishing returns.

TOM Coming or going, I care not, when poised, alert and
shimmering
Like angels on a pinpoint, we stand at the tip of departure.

DICK A point that is equidistant between two fields of attrac-
tion
And thus, for me, the extreme agony.

HARRY   One or the other
Proves always the stronger field. You should regard such
occasions,
Dick, as limberings-up and rehearsals for a deathbed.

TOM Well, God save us all! What a way to encourage the
queasy
Traveller! We go home enriched

DICK   Sobered

HARRY   Lightened:
Lightened of one illusion, and therefore one truth the richer.

TOM Enriched with extravagant draughts of the strange: after
them, soberer.

DICK Sobered through sense of gain, by knowledge of loss
enlightened –
Though what we have gained or lost is not yet apparent to me,
Nor do I get any answer from these implausible word-plays.

HARRY Time will tell. In the meantime, let us inquire what
Tom,
The boyish and indiscriminate collector, has filled our trunk
with.

TOM Sapphires of lakes I declare, a tiara of diamond fireflies,
Emerald valleys aglow in platinum dawns, mosaic of
Noondays, ivory evenings with voices flowing like thick silk:
Illuminated leaves torn from an Italian
Book of hours: frescoes and canvases by the masters;
A landscape with figures alive yet touched by the same genius:
Perfumes of contraband moments, essences of antiquity:
Nightingales, oxen, a hoopoe, cicadas and frogs – miscellaneous
Curios rare as dirt and cheap as gold. I declare, too,
The wines of the country, the olive and maize of women's flesh.

DICK That will do to go on with. And such of these acquisi-
tions
As we get past the paternal customs and heavy duties
Which await our return, I shall unpack in the front parlour
Where Harry will arrange them in the pattern his latest aesthetic

Or ethic requires, to show off to our guests, like any travel-bore.
Presently, chipped and tarnished, or crowded out, they will find
Their way to the attic: and there, one morbid afternoon
When rooks are eddying round a backwater of brackish sky
And a blight smears over the streets, morosely rummaging I
Shall cut myself to the bone on some poignant cobwebbed
souvenir.

HARRY Let it be so. What Tom acquires for us has no absolute
Value; nor, I admit, have the elegant systems wherein
I am disposed to compose it. There's no way even of telling
Which objects are really kin to us, which we've partaken of life
with,
Until, deep buried, they draw blood from us and are eloquent.
Home is where we inter our travels, but equally give them
A chance to germinate beneath the dust and the housework,
The preoccupied face of routine, the protective sleep of the
heart.
Thence, on a gust of travail, something is born, crying
'I am your flesh and blood!' . . . Let us look homeward, then.

TOM I see, as the plane booms into the beetling, vertical dark,
Gold and green and blue, amber and red, the lights of
A city like uncut gems in a jeweller's tray, tempting
And myriad below me. How precious now are the stones of
London!
How deeply caressing the velvet blackness in which they are
bedded!

DICK Soon my bees will be swarming, swirling and swarming
upward
Like bonfire sparks in a gale. Let the early flowers be consumed,
The new cells built. I feel – and my harebell heart windlessly
Quivers with far-flown tremors – the tramp, tramp of Atlantic,
A funeral march plangent upon my uttermost shore.

HARRY I imagine our house repainted by absence, the
windowpanes cleaned,

z   355

A clearer view of the tangled streets, and the flowerbeds tidier.
I return to myself as it were to a son who, in the interval,
Has grown perceptibly older, filled out; or like the astral
Self flying back to a body refreshed by the night's vacation.

TOM Happy the natural nomad, sees home in a series of new
lights!

DICK Blessed the born settler, whom all roads lead to home!

HARRY Can the human animal ever return, though, to its old
form?

TOM Never. The form may remain; but the animal, being a
mere sequence
Of current sensations, could not recognize it.

DICK You're wrong.
The *human* animal carries his form

HARRY Like a shell?

TOM Like a prison –
Where, but for me, you'd be starving in solitary confinement.

DICK Neither a shell nor a prison. Say rather an x, a potential
Within him that cell by cell he has to incarnate, until
It sloughs him off one day and emerges, more or less perfect.

HARRY That is not quite what I meant. I wonder, to be
explicit,
If the home to which our traveller returns may seem, not only
Changed by his prodigal experience, but estranged from him.

TOM Why yes. And that is surely one of the points of
travelling:
The exotic veils we bring back and drape over the form of
The too familiar charmer, reviving her value, her mystery,
Compel us to woo her again.

DICK I cannot take part in such make-believe.
Home, for me, is simply the place you can never quit;
An ideal home, if you like, which you spend a lifetime building
Out of whatever comes to hand – dropped bricks, last straws,

Love's mortar, the timbre and rubble of today, old stones from
                                                                Italy

HARRY I agree with you both, but will add *this*: our going
                                                          abroad is
Only a shift in space, a projection of home's shadow,
Unless it enlarges us with a new concept whereby
We may reassemble the known in a different, more luminous
                                                            pattern,
The better to guide or follow our fateful thread of becoming.

TOM Must every holiday end in a kind of Royal Commission?
I myself, like a sun-warmed stone or a satisfied lover,
Am purely grateful. Cannot one say so, and leave it at that?

DICK Grateful exactly for what? Italy waits a tribute.

HARRY Let us sharpen our recollections and write in her
                                                  visitors' book.

TOM On the sill of languorous autumn a tortoise-shell or red
                                                          admiral
Called by a sunbeam opens the eyes of its dreamless wings,
Longs for a last flutter, rustles against the windowpane
Trembling in the draught of a heliotrope desire.
Italy was the sun that awoke me, the hand that opened
A window and released me into a new playground.
I spread my wings on her basking stones, with her bells I
                                                        quivered,
Then sipped the violet mountains and the lilies of her valleys:
On dome after dome alighting, pirouetting through grave
                                                          arcades,
Dithering over the fruit in a marketplace, pinned to a frieze or
Skimming the dew of flesh, I wilfully everywhere wafted
Like a soul freed from a body yet fraught with the body's
                                                      enthralments.
I have no call to improve myself or the shining hour:
There was only the dance, the butterfly kiss on each of a thousand
Adorable things. That dance is the tribute I pay to Italy.

DICK   On a flank of the hard-faced Apennines, on the threshold
of sheer desolation,
I see a few acres of terraced farmland, ruled with olives
And ridged between for cereal, not a foot nor a clod wasted,
All snug and rooted against the barbarian hordes of boulders.
It is a composite picture: many such have I seen here –
Places where generation on generation labouring
Up to the last instant before the rock takes over,
Ploughing their legends back into the heart's fibre,
Hammering their need to a tool and an emblem of primary
virtue,
Have kept man's nature green. It's here, and not in some
absolute
Immaculate distance or lawn of idyllic dance, I have found
The piety glimpsed by my youth, the deity under the fable.
And whenever, amid the vapours and topheavy crags of the
present,
I feel a handhold or lifeline, and grasp in myself the classical
Lineage of man's endurance, I shall remember Italy.

HARRY   On a lap of the road to Florence we passed a Tuscan
graveyard
Out in the fields at the far end of a cortege of cypresses,
Insulated and distanced from life, yet part of a frieze where
Living and dead are one to love's creative eye,
Embryos each of the other . . . I took our most cherished posses-
sion
And offered her to death. I took a ghost for my glass
And focused through it the inchoate, atomized face of becoming.
Then, from the tower in the sky to the tiniest flower on the
earth's hem,
All was distinct, illustrious, full-formed in the light of necessity,
Time's cocoon fallen away from the truth and kinship of all
things.
For one immeasurable moment the world's hands stood still

And the worm that ticks at the heart of the golden hoard **was**
silent.

Losing my heart to this alien land, I renewed my true love:
Lending my love to death, I gained this grain of vision.
I took my pen. What I wrote is thanks to her and to Italy.

INDEX OF FIRST LINES

INDEX OF FIRST LINES